Praise for *Afterlight*

"Written with powerful awareness and historical heft, the memoir *Afterlight* follows the daughter of Holocaust survivors as she travels to unpack her lifetime of living with the aftermath of a genocide."

FOREWORD REVIEWS

"What a remarkable, deeply moving act of homage Isa Milman has accomplished: a long quest to rescue stories of relatives enduring war-time atrocity from oblivion; a Kaddish performed through personal on-site practice and writing. With candour, humility, and courage, she travels in space and time through this 'scarred landscape,' calling upon imaginative thought experiments to supplement the spare horrifying facts. *Afterlight* is a telling reminder that atrocity thrives in the dark and must be unearthed, whatever the anguish, in order to be overcome."

DON MCKAY Governor General's Award–winning poet

"Marrying dogged research with sharp emotional insight, and storytelling both intimate and poetic, Isa Milman reassembles her brutalized family tree. With palpable love, unflinching horror, and unexpected joy, she reclaims and reimagines the almost unutterable memories that her mother held in silence until just before her death. Meanwhile, Milman gives voice to so many children of the European Jewish diaspora, as she moves toward her own peace with the land that bore and then cast out and swallowed her ancestors."

NAOMI K. LEWIS award-winning author of *Tiny Lights for Travellers*

"In this beautifully written and evocative memoir, Isa Milman takes us with her on a trip back to her ancestral home in what is today Ukraine but was once Poland, as she searches for the writings of her aunt, her mother's twin sister, who was one of the several million victims of the Holocaust. In chapters that alternate between past and present, Milman suggests how the afterlight of historical tragedies can both illuminate and complicate the present."

GOLDIE MORGENTALER professor of English at the University of Lethbridge and award-winning translator from Yiddish to English of the work of Chava Rosenfarb

"In search of a family narrative shattered by war, displacement, and genocide, Isa Milman traverses the past and present in Poland and Ukraine, Israel and Canada, to weave a memoir of profound loss and great love. Time and again, *Afterlight* pierces through darkness and leads, at last, to acceptance, recovery, and hope."

RUTH PANOFSKY poet and author of *Radiant Shards: Hoda's North End Poems*

"Isa Milman's *Afterlight* is as close to a living history as one can come. There is a quality of lucid dreaming in this memoir. Told with a poet's exquisite attention to detail, it is a work of exhumation—a bringing to light that which has always been with us."

EVE JOSEPH author of *In the Slender Margin: The Intimate Strangeness of Death and Dying*

"Isa Milman's *Afterlight* is an absolutely riveting memoir. From her parents' survival in a Siberian gulag to her own investigation of the scarred landscape of Eastern Europe, the author portrays a deeply moving journey across time and space as she searches for traces of history, including her aunt's lost poetry, and explores the meaning of home in the aftermath of the Shoah."

HELGA THORSON associate professor of Germanic and Slavic Studies at the University of Victoria and co-founder of the I-witness Holocaust Field School

"*Afterlight* is a powerful journey. By going to Poland, where her Jewish family was torn apart by war, Isa Milman invests her story with potent force. We are taken into the frozen Siberian gulag; we escape Stalingrad just before the Germans arrive. Compelling and poignant, *Afterlight* is a truly luminous book."

ANNE SIMPSON author of *Speechless*, winner of the Thomas Raddall Atlantic Fiction Award

"Isa Milman brings an artist's eye, a love of the music of language, and a ferocious tenacity to her quest for her family's lost ones, for the survivors, for herself. As the still unfathomable atrocities of the Holocaust retreat from living memory, her story glows in the afterlight of history and memory, deeply personal and ultimately profound."

DIANA WICHTEL award-winning author of *Driving to Treblinka: A Long Search for a Lost Father*

"In *Afterlight*, Isa Milman tells a timely personal narrative of travel and discovery, which is entangled in the twentieth-century calamity of the destruction of Jewish life in eastern Europe. Milman provides a fresh and thoughtful reconsideration of postwar Polish Jewish identity. 'Was I not free,' she wonders, as she seeks out her ancestral story, 'to adjust my own opinions without breaking the codes I'd been brought up with?'"

NORMAN RAVVIN author of *The Girl Who Stole Everything* and *A House of Words: Jewish Writing, Identity, and Memory*

"Isa Milman's powerful book takes her readers on a voyage of self-discovery through the landscapes of Eastern Europe—and Jewish memory. A story of real people and events, *Afterlight* reads like a mystery novel that you cannot put down until the very last page. It will have a major impact."

SERHY YEKELCHYK professor of Slavic Studies and History at the University of Victoria and the author of *Ukraine: What Everyone Needs to Know*

"Combining the threads of memory, history, and imagination with a strong fabric of family stories and research embroidered with recovered maps and artifacts, Isa Milman recreates her Jewish family's tragic fate during the horrific events of wartime Poland. *Afterlight* is a beautiful, haunting memoir that speaks of both devastating pain and abiding love."

LYNNE VAN LUVEN professor emerita, Department of Writing, University of Victoria

Afterlight

Afterlight

IN SEARCH OF POETRY,
HISTORY, AND HOME

ISA MILMAN

Heritage House Publishing Company Ltd.
heritagehouse.ca

Cataloguing information available from Library and Archives Canada

978-1-77203-383-0 (pbk)
978-1-77203-384-7 (ebook)

Edited by Renée Layberry
Cover design by Setareh Ashrafologhalai
Interior book design by Jacqui Thomas
Cover photograph: Sabina and Basia Kramer, Warsaw (Praga), Poland, *circa* 1937 (family collection); background image: iStock.com/duncan1890
Interior photos are from the author's family collection, unless otherwise noted.
Maps by Joe Castiglione

The interior of this book was produced on 100% post-consumer paper, processed chlorine free and printed with vegetable-based inks.

Heritage House gratefully acknowledges that the land on which we live and work is within the traditional territories of the Lkwungen (Esquimalt and Songhees), Malahat, Pacheedaht, Scia'new, T'Sou-ke, and W̱SÁNEĆ (Pauquachin, Tsartlip, Tsawout, Tseycum) Peoples.

We acknowledge the financial support of the Government of Canada through the Canada Book Fund (CBF) and the Canada Council for the Arts, and the Province of British Columbia through the British Columbia Arts Council and the Book Publishing Tax Credit.

25 24 23 22 21 1 2 3 4 5

Printed in Canada

For my children, and theirs
and
For Robert Brooke Naylor McConnell
1942–2019
in loving memory

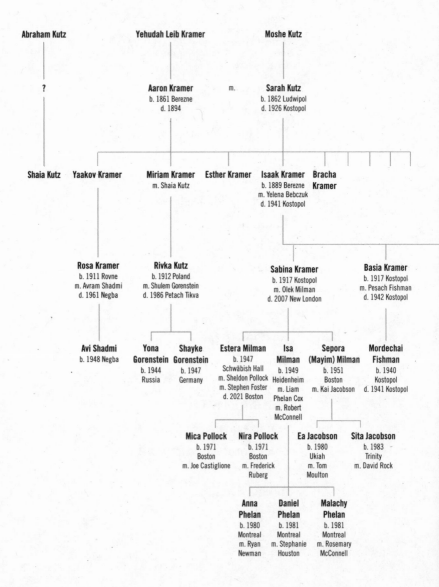

KRAMER-KUTZ-BEBCZUK

FAMILY TREE

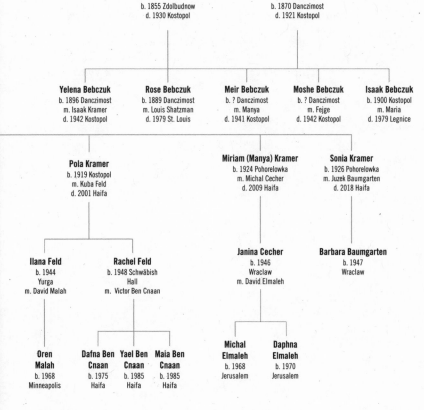

Mordechai Bebczuk
b. 1855 Zdolbudnow
d. 1930 Kostopol

m.

Miriam Roitburt
b. 1870 Danczimost
d. 1921 Kostopol

Yelena Bebczuk
b. 1896 Danczimost
m. Isaak Kramer
d. 1942 Kostopol

Rose Bebczuk
b. 1889 Danczimost
m. Louis Shatzman
d. 1979 St. Louis

Meir Bebczuk
b. ? Danczimost
m. Manya
d. 1941 Kostopol

Moshe Bebczuk
b. ? Danczimost
m. Fejge
d. 1942 Kostopol

Isaak Bebczuk
b. 1900 Kostopol
m. Maria
d. 1979 Legnice

Pola Kramer
b. 1919 Kostopol
m. Kuba Feld
d. 2001 Haifa

Miriam (Manya) Kramer
b. 1924 Pohorelowka
m. Michal Cecher
d. 2009 Haifa

Sonia Kramer
b. 1926 Pohorelowka
m. Juzek Baumgarten
d. 2018 Haifa

Ilana Feld
b. 1944
Yurga
m. David Malah

Rachel Feld
b. 1948 Schwäbish
Hall
m. Victor Ben Cnaan

Janina Cecher
b. 1946
Wraclaw
m. David Elmaleh

Barbara Baumgarten
b. 1947
Wraclaw

Oren Malah
b. 1968
Minneapolis

Dafna Ben Cnaan
b. 1975
Haifa

Yael Ben Cnaan
b. 1985
Haifa

Maia Ben Cnaan
b. 1985
Haifa

Michal Elmaleh
b. 1968
Jerusalem

Daphna Elmaleh
b. 1970
Jerusalem

That your search goes on for something you lost—a name,

A family album that fell from its own small matter

Into another, a piece of the dark that might have been yours ...

MARK STRAND

Introduction

A FTERLIGHT IS AN UNCOMMON WORD that refers to the light visible in the sky after sunset, or to a look back in time, a retrospect. When this word arose unexpectedly, as I was searching for another, I knew at once that it was the perfect title for my memoir.

This is a work deeply rooted in the facts of the history that I tell, but it's an exploration of imagination, too, as I create scenes where I clearly was not present. It's as close to the truth as I could come, given the erasures of history that I encountered during the journey I describe here, and due to the nature of memory itself. I've made every effort to respect the stories and opinions of the people who appear in these pages. Any errors or distortions I've made inadvertently are entirely my own.

The places and people in this book have many names, depending on where the geopolitical and cultural borders are located at the time being described. For example, the city is Równe, in Polish, while Jews called it Rovne; today it is Rivne, in Ukraine. My father was Eljasz in Polish, Elya in

Yiddish; my mother always called him Olek. In America he became Elliot.

To simplify matters, I use common English spellings for place names like Warsaw and Moscow, and I spell smaller cities and towns the way my parents would have done in their time. If a person's name is changed, the original appears in parentheses, when not obvious in the text. Occasionally Yiddish, Hebrew, and Polish words make their appearance; their definitions are provided in the text or in the endnotes, along with other supporting information to assist the reader. I apologize for any undue confusion, but the story I tell is of times and places still tangled and fraught with unfinished business; confusion and bewilderment are its warp and weft.

I began this book in 2013, and I finished it in 2019. As I write this introduction in 2021, it is with a heavy heart. Polish courts now punish historians who write unwelcome narratives about the Holocaust as it occurred in Poland. I sincerely hope my family's story will be received for what it is: another testament about what happened, which cannot be supressed.

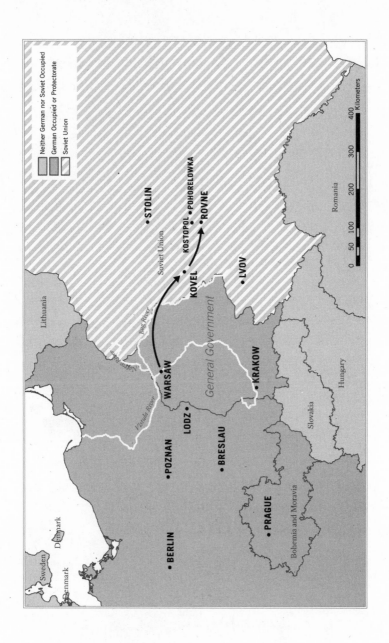

Sabina's escape from Warsaw to Kostopol, late fall, 1939.[1]

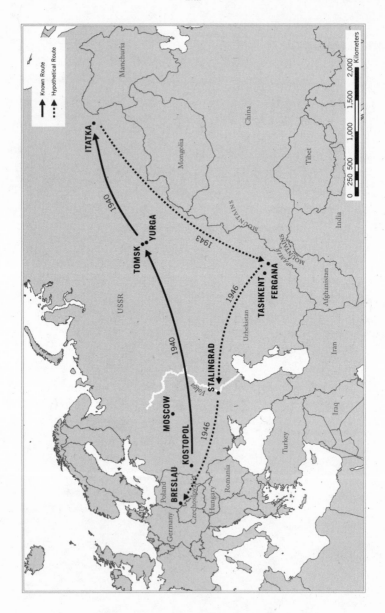

Sabina and Olek Milman's deportation to Siberia,
relocation to Uzbekistan, and repatriation to Poland, 1940–1946.[2]

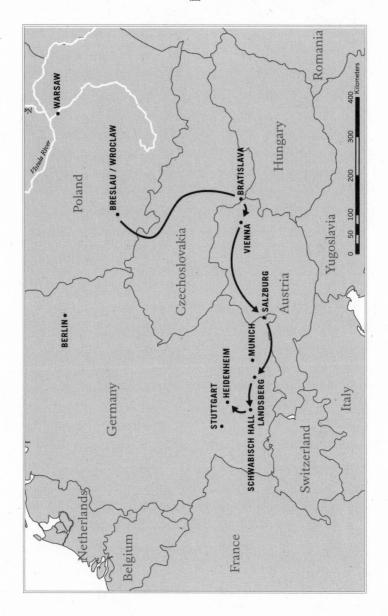

Flight from Poland to US zone in Germany, 1946–1950.[3]

1

Opening the Box of History

2013

THE DAY AFTER OUR MOTHER was expected to die, when all of us gathered in New London, Connecticut, heavy with grief, to say goodbye, she had a change of heart and woke up. She'd heard her great-granddaughter Elea calling *Bobie, Bobie*, and her three-year-old voice was too compelling to ignore. With pillows propped behind her head, her pale face framed by silver-white hair, our eighty-nine-year-old mother began to tell a story that my sisters and I had never heard in the sixty years we'd known her. In a voice that took on a rushing urgency, for she knew she didn't have much time left, she let go of restraint, while I sat at the foot of her bed with pen and paper, madly trying to capture her words.

The story she told was about her twin sister, Basia. She hardly ever spoke of her twin, a published poet, who was killed during the war. The details of her murder, along with almost all of our extended family, were so horrible that our mother withheld them from us for most of our lives, or at least tried to hold them back. But in her newly awakened state, just steps away from the threshold to the next world, my mother returned with a story of her childhood with Basia. She told of her twin's brilliance, her love of poetry and history, and her desire to write a book when she was only fifteen.

I watched the colour return to my mother's cheeks as she explained how Basia was keen to write about Moscow. Her tutor was a Russian Orthodox priest from their village, who had been defrocked and forced to move away because he'd had an affair, yet he remained a close friend of my grandparents. He invited Basia to make use of his library, his knowledge, and offered to take her in to live with his family so she could fulfill her dream. The big surprise was that our grandparents agreed to this, and allowed Basia to live with Bat'ko Ivano in a faraway village for almost a year. Somehow they managed to keep it a secret because it would have been a scandal should the truth become known.

My mother gave us an unexpected glimpse of her family life in a tiny village in Polish Ukraine, and startled us with her unbroken bond with her twin, who had been dead for sixty-five years. (Maybe Basia's spirit prodded her while she prepared to leave her body and finally join her in the next world.) As my mother spoke, I was jostled by bewilderment. I never imagined such warm relations between the Kramer family and their friends in the village of Pohorelowka. We'd always heard a different narrative, of the nightmare of Jewish sacrifice at the hands of neighbours and compatriots. So maybe, in her dramatic return from the dead, our mother recognized her need to add more nuance to the truth of her pre-war experience, in that there were many positive, special memories, too. I can still hear her voice, rising in excitement, saying *Isa, write this down, this should be your next book!*

Those papers where I'd jotted down my mother's words that day in the hospital sat on my desk for years. My grief over her death six months later, in April 2007, marked a profound wound that took ages to heal. Nothing prepared me for the anguish of losing her. At first I focused on poetry to recount the devastation I felt. I read works of poets that inspired me, grabbed a line that was compelling, and used it—a haunting phrase to propel me into my own text; the resulting poems became my next book. Additionally, fibres assumed greater importance to me. I'd always loved piecing fabrics together, sewing quilts, knitting sweaters for babies and friends, and joining scraps of paper and cloth—torn and broken bits that had no business going together yet pulsed into unexpected coherence and beauty. And so I lost myself in quilting and collage. Gradually, the tightness surrounding my heart softened, and I returned to living with more comfort.

As I got on with all the demands of my life, my mother's exhortation that I write this story would come back to me, but I kept saying *not yet*. The seed had been planted, but all the conditions necessary for germination were absent. I needed to build up my emotional stamina so I could support the weight I would have to carry in telling my mother's story. But her voice was gently persistent. I had written many family stories in my three books of poetry, but they were cut-outs, more like pictures thrown into a box, waiting to be organized into an album. Could I possibly compose the book my mother had urged me to write?

One summer morning, my husband Robbie was downstairs, waiting for me to get ready to leave for a trip we'd planned. I pulled out the dusty cardboard box that had been sitting in the back of my closet just as he called out, "Are you coming?" Then I grabbed my bag, tucked the box under my arm, and ran downstairs. I honestly didn't know all that was inside the box, but I knew I had to take it with me.

We were going up to the Cluxewe River, on the northern edge of Vancouver Island, for a week, with buddies from his fishing club. I had long days ahead of me as a fisherman's wife and could only spend so much time on the log-strewn beach. Fortunately we'd snagged one of the few cabins for rent, so while Robbie was fishing for salmon, I would have time to myself. Fishing here was my husband's idea of paradise, when every other year the run of tens of thousands of silvery pinks, thrashing their way from salt water to sweet, was the stuff of miracles. Their migration had to be witnessed to be believed; one couldn't help but marvel at the sight of the salmon transformed from silver to blood red, their backs having grown humps to better swim upriver. Who knows, I thought, immersion in nature's majesty would do me good.

In the morning, I cracked the window open to let in the smell of the ocean, only steps away. Little brown birds flitted and chirped in the salal bushes surrounding the cabin. Fishermen in their waders stood half submerged in the frothy waves, their lines pulled taut by hungry salmon. Everything around me pulsed with energy as I opened the cardboard flaps of the little box I'd impulsively brought. Right on top sat a manila envelope that I'd labelled *DP camp stuff* some fifteen years before. It was full of documents that I hadn't had the heart to examine at that time, a few months after my father had died.

Now I reached into the manila envelope and pulled out a black marbled notebook, the kind that school children used for compositions fifty years ago or more. Beneath the notebook were a variety of loose pages—deeply creased official-looking documents that almost fell apart when I unfolded them, and a few hand-scribbled scraps of paper. Before me was a clamour of languages: Polish, German, Russian, Yiddish, Hebrew, and English; I was only proficient in two, English and Hebrew. The rest of the box was filled with childhood souvenirs, old pictures, and some pages of notes about family that I'd written during conversations with my mother. It was a small capsule of history that I'd gathered up to carry home.

Among the objects was a sepia photo of my mother, who must have been about fifteen when the portrait was taken. Her dark eyes smoulder; her nose is delicate, slightly upturned;

her lips are not smiling nor are they tightly drawn, they're simply full and soft, like her whole round face—a softness hardly seen in today's pictures. She is so clearly a beauty, but there's nothing in her gaze that indicates such knowledge.

I knew a few things about my mother's early life, even before this portrait was taken. She was about five years old when her father bought the flour mill in the village of Pohorelowka, and the family moved there from the town of Kostopol, twenty-seven kilometres away. They were a family of five then, with their twins Sabina and Basia, and younger daughter Pola. It was in Pohorelowka where Manya and Sonia, their youngest daughters, were born. My mother had told me that the Kramers were not terribly religious, more outward looking in orientation, but deeply attached to their Jewish roots. They spoke Polish at home, not Yiddish, which I found surprising. They were far from wealthy, but they managed to live from the flax they grew in their fields, the flour they milled, and the produce of their kitchen garden. They had a couple of cows and chickens. It was a true country life that my mother loved.

In Pohorelowka, the five sisters were educated by tutors because there was no public school. By the time they were ten, Sabina and Basia were already fluent in a number of languages. Their younger sisters followed quickly in their footsteps. They learned Russian from the priest Bat'ko Ivano, while his daughter taught them German. They spoke Polish and understood Ukrainian, and were initiated into Hebrew through prayers. Although they didn't hear much Yiddish around them (there were only three Jewish families in Pohorelowka), they learned to read it and write it, as it was written in the same characters as Hebrew. Orchestrating all their lessons was their mother Yelena, the first woman of her family to graduate from *gymnazium*—an enormous accomplishment, because Jewish women were mostly barred from education back then.

Everything changed when the mill burned down under suspicious circumstances sometime around 1930. Whatever prosperity the family enjoyed vanished overnight. They tried to survive in the village, but with no income it became impossible. At the same time, the sisters were in need of more formal education, which was not to be found in the peasant farming country where they resided, so the family moved back to Kostopol. It was a town of about ten thousand people—a metropolis compared to the five hundred villagers of Pohorelowka. They rented a tiny apartment in the poorest, Jewish section of town, while Isaak, their father, struggled to find work.

In the summer of 1933, the year Hitler came to power, Sabina and Basia were sixteen. That was the year my mother met Olek, my father. They met at the Zionist youth training camp, or *hachshara*, that was based in her uncle Meir's house. Meir offered four rooms of his large house in Kostopol, so that Jewish youth could prepare for a life in Palestine. Zionist longing had seized much of the youth of Poland in these years, because antisemitism was intensifying and life for Jews became more and more grim.[1] My mother was in the kitchen kneading bread when she saw two young men approach the kitchen door. They'd come from Stolin, a town about sixty kilometres away, so they could begin their training, which was a prerequisite for making *aliyah*—a Hebrew term meaning to elevate oneself by going up to the Holy Land. My mother was smitten by my father's handsome face, and excited that his passion for Zionism matched her own. The talk at the *hachshara* that day was about all the hurdles they'd have to overcome in order to leave Europe for Palestine. It was becoming clear that there was no future in Poland for young people like them.

When my mother got home that evening she found Basia sitting in the only comfortable chair in their kitchen. She told her about the two young men she'd just met. One was my father, Olek; the other was his best friend, Pesach. Basia wasn't very interested. She was engrossed in the poem she was writing and barely looked up. My mother remembered her response: "I don't need to meet any *smarcule*," which meant a snot-nosed know-it-all. Someone too young, too stupid, too immature for her to bother with. My mother informed Basia that the men were in fact three years older and perhaps had some life experience that she and her sister didn't have. She didn't remember Basia's reaction, but her rebuttal was enough to make her twin curious, so the next time she went to the *hachshara* at Uncle Meir's, Basia decided to come along.

After that summer, Sabina and Basia returned to their studies. My mother was attending a Russian language *gymnazium* in Rovne, the largest city in their region, and home to a significant Jewish population. I have no knowledge of how much Basia advanced in writing her book about Moscow. Their father had never recovered from the loss of the mill and could barely scratch out a living to support his family. Yelena's three brothers in Kostopol offered no help, while her only sister, Rose, was long-gone to America and had five children of her own. Much as she would have liked, she was unable to help. What's clear is that the family lived in poverty, even with the daughters producing fine embroideries and mending clothes to add a few zlotys to the family coffers. Their greatest wealth was their intelligence and their books. When searching for something good to read, people would say *go to the Kramerovkes.*

By 1936, Sabina and Basia were both living in Warsaw, about five hundred kilometres west of Kostopol. With a population of over a million people, including more than 350,000 Jews, Warsaw was a magnet for many who lived in the economically depressed towns and cities of provincial Poland. The sisters' goal was to earn enough money to live, and find a way to pay for university studies. Their ties to the two young men they'd met at Uncle Meir's had only grown stronger in the three years that had passed. Basia's initial disdain had flamed into a great passion, and she and Pesach would be wed by the time they moved to Warsaw. It took longer for Sabina and Olek.

My mother worked as a seamstress before she married. She described her long days hunched over with needle and thread, creating finely embroidered lingerie, just to earn a few zlotys. But God forbid that the elegant Warsaw ladies discover that their intimates were created by Jewish hands—her Polish boss made it plain to her that that was how it had to be. He appreciated her, perhaps a little more than she could stomach, so she didn't stay with this boss for very long.

While the twin sisters had moved to Warsaw, Pesach and Olek had been drafted into the Polish army and would come to Warsaw on leave. I'm not sure if my mother was convinced that Olek was the man for her; she told me that her mother didn't think so. My grandmother Yelena's first impression of him was of a dandy. The youngest of three, from an Orthodox family, he wasn't big on living a pious, observant life. He liked dressing up in fine clothes, going for rides in fancy cars, and hanging out on the riverbank with young women. Photos I'd taken out of the memory box were proof of my father's youthful inclinations—although how these photos survived the war is a complete mystery.

My mother had other suitors, she told me. One was a medical student; perhaps his name was Sikorski. (I'm not sure, but since it popped into my head, I'll call him Sikorski.) From time to time he'd come over to the sisters' apartment in Praga, the poorer district across the Vistula from the fashionable side of Warsaw. Once Sikorski had forgotten his jacket, left hanging on the back of a chair. My mother made it very clear to me that he hadn't spent the night there, God forbid. But the next day Olek dropped in for one of his infrequent visits, and when he saw Sikorski's jacket there he grew flushed, suspicious, distressed. Perhaps the perceived competition was the trigger that made him express his desire for her and ask her to marry him.

"Your father was very handsome. It was hard for me to resist him," my mother always said. I can appreciate this. His portrait, in his Polish army uniform, shows his dark brown eyes looking out intensely from a clean-shaven, smooth, and unblemished face; his lips, neither thin nor fat, appear lovely, like the rest of him. I'm struck by the beauty of his ears, how they were a perfect size and shape, and entirely visible given his army-cropped hair, which crowned his forehead in a widow's peak.

They didn't have much of a wedding. I don't know what she wore, what flowers she carried, the food they served, who they invited as guests. Perhaps no one at all. There are no pictures. All I know is that Yelena made the long journey to Warsaw from Kostopol to bear witness. Sabina and Olek exchanged their vows and signed their *ketubah* (marriage contract) before a local rabbi. It was May 5, 1938.

I couldn't stop thinking about my parents, newly wed in Warsaw. They would only have a year of marriage before the war began. I know they were keen on going to university, but they couldn't make it happen. Finding work was difficult, even in a large cosmopolitan city like Warsaw. And on top of the general economic depression, the poisonous churn of antisemitism escalated daily.

I remembered a story my mother told of the direct hatred she experienced in Warsaw. She was on a crowded tram on her way to work, squished between people she didn't care to be jostled up against. My mother brushed the hair out of her eyes. The rest of her dark brown hair was gathered in a long braid down her back. In my mind, I don't see her wearing lipstick; she couldn't afford it, and she didn't need it—her lips were naturally rose. Steeling herself for an uncomfortable ride as she stood pressed against the tram's doors, her white blouse and dark pleated skirt losing all their crispness in the sweaty confines, beads of perspiration running down her forehead, she overheard a couple of well-dressed, educated men loudly ranting about ugly, cheating, conniving Jews with piles of money, destroying the Polish body politic. She couldn't hold back her fury. "While Jews work hard for their few zlotys, all Warsaw staggers around drunk every Saturday night," she hissed, or something to that effect. I'm sure it sounded much better in Polish, and she obviously hit the mark. The men, who towered over her five-foot-four frame, shoved her as they moved to step off the tram, slamming the doors on her fingers so hard they nearly broke. I hear her yelping in pain, see her bringing her crumpled fingers to her lips, blowing on them as if she could revive them and cool them with her breath, while the tram was eerily silent. No one came to her aid. No one commented or comforted her.

My father, trained as a machinist, found work repairing radios. He got his vocational training at the *tarbut* school in Stolin, where, along with the technical and secular classes, he continued his demanding Jewish education. He was adept with his hands and loved getting into things and fixing them. It became clear to my mother that she needed a practical pro-fession. Given her nature of taking charge and looking after things, she decided to become a nurse. Her training was at a large Warsaw hospital; when she completed it, a year or so before the war, she began working in a dispensary for new mothers who were ill and needed help to nurse their infants. She made batches of formula and ran around feeding squall-ing babies.

My parents moved farther out of Warsaw, from Praga to the little town of Ząbki, (pronounced *Zombki*) about seven kilometres away. Basia and Pesach moved with them, and each couple had their own apartment. Making a living was a constant struggle. My mother described how they had to choose to forgo dinner if they wanted to go to a movie, because they couldn't afford to do both. About Basia and

Pesach's life together, I know nothing. I'm guessing that their circumstances were similar to my parents'.

There is only one photo of the twin sisters from this time in Warsaw. In the photo, dated 1937, Sabina and Basia are outdoors, standing by a higgledy-piggledy wooden gate. I wish I knew more about the occasion that prompted this photo, or who took the picture. Did Pesach have a camera? Were they going to a gathering with friends, or did a friend who had a camera drop by and suggest an impromptu picture? My mother never filled me in, except to say it was taken in Praga. I look at them, young women getting on with life as best they can, while the earth trembles beneath their feet. What are they thinking, how are they managing?

I could hardly imagine how difficult it was for them in this period of their lives. And this was the good time, the before-the-war time. Living such a protected, privileged life in North America, I have never been subjected to the kind of hatred and brutality that my family experienced. I know that there was, and continues to be, plenty of racism and prejudice here too—we are far from immune—but I have mercifully escaped the sting and rage of it, its murderous extremes.

I sat there in the cabin, at the Kwakiutl fishing camp, completely lost in time, as the press of all the invisible and unknowable mysteries bore down on me. The more I questioned, the greater the weight I staggered under. I felt a strange sensation akin to lucid dreaming, aware of being pulled irresistibly into the past, while knowing this would now be my future. And as I questioned my readiness to embark upon a journey that would be filled with much sorrow, I was startled by the kitchen door swinging open. There stood my husband, his face lit by euphoria, with a couple of silvery salmon dangling from each hand.

2

The Longing for Poland

2013

S O I BEGAN THINKING ABOUT going to Poland—very gingerly thinking about it, because it terrified me. In my entire life, I never heard one kind word about Poland from my mother or my father when they spoke about their past. Going to Poland was for other people to do, and when they spoke of it, I would feel a discomfort that bordered on shock. I was even fearful of voicing my thoughts to my ever-encouraging and travel-loving husband. Shortly after the seed of this idea lodged itself in my brain, I learned about a conference being planned in Poland, about Jewish-Canadian-Polish cultural connections. It would take place at the University of Łódź in April 2014. I wondered if, in an academic conference like this, there was room for a poet like me; I had written a book about Jews who had left Ashkenaz[1] to farm in the Canadian prairies at the turn of the twentieth century, and I questioned whether that subject would fit the conference's theme.

I pulled out my copy of *Prairie Kaddish* and started leafing through the pages, considering which poems might kindle the interest of an audience discussing the history of Jewish flight from European oppression to a country just beginning to cohere.[2] I stopped at "A Few Restrictions Regarding the Jews of Romania, 1885–1900," a list poem that's constructed like a wall on the page, a repetition of devastating momentum, beginning with a restriction forbidding Jews to be peddlers/a restriction forbidding Jews from elementary school—or any school, or creating their own schools; to being barred from all vocations, professions, ownership of business or property, barred from being a patient in a hospital, barred from practising medicine, and finally, from simply existing as a citizen. I remembered how struck I was by the early date—I had thought prohibitions like these originated with the Nazis, but this was fifty years before they rose to power. Life for Jews in Ashkenaz was often oppressive, but in late-nineteenth-century Eastern Europe it became a nightmare, with thousands of Jews murdered in raging pogroms.

Thus began the great immigration of Ashkenazi Jews to North America. Most went to the United States, but Canada invited immigrants too, to settle the west, offering huge chunks of land for a pittance. Somewhat reluctantly, Jews were included on the invitation list. Farm colonies were established in the Prairies, where most transplanted Europeans settled, dotting the map with little pockets of ethnicities from the old countries, as people tried to stick together to survive in rugged land that had never felt a plow.

Reviewing all this history in poetry reminded me of the epiphany I experienced while standing in the Lipton Hebrew Cemetery in Saskatchewan. *As if I heard a drum/struck by an invisible hand,* I realized where I belonged in the great tapestry of Jewish suffering and regeneration; I too had made the ocean crossing, ultimately settling in Canada, after the near extermination of my people, which included so many of my closest family whom I wanted to recover from the dust.

I plucked up my courage and sent an email to the conference organizers, inquiring if I should submit an abstract.

IN MY STUDY, I HEARD the door open downstairs and Robbie kicking off his shoes. I called down my usual greeting: "Hi, honey, how was your meeting?" He'd just come home from his Tuesday Golden Rods and Reels club, which meant that he was most likely more cheerful than usual. "Come upstairs," I invited.

"Sweetheart," I said when he entered the study, "you know how I've been thinking about Poland since I opened the box up in Cluxewe?"

"Yesss," he drawled as he sat down on the couch, waiting for my next sentence.

"Well, I just heard from Concordia, and they'd love for me to send a proposal for the conference in Poland."

"So, yes, you are thinking about it and you want to go, I'm gathering."

"I am thinking about it, and as you know, it's a big deal for me to even think about, so when I picture it, I see us going there together." With a sigh of relief at having got this far, I watched my husband's face, his eyes closed, lips pursed as he considered. After a long silence, he spoke.

"Honey, I know it will be an emotional experience for you, but if you really must go, I won't argue with you or try to dissuade you, even though I don't think it's a good idea. But this time you're on your own. I just don't see myself going to Poland. There's nothing that attracts me there, not even the food."

Well, at least he isn't opposed to me going, I thought, even though I was disappointed that he wouldn't accompany me. But after all, this was my story, and I couldn't expect him to take it up and make it his as well, though he loved my mother dearly and she loved him back. She came to believe that even if he was not a Jewish husband, he was the finest husband I could ever have found. Growing up, any boy who was not a Jew was off-limits. Of course we knew the reason why. Being the miraculous offspring of the few who'd survived the near annihilation of our tribe, we were the living embodiments of the future of Jewish life, so it was our mission to carry it on. This has been true for every generation since the destruction of the Second Temple.

How could I expect my husband to really understand the mission I was embarking on? I felt regret that he didn't wish to come, but what I felt more was my fear and lack of confidence of going alone to the place where all the horror had occurred. To set foot on that desecrated earth. To walk the streets of Warsaw where my mother and father, Basia and Pesach, had lived. My curiosity kept pushing me forward, but at the same time I felt a tremendous vulnerability.

Reading my daily dose of Internet Jewish news, I learned of the new museum in Warsaw, a museum dedicated to the history of Polish Jews. A thousand-year history would be showcased in a beautiful building at the edge of the Warsaw ghetto, on the site where Jews were forced onto trains for shipment to Treblinka and other death factories. The idea of reframing this history, to stretch the story back one thousand years, rather than focusing only on the time just before the Holocaust and its immediate aftermath excited me, as if the museum were a metaphor for my personal quest. I wanted to dig into that soil and unearth not just Basia's published poems that were lost, but the lost history of our family. How far back in those thousand years did we go? I had every reason to believe we went as far back as was possible to go in Jewish time, but I could never find any evidence past personal memory, my mother's memory. I felt as though the edge of memory was a sheer cliff where everything was hurled, shattered and irretrievable. We had a past and I was determined to uncover it, despite all attempts to eradicate it. What about my parents' marriage certificate? Could I find such a simple marker of their life in Warsaw, or anything tangible that proved their existence there?

The conference seemed to be the soft, comfortable entry to Poland that I was hoping for. What's more, I imagined that through the organizers, I could find people sympathetic to my project and connections to translators and researchers essential to my search. The last thing I wanted was to arrive in Poland and feel isolated and shunned, particularly because I was a Jew, given that antisemitism was far from extinguished in the land of my ancestors.

I began talking about Poland with my writer friends, telling of my search for family history, and Basia's lost poems. Sniffing out the ingredients for a good story, they urged me to go. Their encouragement became an earworm, drumming along with my heartbeat, despite my attempts to switch channels when my misgivings and fear took over.

———

I APPROACHED ALAN RUTKOWSKI, A friend from the synagogue, and asked if he could help me find the journal in which Basia's poems were published. Sonia, my mother's youngest sister, had written its name in my notebook when we were visiting in Israel, back in 2000. "It was in *Płomyk Alfa*," she insisted, "a student's journal or magazine."

"No, Sonia, it was in *Nasz Przegląd*," my mother countered, but with a hint of doubt in her voice.

As they argued about it, I sat there, incredulous that I'd been looking in the wrong place. In the nineties, I had searched the microfiche of *Nasz Przegląd*, a Warsaw Jewish daily, at the New York Public Library. With much hope, I'd scanned the pages for Basia's name, and the shape of something that resembled a poem, because I couldn't understand a word of Polish. There were very few identifiable poems to be found in those pages in any case, so I'd given up. When Sonia offered me this new lead, I was reluctant to take it on. So I tucked away the little notebook and it sat in a box on my desk, waiting for the day when I would be ready to pick it up.

Alan was keen to try; he said that it was just the kind of thing that got him going. Being a retired librarian of Slavic languages at the University of Alberta, he seemed the perfect angel of help. He even taught me how to pronounce the name of the journal—it sounds like *Pwomyk Alfa*. It's that 'ł' with the diagonal slash that turns the sound into a 'w.' Just like Łodz, which is pronounced *Woodj*, he explained.

A few days later, Alan phoned with a little miracle in the form of news: He'd located a children's magazine called *Płomyk*, which was published in Poland from the twenties to the nineties, and the New York Public Library had it on microfiche, but not the entire collection. The thirties were missing. "But I'm sure they would be in the Polish national archives," he said, which naturally made my heart jump. I was not expecting this at all. Alan promised to see if he could find the missing issues at another North American library, and get back to me.

"And what does *Płomyk* actually mean?" I remembered to ask.

"A little flame," he replied.

WHEN I GOT THE NEWS that my conference proposal had been accepted, I was excited and happy for a day, then felt down and negative when I realized there would be very few talks I would care to listen to, especially those heavily coded in the indecipherable academic-speak that drove me totally insane. All my ambivalence rose up and assaulted me. I thought I was crazy to even think about spending so much money to go to the conference. There were no granting agencies I could approach as an independent writer, unattached to an institution. In my discomfort, I decided I wouldn't go, and I felt a wave of relief. But not long after, I got the updated program: it advertised far more presentations that sounded interesting, and there would be people from all over Europe and Canada that I would like to meet and talk to. So I was thrust back into the possibility of going.

As I fidgeted, Robbie came up to my study and simply said, "Can I help?"

What a wise man I have for a husband. "If you are still thinking about it, then clearly it's too important for you to dismiss. So just decide that you will go."

Everything accelerated. I received an email from the conference organizer in Lodz, asking me how they should identify me in the program, as I didn't have a university affiliation; I wrote back saying that "writer and artist" would do, and apologized for keeping them waiting. I was working out a means of attending the conference, and now was certain that I would be going. I also asked if she or her colleagues could connect me with a guide and translator in Warsaw, for my research, and she said she'd be glad to help. So now it was official.

I HAD A LONG CONVERSATION with Malachy, the first of my three children that I told I was going to Poland.

"One of the worst antisemitic places on earth," he said, which startled me, as I didn't expect him to be paying such attention.

He told me about the world football championships in Poland and Ukraine not long before, and how British teams refused to attend because of the barbarity of the fans.

"More barbarous than British football fans?" I was skeptical.

He also said that the worst swear word you could utter in Poland was *zyd*.

"Like the 'n' word here?" I asked.

"No," he said. "It's much worse than that."

I remembered my terrifying train ride from Paris to Antwerp for the ferry to England, back in 1975, and how the drunken British football followers rattled the doors on my couchette so violently I was sure I wouldn't make it off in one piece. But Malachy was encouraging when I explained my intentions. I even fantasized travelling with him, my beautiful, sensitive, but often distant son who would be my companion and protector. We could have an unforgettable experience together, learning first-hand about our family origins. My son Daniel was also encouraging when I told him, and his wife Stephanie sent me an email to thank me for my Chanukah gift, with a photo of Daniel lighting the menorah I'd given them, and kind words of support about my latest project. At the time I didn't often hear from Stephanie, so her message was especially meaningful to receive.

When I spoke to my daughter Anna, she was busy and didn't have time for conversation, so we agreed to continue again soon. My sister Estera was somewhat taken aback by my news, while her daughter Mica wrote that her first reaction was that she should go too! That excited me, but I wasn't too surprised. It was Mica who joined me in the home video project to record my mother's story in Boston, in the summer of 1994. Unfortunately, Mica's schedule didn't permit her to join me, but we talked about travelling together another time. She said that she really wanted to go to Kostopol and Pohorelowka, where her Bobie spent her childhood. My younger sister Mayim, who has lived next door since our mother died, was shocked about my intentions, shaking her head and shuddering with near disgust at the idea of Poland. So that, in a nutshell, was the response of my immediate family.

I STARTED LOOKING INTO FLIGHTS to Poland and arranging an itinerary and places to stay. I looked up the Jewish Federation in Victoria with a faint hope that I could find some funding. Although there was no specific grant category that applied to me, the president suggested that I approach the Federation anyway. He said that if we send Jewish kids to summer camp, why shouldn't we support a Jewish writer of national recognition to work on her next book?

Before we knew it, December arrived, and given that it was the twenty-fifth anniversary of sharing our lives, Robbie and I booked a weekend getaway at a picturesque spot not far from Victoria. Perched high up a promontory on the wild Pacific, the resort was dotted with rustic cabins. Wooded trails laced the property, so guests could meander along the ridges, or have a seat on a bright red bench and gawk at the spectacular views. The main lodge, filled with comfortable armchairs where you could enjoy a robust fire by the stone fireplace, was famous for its excellent restaurant. Settling into our cabin overlooking the water, we pinched ourselves for all our good fortune.

That evening at dinner, we raised our glasses and sipped prosecco before our first course arrived.

"Sweetheart, I've been thinking," Robbie said, as his long fingers circled the glass.

"Yes, you've been thinking," I prompted, because his words were slow in coming.

"I've been thinking that I should come with you to Poland."

I sat there, dumbstruck, not really believing what I'd heard.

"I've been watching and listening as you prepare for this trip, and I think that doing it alone is a bit more than you should take on by yourself. I know that it will be emotional and could be overwhelming, and I want to make that experience easier for you to bear."

I don't recall what dishes we ordered for our exceptionally delicious meal, but what I shall never forget is the elation I felt when I heard Robbie's surprise announcement. For days after, I floated, imagining our journey together.

3

Outbreak

M Y MOTHER SPEAKS TO THE camera as she rocks in a Bentwood chair, telling the story of her epic escape from Warsaw.[1] She is almost eighty, an elegant woman in a chic chiffon dress, describing events that could have happened a week before. The immediacy of her experiences is so palpable.

"I was alone in Warsaw because Olek had gone to visit his mother back home in Stolin, five hundred kilometres away, a day before. No one knew when the war would begin, although everyone knew something terrible was coming. We knew it was only a matter of time before the Germans would attack Poland, but people continued to live their lives. No one had a crystal ball. How could my husband have known his simple decision to visit his mother would leave me struggling for three months to escape from Warsaw?"

The first of September was by all accounts a warm, brilliant blue-sky day. If autumn was in the air, it was a mere hint, a golden leaf hidden in calm green boughs—boughs that suddenly shook from the wind of airplanes dropping thunderous smoke and flame. Soon the city was burning, and terror reigned.[2]

I can hardly imagine the fear my mother felt that day, while everyone scrambled to find some safety. There were no clearly marked shelters; no one knew where to run, how to hide. Warsaw was remarkably unprepared for war; it didn't even sink in on this first day that this was it. The beginning of hell on earth.

My mother first says she was alone in Warsaw when the war broke out, but that's not exactly true. She was with Pesach and Rivka, his older sister, in Ząbki, the small town seven kilometres outside Warsaw where they lived. That summer of 1939, Basia and Pesach had returned to Kostopol, where Basia remained when Pesach came back to Ząbki at summer's end. Rivka's presence in Ząbki was unexpected. She had left for Palestine just weeks before, getting on a ship in Romania, but the British, who blocked virtually all Jewish immigration to Palestine, turned the ship back. So she washed up in Warsaw, not sure of what to do next.

"She was thirty-five, unmarried, and like an old woman, more like my mother's generation than my own," my mother says.

The three of them huddled in their apartment, Rivka pacing as though counting each step, wringing her hands when she wasn't washing them, as Pesach grew increasingly annoyed with her. My mother worried about how to prepare a meal when the cupboard was bare, and it was impossible to get groceries. Although September 1 was a terrible shock to them, the next two days were much worse. Warsaw was burning and everyone was panicking, trying to escape the city and run away to the east. All the roads and bridges were clogged with people, and anything that had wheels was dragged into service, piled with whatever could fit.

"By this time, Pesach was out of his mind. He was desperate to get back to Basia, so he decided to take his chances and escape on his own. He asked me to look after Rivka because he knew he would never be able to succeed if he had to take care of her. She was helpless in many ways."

I watch as she pulls on the hem of her dress, straightening and smoothing it perfectly below her knees. It strikes me for the first time, as she tells this part of the story, that Pesach abandoned her and burdened her with the care of his difficult sister so he could make it back to his wife.

"I decided to go into Warsaw to find some friends who might help us escape," my mother continues.

She was lucky, and managed to arrange with them to get a taxi and then go back to Ząbki and pick up Rivka. She couldn't leave her, even though she didn't understand what was wrong with her, why she walked so slowly, and always had to stop and wash her hands. They drove together in this taxi with some strangers to a village near a forest. There were about six of them who stayed in one household, where they were taken in by a local family. They dug potatoes, found a little milk. My mother helped bake bread, and she made a little sweater for the child who lived there. She did anything she could to help out. Among them was a young doctor from Lodz who was an exceptionally lovely man. One day, while out foraging, he was so excited to have found some cocoa. "We were in heaven. Who could imagine cocoa?"

I wondered how she found yarn to crochet a sweater. Maybe she sewed something from cloth. She was always so resourceful and energetic; she was twenty-two years old and very strong. "I grew up in a village," she reminds us, "so I was used to hard work." Nevertheless, it's difficult for me to put myself in her place without feeling panic. My mother and Rivka stayed in this house for about two weeks, but knew they couldn't stay indefinitely. They had no money because zlotys were no longer usable currency. Food was harder to scavenge.

"By this time we knew the Germans had taken over Poland. Soldiers came to the village and told us to go home, so that's what we did."

⁓

MY MOTHER AND RIVKA MADE their way back to Ząbki, on the northeast outskirts of Warsaw. The Germans had come from the west, their tanks and infantry quickly rolling over Poland's rippled terrain. Absent mountains or great bodies of water, it was no wonder that Poland had been ripe game for conquest over the centuries. The aerial bombing of strategic cities cemented Germany's success; although Poland's government was weak and ineffectual, its defence forces fought as best they could. But cavalry was no match for tanks and bombers, which were not plentiful in the Polish armed forces. Warsaw was the prize, and the Nazis, surprised by the city's resistance, were merciless as victory came within their grasp.

As my mother and Rivka rode toward Ząbki, they gasped at the destruction they witnessed. Many familiar buildings were now heaps of rubble. Bodies, some covered by blankets, rotted in the streets because they couldn't be buried. The stench in the air was inescapable.

"Rivka, no matter what, we have to make the best of it. We have no choice but to survive," my mother said, trying to shore up her own courage.

"Sabina, I'm not strong like you," was all Rivka could manage.

They held their breath as they approached my mother's apartment building and exhaled when they saw it still standing. Climbing the stairs, they heard unexpected sounds behind the door of my mother's apartment. She inserted her key and gingerly pushed open the door. Three German officers stood there facing them, apparently as surprised as my mother and Rivka were. One of the officers spoke.

"What are you doing here?" he asked.

Her heart beating loudly, my mother answered, *"Das ist meine Wohnung."* (Olga, Bat'ko Ivano's daughter, had taught her German as a girl in Pohorelowka, but never had she needed to use this language in her daily life until now.)

He glanced at the other officers and back to my mother.

He proposed an unusual arrangement: my mother and Rivka would be allowed to stay in the apartment during the day, while they were out, but the officers would sleep there at night. The women would have to find other accommodation. Fortunately, some friendly neighbours offered my mother and Rivka a place to sleep. As unexpected as it was, their arrangement worked, and the women didn't have to be out after the five o'clock curfew.

During this time, my mother got to know the officer in charge, whom she always referred to as "the kind one." I wonder how my mother and this officer had their conversations. Did they sit down and have cups of tea together? How did they have this connection, where they shared their pain at being separated from their spouses and their fears of what lay ahead? This was wartime. Amid all the horror and destruction, how was this friendship possible? It's so difficult for me to imagine this.

Their days developed a certain rhythm and included the blessing of adequate food supplied by the officers—there was hardly anything to buy and no money to buy it with. Their arrangement worked until the daughter of one of their neighbours, a beautiful young woman, attracted the attention of another of the German officers, and they started to go out together. As their romance blossomed, this beauty asked him, "Why are you staying in Sabina's apartment and giving them food? Don't you know she's a Jew?"

My mother tugs on the hem of her dress as she recalls this betrayal. "But the good officer, who was in charge, did nothing bad to us. On the contrary, he told us that the three of them would be leaving us in any case. They were being posted elsewhere."

Shortly after, they were shocked when thirty drunken German soldiers tried to get into their apartment. She and Rivka knew they could delay no longer, and had to get back to Kostopol. It was five hundred kilometres away, and like the whole region of Vohlyn, now in Russian hands.

Leaving Rivka with neighbours, my mother decided to walk the seven kilometres into Warsaw, to find friends who might help them escape. When she arrived at Most Kierbedzia, the bridge connecting Praga to Warsaw, she was startled to find it blocked. Stranded along with what looked like hundreds of others, there was no way she could get across. Curfew was approaching, and she knew she'd never get to shelter in time.

She was sitting there, literally shaking with fear, certain that her life would soon be over, when suddenly she heard someone call, "Frau Milman!" Startled, she turned to see her friend, the German officer.

"Can you help me?" she asked.

He glanced over his shoulder, checking to see if anyone was listening.

"What are you doing here? Where are you going?" It was late afternoon, and soon it would be dusk.

"I'm trying to get to my friends in Warsaw because we have no money and no food."

"You picked a terrible day to come," he chided.

"Why is the bridge blocked? I will never make it to my friends before the five o'clock curfew, and it's impossible for me to get back home in time."

He looked at his watch, he looked back at her face, then he looked around, exhaling hard.

"Just wait here. I'm not allowed to leave my post, but I'll see what I can do," he instructed, as he left her with some bread and a big piece of cheese.

It felt like hours had passed as she sat there shivering, when he finally returned with a paper permitting him to cross the bridge from Praga to Warsaw.

There were about a thousand people stopped at the entrances, watching as the German officer escorted my mother across the bridge. Just the two of them, walking alone, with all eyes glued to the spectacle.

"They must have thought I was a prostitute because why else would I be getting such special treatment?" my mother explains, blushing at the memory of this unforgettable moment. After a pause, she collects herself and continues. "He saved my life."

It turned out that the bridges of Warsaw were blocked because, unbeknownst to my mother, Hitler had come to town to review his troops as they triumphantly goose-stepped through the city. I find it surreal that seventy-five years after the fact I can sit in my study and watch a scene that's so iconographic it's almost a cliché. How many of these scenes have we all witnessed, short clips of history made into chunks of video, seen so often that they lose meaning because of their familiarity? The grainy black-and-white footage, the bewildered crowds, fear permeating the screen as if we could actually smell it, but the odour is now completely faded.

Off camera, my twenty-two-year-old mother is oblivious to this scene. She's starving and desperate, in a cold panic because she knows her life could soon be over, stuck on a bridge she needs to cross to get to the shelter of friends before curfew. But Hitler has come to feast on this great, vanquished city. On camera, his triumph is palpable, while Warsaw's people are dumb with dread; they believe the worst has already come, still unaware this is only the beginning.

But my mother had her angel of rescue, her German officer, whose name she never did remember. She wondered about him for the rest of her life, never believing he had survived the war. "He was too good a man," she always said.

Thus began my mother's second escape from Warsaw. It was October 5, 1939.

"After I crossed the bridge, I ran to my friends' place, and we made a plan," she tells me. They knew they had to get to the Russian side of the border and had little time to lose before the German vise locked tight around Warsaw. My mother spent the night at her friends' and returned to Ząbki the next day. She packed a rucksack with essentials and gave away everything else she had. "What could I take with me?" she says. Then she and Rivka waited for her friends who would come in a taxi to pick them up and drive them all to the border. But the taxi never came.

Worried and uncertain, my mother walked again to Warsaw to find out what happened to her friends. When she arrived at their apartment, across the street from the infamous Pawiak prison, she discovered they were gone.

"I was shocked. They wouldn't have run away without a good reason, I knew, but I thought that I was doomed."

Again she walked back to Ząbki, not knowing what to do next. Struggling for a solution, she suddenly remembered some business friends of her father and uncle who lived in Praga, and her meeting them when her Uncle Meir had visited during Passover a few months before. She pictured their home and recalled exactly where they lived—it was a clear message that entered her mind, telling her to go there.

Her father's friends were as good to my mother as she'd hoped. Like so many in Warsaw that October, their son was also planning to run away to the east, but he was delayed because his wife had just given birth and was unable to travel. By this time, they thought it prudent for him to take his four-year-old daughter and figure out how his wife and baby could follow them later. My mother was happy to snuggle the little girl on her lap, enveloped in her fur coat, her prized possession, as they rode in the taxi to Ząbki to pick up Rivka and aim for the Russian-controlled border, about one hundred kilometres away. As of September 17, when the Soviets had invaded from the east, Poland had completely disappeared from the map.

"*ACHTUNG!* STOP THE CAR," THE German soldier ordered. Leaning in through the driver's open window, his menacing face appeared to fill the entire frame.

"Get out," he snarled. "Take off your coat. Open that suitcase."

As my mother watched from her seat, hugging the little girl, the soldier tipped everything out on the half-frozen ground, kicking her little dresses with his polished boot. The father stood there, trembling from the cold and his fear that next he'd be forced to remove his shoes. My mother knew that meant he'd lose the dollars and gold jewellery he had hidden there. She could barely breathe as she waited for her turn. But the soldier had enough booty, and let the father, dressed only in a thin shirt, get back into the taxi. They drove away with as much calm as they could muster.

They were heading to the new no-man's land, where the Vistula, Narew, and Bug Rivers joined to form a sharp triangle. When Molotov and Ribbentrop had signed their pact back in August, they agreed that this geographic confluence was a perfect place to draw their dividing lines. By this time, hundreds of people had already reached this spot, all of them clamouring to cross to the side belonging to the power of lesser dread—the Russians.

It was chaos. It was snowing. Children were crying. Old people were dying. There was no shelter. No food. No place to sleep except the ground. Eleven hundred people were trapped there.

"You can't imagine how terrible it was," my mother says, with a look of pure anguish as she remembers.

On the third day of this hell, a Russian officer rode up on his motorcycle, surveying the ugly scene spread out before him. My mother was there to greet him.

"Look, you can see where I was born, where I grew up," she cried in Russian, waving her passport and papers under his nose. "I'm trying to get back home to my husband and family." (Now I imagine her thanking Bat'ko Ivano for tutoring her, and her Russian *gymnazium* in Rovne for perfecting her fluency in this language.)

The Russian officer stared at her, stone-faced. "Go back to the Germans," he finally said.

"You want them to kill us? I can't believe that the Russians would treat us as cruelly as the Germans do."

After a long silence, he said, "Wait here," then revved his engine and rode off in a plume of exhaust.

A few hours passed, and with each minute another grain of hope emptied from the top of her hourglass. Her stomach growled. During those terrible days, finding a frozen potato in the trampled earth was a major cause for celebration. There was nothing else to eat. Her legs had swelled so much it was painful to walk; her face was swollen too. She was filthy, exhausted, and wishing for a bath almost as much as for food. Beside her, Rivka couldn't even speak; she sat stone still, except for the wringing of her raw, red hands. As my mother sat there, thanking God for the warmth of her fur coat, she heard the low din of a motorcycle engine, getting louder as it advanced. It was the Russian officer.

"I have received orders," he announced to her. "You may now cross the border."

Listening to my mother speak, I can feel the pandemonium that erupted with this news. My mother tells this part of the story with much pride because the orders included all eleven hundred people stuck there with her. She was their heroine because she managed to convince the Russian invaders that they had a duty to accept those who'd been invaded.

Once again, her skill with language rescued her—and this time, it rescued all the people there with her. I'm sure her charm contributed too.

———

ZORLEVY COSHTELI IS WHAT IT sounds like—the name of the castle rest stop not far from where they crossed the makeshift border. I've listened repeatedly to this moment on the video when my mother names the place that figured prominently in her story, and with help have discovered Zeliszew Koscielny.[3] I picture a thousand people hurriedly cramming into and onto every available space. The abandoned palace had about one hundred rooms, my mother said, and was now a Russian stronghold, complete with food.

But in the confusion and chaos of their arrival, when everyone clamoured for a spot to lie down and collapse, my mother lost her companion and his little girl. She managed to stake out a table on which to sleep—all the floor space had already been grabbed. The first night, nestled in her fur coat with her rucksack as a pillow, she felt a man climb up and try to lie next to her. On top of her, more like it.

"I will kill you," she hissed as he reached for her, and kicked him off her table, waking all the surrounding sleepers. "I was very strong," she tells me.

As she speaks, I'm madly cheering her on, knowing she meant every word. I feel a pride in her strength and courage that's hard for me to describe. I know I'm a chicken, so much weaker than her, and lacking in her fortitude, her powerful determination. Whenever I try to put myself in her place, I don't see myself overcoming all that she had to endure and outfox. I honestly don't think I would have survived.

———

AT THIS POINT IN HER story, I'm having a problem with time. My mother said it was already December, but in her telling, it couldn't be any later than November. She was very clear that the bridge she had to cross in Warsaw was blocked because Hitler came to exult in his victory, and that was October 5. Perhaps the month-long gap is because she couldn't include every detail of what happened over those frightful days. During our filming, she even stops to ask us if she should include so many details. We say yes, and thankfully we now have so much of her story recorded. Maybe she was confused by the dates—after all, it was fifty-five years later that she was telling this story. She always maintained that it took her three months to escape from Warsaw, and she arrived in Kostopol in December 1939. Even though I want to be as accurate as I can, I completely believe she had a three-month ordeal, and what she's telling are the highlights.

MY MOTHER AND RIVKA, ALONG with everyone else, rested at the "castle" for about three days, after the nightmare at the border, but then had to set off for their destinations. Yes, they had crossed onto the Russian side, but they'd only travelled a few kilometres. They still had four hundred more to go to get home to Kostopol.

Zeliszew Koscielny was about three kilometres from a train station. Their first destination was the city of Kovel, a major transit point where they could connect with a train to Rovne, the city closest to Kostopol. When they arrived at the station, the scene was awfully familiar: hundreds of people stuffed into the building with no room to even stand. Hundreds more collected outside, all desperate to get on a train.

"We were there three days, waiting," my mother says, rocking in her chair. "On the second day I lost Rivka, but she made herself lost."

Rivka still had her zlotys. Even though they were useless, because Polish currency was now worth nothing, she thought she could get food with them, and didn't want to share with my mother. Here, there's no masking the bitterness in my mother's voice as she described the situation, risking her life and enduring so much hardship to take care of this woman. Now she was far from certain that she'd ever get home. I know she felt relief at no longer having to worry about Rivka, as though a thousand-pound weight had been lifted from her. My mother didn't have the energy to be angry; what little energy she had left was focused on getting herself home alive. We have no idea what happened to Rivka. Where and how she perished remains a mystery.

HOW DID ONE BUY A ticket for the train when there was no access to currency? Zlotys were useless, and very few had rubles. The Russians set up a ticketing system, giving tickets to travellers who met certain conditions. What these conditions were are as vague and random now as they were seventy-nine years ago. As my mother sat and waited, next to her sat a man who asked her where she was heading. It quickly became clear that he was Ukrainian, and came from the same region as my mother. So they conversed in Ukrainian. When she got up to try to acquire a train ticket, he asked her to get one for him too. "Tell them I'm your brother." It started well, with the Russian ticketing official who was ready to give her a ticket, but when she said she needed one for her brother, too, the official took one look and said, "If that man is your brother, then I am your father. Because you lied to me, neither of you will have tickets."

When the train finally pulled into the station that evening, the wave of surging humanity picked up and pressed my ticketless mother onto the train. Despite her fright about what would happen when she was discovered aboard without a ticket, she sat herself down in one of the compartments. Opposite her sat a well-dressed elderly man and his adult son, who noticed her obvious nervousness. She told them her worry that she would be kicked off the train in the middle of nowhere when she was found to not have a ticket, and explained what had happened to her at the station. As they sat and talked, Jewish radar was fully operating.

"Well, my dear, you can cease your worries, because I will buy you your ticket," the father said. "We live in Kovel. It's Friday night, and if you'd like, we invite you to be our guest for Shabbos, and after, we will get you a ticket to Rovne." Good as his word, when the controller stopped at their compartment, the father reached into his pocket and pressed some rubles into his hand, along with their tickets. My mother was now safe and secure.

Entering their elegant home, the Shabbos candles glowed; the aroma of delicious cooking lifted my mother's spirits as nothing else could. She couldn't believe her good fortune. In kindness, her hostess suggested that perhaps she'd like to have a bath before dinner. It had been over two weeks since she'd last bathed, so I can appreciate how grateful my mother was for this invitation. Soaking in the deep tub, she let her limbs float in the pure pleasure of hot water, soap, shampoo. She had one elegant dress in her rucksack, navy blue with a white collar, that her sister Pola had left behind in Ząbki. When she emerged from the bathroom in this beautiful dress, her hair braided long down her back, cheeks pink and fresh from the steam, she was unrecognizable. "They thought they'd brought an old woman home."

As promised, they bought her a ticket for Rovne after Shabbos, and their smitten son insisted on accompanying her there. How could she refuse his company after all his family's kindness? Entering Rovne station, so familiar from her schoolgirl days at the *gymnazium*, she could almost taste home. Again, the station was teeming with people, and as she tried to get her bearings and move on to the next train to Kostopol, only four stations away, she heard someone call "Pitzie, Pitzie." In all the years I'd known her, I can barely recall my mother ever telling me about her nickname, most likely derived from Shprintze, her Yiddish name, which comes from the Sephardic Esperanza, meaning hope. Turning around, she recognized one of her mother's cousins rushing to embrace her, not quite believing that she was alive. She collapsed in his arms.

Now I picture the train, and the relatively short distance of the last leg of her epic journey. I can feel her mounting excitement as she drew nearer and nearer to home. I can imagine the heightened recognition of the familiar details that she'd always taken for granted. Now each tree and field, pitched-roof house, and wooden barn shouted out to her as the train passed by, and finally she pulled into Kostopol station.

It was early morning. She stepped down, her tattered rucksack on her back, and began walking the final stretch to her parents' home. On her route, not far from the station, she came upon her uncle Meir's house, about a kilometre away from the Kramers' small apartment in Kostopol. Stepping into his warm, loving home was overwhelming. No one could believe it was Pitzie, with her swollen face and legs twice their normal size. Their prayers were answered. She had survived the bombing and hell of Warsaw and made it home, after three months and five hundred kilometres, in one piece.

As my mother speaks, I can hear the screams of excitement and joy in this scene. I am her companion on this journey, feeling the waves of shock, disbelief, relief, and joy all rolled into a great package of heart-thudding emotion. She'd spent so much time in this house, with her favourite uncle and his family. It was here that she worked, baking bread and preparing for her life in Palestine. Under this roof she had met Olek and Pesach, in what felt like a lifetime before. Everything had changed so drastically in such a short, dreadful time. But it was obvious to her that they were safe in Kostopol. The Russians were causing no harm, she learned. There had not been any killing. If anything, life was a bit better since they had invaded.

My mother regains her composure and tells of how she continued down the road to the crowded Jewish neighbourhood where her parents, Basia and Pesach, and her three younger sisters all lived. Yelena and Isaak were in the kitchen of their cramped apartment, preparing breakfast, when she stepped inside. "You can imagine what went on," my mother says, and of course I can: I see her ecstatic parents hugging their oldest daughter as though their lives depended on it. Against all odds, she was alive. Basia, Pola, Manya, and Sonia reach to embrace her, tears streaming down their cheeks. At this moment in her telling, I'm blinded by her intense joy.

As she tries to remain composed, I can see her picturing each one of them; she's back with them, flesh of her flesh, as she feels her deepest human bonds so brutally ripped away. It's clear to me as I watch her face—observe her seeing her parents, her twin sister, her beloved family in her mind's eye—that she's not reliving the pain of loss in these moments. I realize that this is where she lives, that pain is her dwelling place, and no matter how hard she tries, she cannot escape her fate.

4

Mistletoe

2014

I T WAS THE MISTLETOE UP high on the bare branches of ash trees that caught my eye as we rode the train from Warsaw to Lodz. I didn't know what the oval, filigreed capsules were. Nest-like, I thought that they were built by strange birds. After nearly a year of imagining, planning, cancelling, then reviving my plans, here I was in Poland: my strange, frightening, almost-home. A home carpeted with the bones of my closest family, and my awesome, formidable tribe. Enough bones to fill a thousand cathedrals, maybe more. A land shrouded in sooty mist, in a fairy tale where terrible things happen, and your child-heart clutches, knowing that pain is about to seize you. Before this trip, Poland did not appear to me in colour, nor did it appear in black and white. If I had to describe how it looked in my mind's eye, it would be the contour of a sheet of photo paper floating in a developing tray, in a black room where no light must penetrate. As I readied myself for this trip back to the ancestral land, I felt that I was in the darkroom, waiting for some image to start forming on the milky paper. It was a hold-your-breath kind of anticipation, the sort that rises with the gut-tickle that you've captured a good shot with your camera, or that the print sliding through the press on its inky bed will be lifted out a beauty. That special moment of emergence of something never before created. It was time, finally, to allow a real place to float up from the bath of my consciousness, which up until now had been quietly bubbling with the stories my mother had told me.

The train was crowded with commuters, everyone plugged into some device. No one was speaking, except me, to my husband. "What is that growing on the trees?" I asked. "They look like nests, but they're more like eggs." My naturalist husband, my walking-encyclopedia husband, tells me about mistletoe, its mythic holiness, worshipped by Druids and other ancient peoples because it protected its possessors from all evil. It had healing powers. It was an evergreen holy parasite, the hardwood tree its perfect host. How it became a Christian symbol of love, a shrine for public kissing, he wasn't sure, but we would find out soon enough. We had our devices too.

The sight of mistletoe, repeating on bare, upper branches of trees I couldn't name, as we rocked along the rail-bed, riding past fields and towns with unpronounceable names, all intertwined and created an odd dizziness. I felt with each passing kilometre the shrinking of disbelief that I had on the first of April, when we entered this mythical country, and it was becoming more real with each breath. I'd stepped out of the darkroom. How could I have lived on this earth so long and never seen mistletoe? Was I imagining that my heart was beating differently, as if, almost imperceptibly, its muscles were stretching open to this landscape?

As the train rolled closer to Lodz about an hour away, the buildings dotting the landscape told me that we were in Northern Europe, but the distinctive rooflines of many of the houses, with their thumbed-down corners that softened the angles on each side, reminded me of the images of wooden synagogues I'd seen in books and exhibitions. Virtually all had been destroyed. Suddenly, on a creamy yellow, stuccoed building, I glimpsed ancient Hebrew characters that looked like they'd been lifted from a Torah scroll, complete with curlicues and sprouts rising from the letters. I had no time to register the words they spelled; it was just a blink as the train sped by, but it startled me out of my dreaminess. I couldn't believe my eyes. I was indeed in Poland, and hints of its Jewish past rose up to tantalize me.

By the time we arrived at the conference centre at 8:00 PM, exhausted after two days of travel, we were ravenous. The centre's dining room was still open, and the staff were happy to accommodate us. Tucking into cabbage and mushroom perogies, cold cuts, and potato salad, it struck me that the food in my mouth tasted like home, almost like my mother's kitchen. Robbie murmured his agreement as he relaxed and happily savoured the flavours of our simple meal.

The sound of Polish surrounding me created that peculiar sensation of simultaneous familiarity and strangeness. I recognized those sounds, but my brain couldn't comprehend them. I was now in the land of my parents' secret language, a language that I was never invited to partake in, except for a stray word here and there. Here I was, a sixty-five-year-old woman thrust back to my child consciousness, enjoying mouthfuls of perogies, while all the baggage of growing up with genocide was unpacked with each bite.

Up in our clean, spare room, with its single beds and gold taffeta bedspreads—a holdover from Communist-era décor—I managed to say, "Honey, this is going to be a very interesting experience" with my goodnight kiss.

"Yes indeed," I heard him reply before collapsing into sleep.

THE CONFERENCE CENTRE WAS ABUZZ the next morning as we participants collected for breakfast before the first sessions of *Kanade, di Goldene Medine*.[1] We were a gathering from many corners of Canada, Poland, and Northern and Central Europe—England, France, Belgium, Austria, the Czech Republic. A few had direct ties to Lodz, and to Poland, or what was Poland until 1939. We were a mixed group of Jews and non-Jews, perhaps fifty in total, all deeply interested in Jewish history and its impact upon the literature and culture of our times, in Canada and Poland.

The first person to greet me was Norm Ravvin, a writer and academic from Concordia in Montreal, who was the Canadian organizer of the conference. In our communications he'd helped calm my fears about going to Poland. He'd already been quite a few times, he told me, and by now he had many Polish colleagues who were extremely sensitive and interested in Jews and their complicated place in Polish history. Some even had Jewish ancestry themselves. They were good people, doing good things, living antidotes to antisemitism. I knew on the top of his list were his co-organizers, Krzysztof Majer and Justyna Fruzińska from the University of Łódź, who were rushing around making sure that everything was in order.

"There's Krzysztof now," Norm pointed out, bringing me over to quickly introduce us. As Krzysztof hurried on, after his warm handshake, I was taken aback to see a copy of *Prairie Kaddish* tucked under his arm. I hadn't brought any books with me, nor sent any in advance, so it must have been his personal copy. I couldn't imagine anyone in Poland even knowing about my book, let alone owning a copy.

I TOOK OUT MY NOTES and scanned them nervously as I waited to be introduced. Although I'd spoken about how I'd

Mistletoe

come to write *Prairie Kaddish* many times to many different audiences, I was acutely aware that this time was special. I'd written the book while my mother was still alive, and her stories about growing up in the little village of Pohorelowka resonated between the lines and poured onto the pages. She was excited about my book and helped me as best she could, even reading a Yiddish memoir with me so I could understand it better. I'll never forget how she pulled Usiskin's book[2] out of my hands because I'd exhausted her patience and she couldn't bear to listen anymore to my tortured reading. She took over, and we laughed together at the poignant, humorous stories of early life in a Jewish farm colony in Saskatchewan. It's one of my favourite memories, one of the last experiences we shared together.

The conference room leaned toward intimate, crowded yet roomy enough for fifty people. As far as conferences went, it was a perfect size, with no need for simultaneous sessions. Everyone could partake in everyone's work. Now I stood at the podium, an image of the grave houses in the Lipton Hebrew Cemetery in Saskatchewan behind me, and began to speak:

My parents would not believe this; they would have been horrified at the thought of their child stepping foot upon this blood-soaked earth, the place where so many loved ones were forced into oblivion—the ultimate humiliation of disappearance from history, with not even a grave to pronounce their humanity. But here I am, excited to be in the land of my ancestors, and to feel the reality of what has always been my imaginary home, in my dreams, fantasies, and nightmares.

Thank you for welcoming me back.

Prairie Kaddish began with a chance suggestion to visit an obscure Jewish cemetery in rural Saskatchewan and became a pilgrimage to learn about Canadian Jewish history, Jewish death and burial practices, and an exploration of Jewish history from the mid-nineteenth century to now. I'd started from a belief that I'd stumbled upon an interesting story that I had no personal relationship with, yet came to realize that my personal and family history was absolutely a part of this story, and to appreciate more than ever that Jewish history is one long, complex, and fecund story of survival and triumph over near annihilation.

As I delivered my talk and showed my images of the farm colony sites in the Canadian Prairies, virtually all abandoned now, I felt myself transported back in time, but in reverse because now I was imagining the landscape of departure, the landscape I'd viewed for the first time as we rolled through the Polish countryside the day before. I can't call it nostalgia for what was left behind; I don't really know what to call it, but an experience of exhumation. My notion of Poland was born from a deliberate burial of this place by my parents, who dug a deep hole and interred their childhoods and young lives along with it. They blanked it all out because it was in this place where prejudice greened and fermented into hatred so vile that neighbours turned into monsters that hacked you to death, who buried your children alive.

Reverberating through my mind was the question raised by Robert Pogue Harrison when I was researching *Prairie Kaddish*: Why did the living house the dead before they housed themselves?[3] For Jews, care for the dead is sacrosanct. In every community, the *chevra kadisha* (holy burial society) would always be organized first, even before a synagogue would be created. After all, one could pray anywhere, but the dead depended upon the living to be returned to earth. It struck me that having no place to go to remember my dead, nowhere to say, *here they lived and died, and here I am, come from them,* was the worst banishment. Pogue Harrison's answer is that "to inhabit the world humanly, one must be a creature of legacy. We, the living, are but a ligature between the dead and the unborn." This explained it all to me. Not only was I robbed of my family, but I was also robbed of their

deaths, robbed of my human legacy. Even if I'd never visited the graves of my ancestors, I needed to know that their
graves existed, for it proved their existence. All my life I'd felt
this rootlessness. I'd come from the Shoah's fire, come from
vapour, but not from earth. And now I was standing on the
very earth where they came from and disappeared.

Not surprisingly, much of the discussion after my talk
addressed the issue of Jewish attitude toward Poland. Most
Jews of my vintage grew up with similar experiences, but others spoke of breaking out of this mould, of feeling that they
had a rightful heritage in Poland, and while not denying the
horror of Jewish annihilation that took place here, they could
also celebrate Jewish achievements and re-emergence in the
Polish present.

My heart thumped. With this risky, emotional talk it was
exhilarating to feel the loosening of strictures and command-
ments I'd lived with for so long. Was I not free to adjust my
own opinions without breaking the codes I'd been brought
up with?

AFTER A COUPLE OF DAYS, having spent enough time in con-
vivial conversations that flowed in a comfortable stream from
one language and subject to another to have already formed
bonds of friendship, we took some necessary air from the
hothouse of the conference centre.

Our first outing was to the Lodz Jewish cemetery, an
enormous forty-acre expanse dating back to the last decade
of the nineteenth century. It was the largest existent Jewish
cemetery in Europe. Our guide was Milena, a young Polish
woman with fiery red hair, green eyes, and excellent English.
She clearly revered the place. She was familiar with many
of those buried there, filling us with their stories, and
explaining some of the Jewish symbology: the splayed fin-

gers representing the priestly benediction of the *Cohanim*; the water jugs of the *Levi'im*, the assistants to the priests; Shabbos candles for the pious women; the open books of the learned men.

We walked section by section, examining the tremendous variety of graves that ranged in size and design, from modest stones to mausoleums, simple carvings to impressive sculptures. It was here I first heard of the great poet Tuwim, when we stopped at his mother's unusual tomb, carved in the shape of a large hope chest. It looked like the fine furnishings of the family home were brought to the cemetery, elevated on a pedestal, and protected from all bad weather for eternity by a carpet of rose granite unfurled on top.

Miraculously preserved, these Jewish graves represented natural death; of the 180,000 buried here, most predated the Holocaust. The bent, sometimes severed oak tree declared the end of life, as people were lovingly returned to earth, their names and those of their parents, the dates of their entry and exit from this life, their Jewish standing, all inscribed in stone to be remembered for posterity. Yes, I envied them the simple dignity of a grave. It didn't matter that most were overgrown with moss and scrub, half-buried in debris. Pockets of forsythia blazed in spring glory. Common ivy scrambled over everything, madly tangling up the trees. Ivy, we learned, was a protected species in Poland, prohibited from removal. With excitement and humility, Milena told us about her brainchild project to remove the scrub and brush, plot by plot, with teams of volunteers. This cemetery, and other Jewish cemeteries across Poland, were being cleaned and tidied, even as the ivy remained.

Taking this in, Robbie and I nodded in appreciation of this tenderness and respect. Milena seemed to represent a Polish generation that deeply, honestly cared about Jewish history, and actively honoured it. Needless to say, it's not what I expected.

"Sweetheart, look," I said, pointing up from where we stood. In the distance, clinging to the upper branches of budding oaks and maples, I'd spotted more mistletoe.

During the war, more than 43,000 Jews were buried in this cemetery (which bordered the ghetto), their mean flat concrete slabs spread out over acres—a haunted city of its own within the necropolis. After Warsaw, the city of Lodz contained the largest Jewish ghetto: approximately 160,000 people squeezed into a few city blocks. Known for its textile manufacturing, the Nazis continued this specialty by having most of the uniforms for the German army produced by Jewish slave labour. In addition to the local Jews of Lodz, they shipped many Jews from Western Europe there for forced labour, then death.

Of course our next stop was the *Umschlagplatz* memorial, on the edge of the ghetto. It was from here that Jews were packed onto trains and shipped to Chełmno and Auschwitz. A couple of refurbished cattle cars sat on the rails and we were free to step foot in them, so I did. There was only one narrow rectangular window high up in the corner; the crisp early spring light refracted in rays, illuminating the oxblood-stained walls. Close by, beside a huge smokestack, the memorial continued down a long tunnel where the story of what happened there was written in stone on the walls. Advancing year by year, the history was illustrated by photographs and framed collections of broken, rusted scissors and buttons. Bits of common, everyday objects of human activity had been raked up and displayed as if they were precious fragments from a lost civilization. And they were. It's difficult to convey the eloquence that they expressed; the best I can do is compare them to a Leonard Cohen song, lyrics of human fragility soaring with incomparable dignity in a tube of pain and ruin. Exiting the tunnel, an intensely sweet fragrance enveloped me. It was coming from the white chokecherry blossoms on a tree in full bloom. All I remember is staring at those dense button-sized flowers and inhaling their perfume as the sky behind the tree pulsated blue. I could hardly breathe.

OUR FINAL EXPERIENCE OF LODZ was a Kabbalat Shabbat service and dinner at Lauder House[4] on Friday evening. All the conference participants were invited. We tramped up the rickety stairs of the old building to enter the main room that was fitted with bookshelves filled with holy books, metal folding chairs, and a gauze curtain separating the men's section from the women's. I swallowed my distaste for this Orthodox practice and allowed myself to enjoy the Shabbos prayers that I hardly ever heard anymore. I felt my father close as we sang "Shalom Aleichem," his favourite Shabbos hymn, saw him standing with his *siddur* (prayer book) in one hand, Kiddush cup in the other, welcoming the Sabbath queen. But at this moment I was so very far removed from our dining table in Ashland, Massachusetts. I was in the land of my father's birth, joining voices with a collection of strangers from all over Europe and North America who respectfully—no, joyously—raised their glasses to thank God for the blessed fruit of the vine.

We sat shoulder to shoulder in a room far too small for comfort, passing plates of fish pâté, chopped egg, stewed beans and carrots, surprisingly tasty vegetarian dishes, as the sound levels rose to a great, pleasurable din. Behind me, Gloria from Toronto started to sing "Ikh Dermon Zikh Oyf Der Fraytik Oyf Der Nakht" ("I Remember How It Was on a Friday Night"). Her strong voice lifted this Yiddish song into a realm where memory and tears coexist, and we could appreciate that despite everything, Jewish life continues, even here at the epicentre of destruction.

5

Warsaw

2014

A FTER LODZ, WARSAW WAS A true metropolis. Exiting the train, the first things that Robbie and I saw were a giant neon guitar, and an imposing Stalinesque skyscraper that seemed to take up a city block. A socialist-realist concoction, an unwanted gift to the people of Warsaw from the nations of the USSR, we learned. The Beatles' *White Album* and "Back in the USSR" blasted away in my mental soundtrack. We'd already heard so much about how the end of communism in 1989 changed everything in Poland, and this first sighting of what the Russians left behind in Warsaw was sobering.

We looked for a taxi to take us to a part of town that was not on any tourist map. We were going to meet Katarzyna Kacprzak, whom I knew only through email. She was the researcher that the Lodz conference team had connected me with, back when I was beginning my efforts to search for my Aunt Basia's poems, and to find my parents' marriage certificate or any other evidence of their lives in Warsaw. She had invited us for dinner.

"Do you see any taxis?" Robbie asked.

"Yes, sweetheart, I see taxis, but how do I hail one?" At that moment, my competent husband outstretched his long arms—bingo.

Inside the cab, we showed our driver the address that I'd written on a piece of paper. Now it was the cabbie's turn to throw up his hands. Over the static of his radio, he got some directions, and off we went. Blocks of ugly communist apartment towers loomed in the night sky, with little light to illuminate the sparsely populated streets. After circling a few blocks, our cabbie finally deposited us outside a three-tower complex while gesticulating incoherently in their direction. Kasia lived on Abraham Street, which I found symbolic. I couldn't really believe that a street named for the father of the Jewish tribe would be found in Warsaw. There were no numbers or any address indicators on the first building we approached, but some kindly women in the ground-floor beauty parlour pointed us in another direction. After wandering like Abraham's lost children in the deserted boulevard for nearly half an hour, I sheepishly phoned Kasia to tell her we were somewhere close, but hopelessly confused.

"Don't worry," she said, "I'll guide you."

We followed her instructions to head toward the nearby grocery store, and as we spoke, she told us to turn around. Before us stood a slight young woman in a white raincoat, with a phone held to her ear. Her short dark hair framed her pale face, while her blue eyes shone. "Welcome to Warsaw, and sorry for your trouble finding me," she said. A huge smile lit up her face.

Entering her small apartment, we were greeted with the rich aroma of stew cooking. She invited us to take a seat.

I haven't fully introduced Kasia yet, so let me describe our email correspondence and the events that transpired to bring Robbie and me to this apartment in the boondocks of Warsaw: In addition to searching for the marriage certificate and Basia's poems, I also needed help with translations of Polish documents that I'd discovered in the box I'd taken to Cluxewe all those months before. When I first emailed her, she replied immediately and with great enthusiasm, and embarked upon a search before I'd even confirmed with her to go ahead. Just as I was writing to her, she sent the first bit of news: no marriage certificate could be found. I knew that my parents didn't have a public wedding; they simply went to a rabbi who recorded the marriage, with my grandmother Yelena present as witness. It was in May 1938. Kasia, because we were quickly becoming intimates, explained that Jewish records, like the records of all religious groups, would have been kept separately; Jews were not required to record their marriages in the vital records. To do so, they would have to go to a Komisariat at a police station in Warsaw and pay a large fee.[1] I strongly doubt that my parents had the funds or the inclination to do so. Given that our family roots were long-planted in the east, in what is now Ukraine and Belarus, there were no other vital statistics to be found in Poland at the time. If any such documents survived the war, they would be somewhere in Ukraine, perhaps Rivne, the closest city to Kostopil, where my mother was born, Kasia explained.

As for Basia's poems, Kasia wrote that *Nasz Przegląd* indeed had a weekly supplement called *Mały Przegląd* (*The Small Review*), founded by Janusz Korczak, which was almost uniquely for children's writings.[2] She had a look at the digital library and checked all the available issues from 1930, 1931, and 1932 (only a few pages were missing), but there was no sign of Basia's poems. Actually, there were not many poems at all. So if there was nothing in *Mały Przegląd*, Kasia said that the other possibility, *Płomyk Alfa*, was most probably a school magazine; if so, the chances of finding a copy of it nowadays would be very unlikely.

After my hopes had been raised by Alan Rutkowski's initial search in Victoria, this news from Kasia shattered my expectations and left me back at the edge of the cliff of lost memory. But Kasia was optimistic and not ready to let go. Perhaps there were other avenues to explore, she offered, and she was willing to keep looking. She wanted to give us a tour of Warsaw and especially Praga, which was the district her family was from. She even suggested that somewhere in the past our families might have crossed paths, if only for a second. She insisted on inviting us for a meal of Jewish food that she would cook, so we would feel at home when we arrived in Warsaw. She knew so much about Jewish history and culture that I had to gently inquire if she was Jewish herself. I was starting to understand that many Poles had Jewish ancestry and were just beginning to uncover the buried roots of their family trees.

"I'm still looking for the details of my history," Kasia wrote, "because there are many stories that lead me to suspect Jewish connections, if not by blood, then by close friendship."

KASIA HAD PREPARED *CHOLENT* FOR us—the classic Jewish dish of beans, meat, potatoes, onions, and eggs that stewed for hours and got better the longer it cooked. It would traditionally be prepared on Fridays, before Shabbos arrived, and would slowly simmer in a warm oven overnight, to be served for the Shabbos afternoon meal. Jewish law prohibited any kind of work on Shabbos, so lighting a fire, even for cooking, was forbidden. Cholent was not a big menu item when I was growing up, as we did not observe all the rules of Shabbos. What I loved best about it, when I had it, were the eggs that had cooked so slowly in their shells that their whites turned ochre brown and tasted otherworldly, infused with the flavours they had nestled in for so long.

What impressed me most about Kasia's cholent was that she had taken so much care to prepare it as an entry to the

Jewish past of Poland that I was seeking. She imagined this was the food of my family, and though she couldn't bring them back, she could bring me back to them. Did my mother and Basia make cholent on Fridays in Praga or Ząbki? I don't think so, but I'm sure the streets of Praga were filled with the aromas of cholent stewing, chicken soup simmering, and challah baking every Friday afternoon.

The meal gave us a chance to get to know Kasia better. She explained that as her interest in Jewish history in Poland deepened, she felt the need to truly study it, and as she studied, it became clearer to her that she should give up her unsatisfying job in high tech and train to be a guide for Jewish Warsaw. She told us that it was the hardest program she'd undertaken, much more demanding than her university studies, but the best decision she'd ever made. Well, almost the best. She'd also decided to be a single mom because her relationship had just broken up when she got pregnant. Two-year-old Cyprian was visiting his grandparents that evening, so we didn't have the chance to meet him. Of course we spoke about our impressions of Poland, our eye-opening visit to beautiful Krakow, and described our experiences in Lodz, especially our tour of the Jewish cemetery, and how impressed we were with our guide Milena.

Kasia chuckled. "Oh yes, Milena is wonderful. We trained together and are now good friends. She gave my name to Justyna, the conference organizer in Lodz, when you'd asked her for a researcher and guide for your project in Warsaw. That's how we got connected."

We basked in the small-world sweetness of it all and made plans for our tours of Praga and Warsaw in the coming days.

Snuggling down in our comfortable bed in our Praga hotel that evening, Robbie and I had much to talk about. I couldn't get over Kasia's welcome, and being in Praga felt unreal.

"I wish I knew where my parents and Basia and Pesach had lived," I ventured. "It could have been on this street for all I know, but I'll never know." With eyes closed, I pictured the crumbling old buildings surrounding our hotel. Unlike the parts of Warsaw we'd seen across the river, Praga had not recovered well since the war. Destruction was still visible, while urban renewal had yet to arrive.

"Honey, I fear your high hopes," Robbie gently said. "I know you want to find treasures here, but be prepared for disappointment." We'd heard enough about the destruction— well, obliteration—of history to know that the chances of success in my hunt for clues about my family's lives here were very slim. To think that even a marriage certificate—such a fundamental piece of social legacy—was beyond reach made me weep. And as I wept over the absence of paper, while my husband held me in his arms, the deeper wounds of my life-time of profound loss shook me. I was back in my child-self, reliving the time I asked my mother what was a Bobie, and watching her face collapse.

I'd never even seen a picture of my grandfather until the year 2000, when I was in Israel with my mother and my sister Mayim. My mother was eighty-three years old then, and we knew there would be precious few opportunities left for such a visit, with the four surviving sisters still alive and relatively healthy. It was on this same visit that Sonia had told me about *Płomyk Alfa* as the publication of Basia's poems.

I was in Pola's bedroom one morning when I noticed a small, framed photo on the wall, of someone I'd never seen before.

"Who's this?" I asked Pola.

"That's my father," she answered, so casually that I expected her to end the sentence with, "Surely you must rec-ognize him?"

"Oh my God, I can't believe it! This is Isaak Kramer," I said.

She had no idea that this was my first sighting of my grandfather. I was fifty-one years old.

KASIA MET US AT OUR hotel the next morning to begin our exploration of the landscape of my parents' young adult lives before the war. The district of Praga was full of Jewish landmarks during their time, but they were well camouflaged now. Kasia walked us to sites of synagogues, schools, residences, and orphanages. Those buildings, in varying states of decomposition, now served as housing, or children's theatre, or offices, with little public notation indicating previous use. Windows constructed with Stars of David, and iconic tablets engraved with Hebrew letters, were still visible if we lifted our eyes to roof level. Remnants of the war could still be seen on the streets, which surprised me. We passed the roof of an armoured bunker that rose like a giant mushroom from the sidewalk of a street corner. Occasional bullet holes polkadotted stucco façades. Kasia took us into what had been a Jewish orphanage and was now, for all intents and purposes, a squat. "Don't be afraid, it's very safe here," Kasia said as we tiptoed around. It wasn't the people that scared me; I just couldn't imagine it not collapsing on us. Kasia pointed out the pre-war iron railing decorations of little houses and animals that were meant to lift the spirits of the children who had once scrambled up and down the stairs.

We made our way to the zoo, where Antonina and Jan Zabinski had hidden a few hundred people, mostly Jews, in their villa and the abandoned animal dens, after all the animals had been released or killed by the German occupiers. I'd read the incredible story in *The Zookeeper's Wife* by Diane Ackerman, and it left an indelible mark on my psyche. Roaming around this special site—now populated with pink flamingos preening by a shallow pond, then Australian wallabies hopping around a grassy lawn outside their spacious bunkhouse—felt somewhat unreal. A small, frosted glass window poking up from a pebbled bed of the grounds nearby was meant to be the memorial to what the heroic zookeepers had done here. The Nazis had made it clear that anyone caught rescuing Jews would be executed, along with their entire families. The courage it took to act as a moral human being during this nightmare time is impossible to reckon. I honestly have no idea if I would have had that courage, especially if it meant endangering my children. Having had a serious meltdown at the exhibition about Polish rescuers at the POLIN Museum the day before, when I could not control my sobbing, my sore heart was still trying to recover. Surely the Zabinskis deserved more recognition than what we saw here. They were honoured as "Righteous Among the Nations" by Yad Vashem,[3] the World Holocaust Remembrance Center in Jerusalem, but what about here at the actual site of their righteous deeds? What kind of monument could honour the audacious bravery of these people? An enormous garden ringed by trees that form a leafy dome of shelter? A labyrinth of giant topiary animals, with an eternal lamp at its centre? Perhaps an animal den with a glassed-in cage that you could step in, take a seat, and contemplate while a sound and light show tells the story of what happened here?[4]

Not far from the zoo, we approached the bridge to cross over to Warsaw. The Most Kierbedzia had been destroyed by the German army during the Warsaw Uprising in September 1944, but the remaining stone pilings were used to construct a new bridge, renamed the Most Śląsko-Dąbrowski. Far beneath our feet, the grey-green Vistula lapped up against its shore; with each step I took, I heard echoes of my mother's footsteps, in rhythm with her German officer.

We continued our tour of the Old Town of Warsaw, which was so well reconstructed that it was impossible to believe it had been ground to rubble by the Germans in 1944. Using antique architectural drawings and plans still existent postwar, the buildings surrounding the large market square and lining the narrow cobblestone streets that radiated out from it were beautifully recreated—even painted in medieval colours of dove grey, mustard, soft mint green, turquoise. Sniffing out an opportunity, I asked Kasia if there might be a shop where I could find an authentic Jewish souvenir to take home from Warsaw. "I know just the place," Kasia said as we turned a corner and nipped into the Lapidarium. There were a few pricey objects, like small silver Kiddush cups, but what caught my eye and stopped my breath momentarily was a little glass bowl filled with tiny bronze figures of menorahs and lions all jumbled together. They were clearly damaged by fire and coated in ochre dust. I had no time to look closely at all the pieces, and there was no story that accompanied them; I just paid fifty bucks for the lot and tucked them into my bag. We were on our way to meet Anna Przybyszewska Drozd at the Jewish Historical Institute.

I'd written to Anna, a genealogical researcher, to let her know that we'd be in Warsaw in early April, and she sent a gracious note back, inviting us to meet with her. Her office was in a nondescript modern building, opposite the Jewish Historical Institute—one of Warsaw's rare surviving Jewish buildings. Built as a companion to the Great Synagogue, it had housed the Jewish Library and Institute for Judaic Studies before the war. Robert and I entered Anna's office, which she shared with another researcher, and introduced ourselves.

A tiny, wiry woman of indeterminate age, dressed in jeans and an *I Love New York* T-shirt, sat dwarfed by two giant computer screens before her.

"Yes?" she said, turning her head away from the screens, with an expression so flat she gave no indication of her interior life.

"Katarzyna Kacprzak connected us to you," I began.

She appeared accustomed to people dropping in out of the blue, from the great Jewish diaspora, and wanting help with family research. That was her job, to stop whatever she was doing and deal with people like me.

"No, I do not know who is Katarzyna."

"She wrote to you about me, and then I wrote to you, say-ing that I'd be coming to do some family research."

"Ah yes, I vaguely remember," she murmured, "but it doesn't matter. You are here now, so how can I help you?"

I was suddenly at a loss for where to begin, so I started with a chaotic expression of all my desires. Family stories tumbled out—about my parents' marriage in Warsaw, my aunt's published poems that I was hoping to find, my grand-father's flour mill in Pohorelowka, my great-uncle's life in Ukraine after the war, and would it be possible to find his sons—but she quickly interrupted me.

"One thing at a time. Let's start with your mother. Where was your mother born?"

"Kostopol, in what is now Ukraine."

"Her parents?"

"Danczimost, Berezne, also now in Ukraine."

"Oh."

When it became clear that most of my search involved present-day Ukraine, she knew we wouldn't find much here in Poland.

"Records are hard to come by from Ukraine," Anna warned. "Hardly any survived after the war, especially Jewish records."

I'm sure my disappointment flashed out from every cell of my body. Here I always thought of my family roots as Polish, but this was not remotely in accord with Polish assumptions. That my parents were Polish citizens, that they studied and worked and married in Warsaw, that my father served in the Polish army, that Polish was their everyday language, that my mother nursed sick mothers and made baby formula for their Polish infants did not matter. That they lost every record of their identity, or did not merit a record because they were Jews did not really matter in the Polish body politic. Borders were destiny.

I unbuttoned my sweater and fanned myself with my crumpled map of Warsaw.

Anna was undaunted. "Let's see what we can find."

She sat me down next to her screen as her fingers danced across her keyboard. She began with Kostopol and Pohore-lowka. Now it's Kostopil, but she had no idea how Pohore-lowka would be spelled in Ukrainian or Russian. Did it even still exist on this earth? Such a tiny village. In short order, she'd located a *Geographical Dictionary of the Kingdom of Poland and Other Slavic Countries*, dated 1927. Created with exquisite detail, it depicted every road, track, rail, stream, marsh, river, and structure to be found on the ground. There indeed was Pohorelowka, its eighty-four houses, one church, and three mills, twenty-eight kilometres from Kostopol. My mother had told me twenty-seven.

Given that Isaak Kramer had owned a mill in Pohorelowka, she looked in the *Poland and Danzig Business Directory*, typing in the year 1926. Clickety-click. "Have a look," she said, turning the screen so I'd have a better view. She pointed to the small print as she translated from Polish. In the listing in the region of Ludwipol, Kostopol, and Berezne (the towns of origin of my great-grandparents) three mills were noted in Pohorelowka, along with their owners. There, in black and white, I saw "Kramer I" and beside his name, in parentheses, *"par"* which translated as the abbreviation for *parowy*, or steam mill.

POHORELÓWKA.
Wieś, gmina Lud-wipol, powiat Kostopol, sąd pok.Bereźne,sąd okręg. Równe, 1709 mieszk. (28 km) Kosto-pol Lud-wipol Bere-zno, 1 gr. wsch. Młyny.
V-ge, commune d-Ludwipol, distr. de Kostopol, just. de paix Bereźne. trib. d'arr-t Ró-wne, 1709 habit. (28 km) Ko-stopol Lud-wipol Berezno. 1 orthod. Mou-lins.
Kowale (forgerons): Trofimczuk K.
Młyny (moulins): Bagiński F, (wod.)
— Kramer I. (par.).
Wiatraki (moulins à vent): Kesler K. — Trofimczuk K.

Listing in the 1926 *Poland and Danzig Business Directory.*[5]

In that moment, a dream became flesh. This was the first time in my life that I experienced my grandfather's existence on public record, in a tiny, digitized notation, from an obscure book that seemed a miracle of survival in itself.

So there in Anna's office, looking at the entry in the 1926 Business Directory, I had one of my fainting moments, psychologically speaking. I actually did feel dizzy from the mix of surprise, excitement, and grief all stirred together. I'd been searching for the closest members of my family, whom I'd spent my life imagining, and this was the most concrete evidence I'd found so far. When Anna clicked onto Google Earth and took us to modern-day Pohorelowka, now called Poliske, and we looked down on the village from outer space, my dizziness turned to vertigo as she zoomed in and we landed in a farmer's field, near a huge haystack, a horse and cart in the background, a red barn with a steep-pitched roof in the farther distance—a scene that could easily have been recorded in 1926.

Taking a huge breath, we concluded our visit with Anna in an exhalation of gratitude. Yes, she would email me the map and the photos she'd found on Google, and yes, she would inquire about any family documents that might be found at the Institute—perhaps registrations the Kramer sisters could have made after the war, when they were refugees. We thanked her for everything she'd done. As we left, we glanced back to see her petite frame juxtaposed against her large computer screens, her fingers busily tapping away.

EVERYONE TOLD US THAT WE couldn't leave Warsaw without visiting the Warsaw Uprising Museum. I never knew it existed—a museum that tells the story of the total destruction of the city of Warsaw in late 1944, on the verge of what could have been liberation from the Germans. We'd bought our tickets and were about to begin touring the museum when I overheard a small group of men speaking English with a British accent. They appeared to have been attending a conference and were taking time out for some Polish culture.

"It's nice to hear your British English," I ventured, not shy to engage in some friendly tourist banter.

Robbie rolled his eyes. He was accustomed to me embarrassing him in public.

"It's nice to hear your American English," one man said.

"Well, Canadian, actually."

He put his hand on his chest. "And I am actually Polish. Is this your first time here?"

"Yes, it is. First time in Poland, first time in this museum."

"Why don't you join us on our tour?" he generously offered. "Having an English-speaking guide will certainly enhance the experience."

I took Robbie's arm and we joined the group. We stopped first to look at the weaponry that the Polish resistance had put together to fight the German army. But weaponry is not quite the appropriate word because the guns looked more like toys held together with scraps of wire and tape; they used whatever they could make to arm themselves against the German fighting machine that ruled Warsaw. Our guide told the story of the Uprising, as he brought us from room to room. The museum was well designed and very interactive. We stooped low and entered sewers (the only way the Polish fighters could get around was underground). Like the Jewish ghetto uprising the year before, the Polish resistance knew it could be a fight to the death. What was expected to take a few days, or a week at most, became a struggle that lasted more than two months because the Russians refused to cross the Vistula, leaving the Germans free to kill, starve, and finally capture the Poles, then dynamite and bulldoze what remained of the city. As we toured, the horror of what had happened in Warsaw sunk in for the whole group.

"My mother was in Warsaw when the war broke out," I announced to Damian. By this time, I was on a first-name basis with the young Pole who'd invited us to join his tour. "It took her three months to escape."

"Ah, so your mother was Polish," Damian responded. "I knew there was more to your story."

"My mother was a Polish Jew," I replied. "So Poland didn't think she was Polish."

"Well, that is nonsense," Damian huffed. "How could anyone say your mother was *not* Polish," he added, as though he couldn't imagine such prejudice, and it needed serious correction. "I know some of my people don't share my attitude, but they are the minority." As far as he was concerned, my mother was as much a part of the Polish fabric as he was, and he was ready to include me too. Our parting from the group was surprisingly poignant.

I can hardly say how much this encounter still resonates with me. We were in an experience of deep compassion, recognizing each other's suffering. More than anything, it's this recognition, this empathy that goes so far in soothing the wounds that have yet to heal. I know one of the greatest challenges for Jews is to acknowledge Polish suffering during the war. Before coming to Poland, I was one of those Jews. Now something was shifting.

———

AT THE END OF THIS memorable day, at dinner that evening, when we tasted the most delicious, velvety borscht I'd ever had, Robbie and I tried to make sense of all our experiences.

I pulled out the little bowl of dirt-encrusted bronze figures that I'd purchased. One by one, I placed each piece on the table: two lions of Judah, one bent at the torso as though folded in half; a seven-branched menorah missing its stem; four tiny, squashed Chanukah *dreidels*, with their Hebrew letters still legible; and a medallion about an inch round, featuring a tree-like menorah flanked by two tiny doves. They looked like they'd been burned in a bombing, then dug up from Warsaw rubble. They must have been adornments of some kind of Jewish celebratory object—the folded lion still had a little screw in its back. I tried to imagine their original home. Underground for unknown decades, they still throbbed with Jewish energy. I couldn't have found a better metaphor of plucking Jewish life from the ruins of Polish history.

"What are you going to do with these, my love?" Robbie asked.

"I'd like to do something special, but I'm not sure yet."

I sat there almost dumb with wonder about all that I'd taken in that day. I had no room for even one more iota of experience. I was filled up to the brim, trying to sort out all my conflicted beliefs while attempting to calm the emotional sea I was tossing in. It reminded me of the time I nearly drowned in the crashing waves at Zuma Beach in California, a lifetime before. I had to will my body to relax so I could lift myself out of the undertow. I was never so happy to stand upright on firm sand. This seemed like the emotional equivalent. I had finally experienced *Varshe*, as my parents called it, and *War-sza-wa*, as the writer Melekh Ravitch described those three dark syllables fraught with danger and destiny.[6]

I had found a minuscule bit of evidence of my family's life here, evidence of my grandfather's mill, and felt as though I'd unearthed the Dead Sea Scrolls. The people I'd met had welcomed me with great warmth, dignity, and friendship. My encounter with Damian kept replaying in my mind—the words we exchanged, the deepening of appreciation of each other's suffering, and the recognition of how fortunate we were to live in peace and acceptance of each other's humanity.

Robbie put down his spoon, reached across the table and touched my arm. "What are you thinking?" he asked.

"I'm thinking about how complicated everything now seems. Trying to understand the incomprehensible. And I'm thinking about the notion of 'attitude' as I'm trying to make sense of it all. How do we make meaning of experience, especially when we suffer?"

"Reality's not always black and white, much as we want to simplify things. It's easier that way. It takes courage to change our attitudes. Am I detecting some attitude adjustment going on, my dear?"

I picked up the bent Lion of Judah and held it in my hand, felt the rough contours of its outstretched paw and flowing mane, still insistent on its vitality after being buried for half a century. This little artifact of pain and survival, this representation of Jewish history and continuance pulsed in my hand. A more eloquent metaphor of Jewish experience I could not imagine.

6

Five Good Months

1940

I T IS DECEMBER 1939, A week after my mother's return to Kostopol, and she is at the cinema. They'd all gone together—my aunt Pola and her boyfriend, my aunt Manya, some other friends—for a welcome evening out. When the intermission came, they got up from their seats and went to the lobby of the theatre. Back then, the cinema was a substitute for theatre, and a break in the program was necessary. So the sisters sat in the lobby chatting while people milled about.

When my mother tells the story, she pauses dramatically.[1] "I was looking down, when suddenly I saw two feet stop in front of me. I picked up my head and there stood your father."

I don't know very much about this moment in the cinema between my mother and father, but I can imagine the flood of emotion. I can hear my mother gasp, see her jump up as they reach to embrace each other, barely able to breathe. They are swept away, oblivious to their surroundings, not caring about breaking the social code in such a public display of intimacy. My twenty-two-year-old mother and twenty-five-year-old father hold onto each other as time stands still.

It had taken my father a couple of hours on the train to get to my mother in Kostopol. He'd left Stolin soon after he'd received the telegram that my mother was finally home with her family. Pesach, his brother-in-law who worked in the Kostopol post office, managed to send the miraculous news. After living three months in a fog of anxiety and fear, wondering daily if his wife was still alive, and completely helpless to do anything to find her, my father's jubilation would have been palpable as he read the telegram; I picture him running around his mother's house, trying to pack up a few belongings. What did he take with him? Whatever clothes he could fit into his bag, some family photos, and papers to prove his identity—two school report cards, dated 1931 and 1934, attesting to his vocation, and his Polish army record book. He endured a tearful goodbye with his mother, hugged his brother Aaron and his sister Michal, and hurried to catch the train. Kostopol was only sixty kilometres away.

I'm sure that as soon as they were able to collect themselves, they left the building to find a quiet, private place to talk. And what did they talk about? How could my mother possibly convey all that she had endured? How could she speak of all the near misses and constant fear, the dead bodies in the streets of Warsaw, the pain and frustration of taking care of Rivka, her amazing luck with the German officer, the hunger and deprivation while waiting to cross the border, and her startling success in convincing the Russian officer to let her and everyone with her across? I do remember her telling me how she had never seen my father cry until that night, when she described how she had had to dig for some frozen potatoes to stave off her starvation.

Over the next few weeks they set up their life together. They found a tiny apartment, not far from her parents and younger sisters, and furnished it with some basics. Basia and Pesach lived in their own apartment close by. From what I've gathered, life in Kostopol immediately after the

Russian invasion was livable; for Jews it seems the situation had even improved after the long decade of economic disaster and intensified antisemitism they'd just experienced. An eyewitness account I read described members of the Jewish community greeting Russian soldiers with flowers and baked goods when they arrived in Kostopol.[2] Although my mother's family was not part of this welcome delegation, for them, life was certainly better. My grandfather Isaak was finally working again, in a mill, after years of destitution.

My father worked in a quarry. It's difficult for me to picture him, a relatively slight man, not particularly muscle-bound, hacking at granite with a pickaxe. He was a man who liked to dress in fine clothes, a man who loved language, who enjoyed fixing things with his clever hands. His machinist trade suited him. He was a swimmer, a runner, but not a sporty guy who took pleasure in his physical prowess. I'm gathering that he didn't have much choice in the work he did; since the Russians were in charge, there was probably no arguing. The quarry needed workers and he was sent there to work.

My parents passed the winter of 1940 in relative calm, and welcomed the return of spring. In April, the family had just celebrated Passover together; while reading the *Haggadah* my mother must have compared her escape from Warsaw to the Israelites' escape from Egypt. As I try to set the scene of their lives at this time, I'm confounded by how complicated the political and social circumstances had become. At the start of the war (as we Westerners mark September 1939), Kostopol was a small, provincial town with a population of approximately ten thousand people. Four thousand of them were Jews; Poles and Ukrainians made up the rest. Tensions between these three ethnicities were always present, although they had managed to live together in an uneasy truce until the war began. In their little corner of the planet, my parents knew the Nazi war machine was raging very close by, but their neighbourhood was still relatively safe, even for Jews. They were living in a bubble, protected from the Nazis by their Soviet masters. Many Jews had been committed communists in the turbulent years leading up to the war, but not everyone was enamoured of the Soviet takeover. My mother and most of her family were not. They certainly weren't believers in communist ideology; if anything, they were Zionists, and Zionists were despised in the Stalinist world.

Kostopol, like most of the towns of the Polish Ukraine now under Russian control, was overflowing with foreigners. The majority were refugees from what had been central Poland but was now Nazi-governed territory: "The General Government," ruled by the infamous Hans Frank, Hitler's personal lawyer and Nazi ideologue. Life was far from easy for most of these Jewish refugees. With no family, home, connections, or opportunities to make a living, some had no choice but to consider going back to their hometowns, even if it meant returning to Nazi terror. Although Hitler and Stalin were allies at this early stage of the war, there was no trust between them. Stalin considered anyone who would choose to return to German-held territory a traitor to Russia. It was not surprising that as soon as the Soviets set up the administration of their newly occupied territories, they ordered everyone to accept Soviet citizenship. To refuse because you wished to remain a Polish national marked you as an enemy. Your name would be put on a list and your fate could be deportation.

Amid all the hardship and loss of personal freedom that characterized Soviet rule, there glowed one bright lamp of enticement: universal education, including free university enrolment. My father lit up at the prospect. He put his name on a list. His mother's sister lived in Kiev, and he would be happy to go there for his education. Manya, my mother's seventeen-year-old sister, was already benefiting from this largesse, and attending university in Rovne.

ONE MAY MORNING, A COUPLE of hours after my father had left for work at the quarry, my mother heard a knock on her door. There stood a Russian soldier.

"Your husband asked me to come here to tell you that he wants to see you to say goodbye."

"But he's just left for work," my mother said. "What do you mean he wants to say goodbye?"

"He's down at the train station and wanted you to know that he's going away."

As I write, I wonder how my father convinced this soldier to go find my mother and tell her what was happening. Would he have gone out of the goodness of his heart, or did my father have to bribe him? Whatever the answer, here is another moment of unexplainable good fortune.

My mother, her head swirling with incomprehension, got into the soldier's truck and they rode to the train station. Soldiers with machine guns guarded the entrance; the platform was surrounded by barbed wire. She spotted my father among the hundreds of people corralled in the distance.

"Why is my husband being sent away?" she asked. "What has happened?"

"Your husband put his name on the list. He wants to go back to the Germans."

"He did no such thing," my mother insisted, but there was no convincing the soldier, who could do nothing but follow his orders, and was actually stretching them by bringing her the news.

"I want to go with my husband," my mother insisted.

"You can't."

"Please, let me go with him," she repeated. Although the air was still cool, large circles of damp stained my mother's armpits. She panted for breath; her unbraided hair blew wild, stuck to her forehead. By this time, my father managed to get close to her. "I don't think you should come with me," he cried. "It's safer for you to stay here with your family."

"You will have to sign a confession that you too want to go back to the Germans," the Russian pressed.

"I can't sign anything like that. That is absurd. How could I possibly choose to do that?"

The Russian soldier wouldn't budge.

"The only thing I will sign is that I choose to go with my husband."

My mother was allowed to go home and pack some things. She looked around at their meagre possessions and didn't have to make many difficult decisions about what to take. Food was a priority. Warm clothing, whatever they had, because she'd already experienced winter on the run. Documents. She found my father's passport, then found her own. Somehow, she managed to get word to her parents. They lived close by, so maybe she ran to their apartment. I hate to think how excruciating it was to tell them what had happened, and how wrenching it was for her to leave them and her sisters. Basia burst into tears and sobbed uncontrollably. She couldn't bear the thought of losing her sister again, after only five months together.

My mother always maintained that her parents told her to go with her husband. Was it courage or folly for them to give such advice? At the time, it looked like a death sentence, if they were being sent to Nazi-held territory; this seemed to be the story my mother was told when she was forced to sign her "confession." My mother, laden with her packages, was now ready to return to the train station. Word of my parents' calamity had spread to the rest of the family. Neighbours stood outside her door, witnessing her shock and humiliation. The most devastating story she told of this moment was how one of her neighbours grabbed at her purse. "You won't need this where you are going," she taunted. Everyone came to the station—Isaak and Yelena, Basia and Pesach, Pola, Manya, Sonia, Uncle Meir and his wife, Manya, Uncle Moshe and his wife, Fejge.

Pointing with his machine gun, the guard motioned for her to pass through the gate and enter. From a distance, my father spotted my mother's arrival at the station platform. Now they were both behind the barbed wire, as my father helped her with her bags. Kept far from their loved ones, they could only wave their goodbyes. It was Shabbos, my mother always remembered.

I don't know when they found out that they were being deported to Siberia.

During this period, all over the Polish territory conquered by the Soviets in 1939, Poles, Jews, ethnic Germans, men, women, whole families were being rounded up and crammed onto trains. Some were arrested and charged with crimes, but most were just scooped up in a big net, forced to sign some document attesting to an intention deemed unacceptable by the Soviets, and shipped to Siberia, Kazakhstan, Uzbekistan. To this day there is argument about how many were deported, but the figure goes as high as 1.5 million people.[3]

TWENTY-SIX DAYS PACKED IN A cattle car. They stepped on board as human beings and were immediately transformed into beasts. My mother described a moment when she looked out the small, slatted window of the train and saw a woman carrying a bucket of water: "How I envied her. All I wanted was to trade places with her," my mother said, "to simply walk down a road carrying a bucket of water." This was her dream of freedom.

I'm not sure how many days they were on the train when the tears became unbearable. There was little air, hardly any food or water, just intense misery. It was impossible to wash. My mother's long braids were so dirty that my father cut them off. An old woman sitting next to them spoke. "*Kinderlekh*,[4] don't cry so hard," she consoled. "Who knows the ways of

God?" she murmured. "Perhaps it is *bashert* that we are on this train. Despite all appearances, maybe fate will be kind to us."

"Of course we didn't pay attention to her," my mother said. "We were young and facing this horrible reality; how could we take her seriously?"

After 4,350 kilometres, the Russians stopped to let them have a bath in Novosibirsk. "But they were so cruel," my mother said. "They sent male guards to supervise the women, and female guards for the men, to humiliate us." It was more a hose-down than a soak, then back into the cattle cars for the remainder of the journey. At this point, I'm not clear about how much farther they had to go. I know they continued on to the city of Tomsk, the last outpost of civilization in Siberia, 265 kilometres away. My mother said they travelled another thousand kilometres to their destination of Itatka. It was the second-to-last stop of this railway line, the farthest prison camp of the Soviet gulag. When I searched for it, I couldn't seem to find it on any map, until a helpful scholar found a Russian website with photographs of the virtually abandoned settlement.[5]

I try to picture my parents stumbling off the train, looking around the bleak, isolated expanse, so far from any civilization they could recognize. Crude log buildings, barbed wire fences dominated by a tall watchtower, made it clear that this was a prison. Originally used to incarcerate criminals, it was now part of the vast network of camps for Russia's political prisoners. They were greeted by the camp's commandant. "You are here to work," he announced, "and the work here is cutting trees." He read the list of prisoner names, and barked out the rules of how life was lived there. When doing his rounds, the commandant stopped in front of my mother. "Who are you? Your name is not on my list."

"I volunteered to come with my husband," my mother explained in Russian. "Maybe I can help with translation," she offered, as she looked around at the blank stares of her fellow prisoners. They spoke Polish, or Yiddish, perhaps Ukrainian or German, but none had a grasp of Russian. My mother was fluent in all.

"I think your talents will be very useful here," the commandant said with a smile.

THEY WERE BROUGHT TO THEIR barracks, which housed two hundred people in one large room, and told they had eight days to rest, after their three-week ordeal in the cattle cars. The first good news my mother got was that she would share a tiny, private space with my father; she was not a prisoner, after all. It was the anteroom to the barracks, usually occupied by a guard. (I can estimate the size of the room as no bigger than fifty square feet because my mother described the tiny basement room in our Montreal apartment as about the same size as the space she lived in with my father in Siberia.)

Everyone was interrogated about their skills so the labour assignments would be most appropriate. There were many professional people in this batch of 850 slave labourers who'd been deported to this particular camp, including engineers, doctors, and nurses. My father's machinist skills were very welcome, and he was assigned to drive the tractors for tree removal, and to make sure the tractors were in good working order. My mother was made the commandant's translator and secretary, which included the task of supervising the roll call. It meant that every morning at 5:00 AM, each prisoner had to appear at the assembly spot, on time, to report for duty. Anyone late would be punished with two or three days in solitary confinement. Her job was to report those tardy.

My mother couldn't stomach this job. Old men and women who could barely walk upright, those who were sick and needed bed rest—she had to report them for punishment, and couldn't bear it. "Please, Commandant, give me another job," she begged. "I'd rather go to jail myself than send these poor people there." After she'd complained for some time, not just to the commandant, but also to his young wife, with whom she'd developed a friendship, the commandant sat her down and asked her to work out some math problems—simple arithmetic, mostly—which she did with ease. He put her in charge of the dining room for the Russian officers, where she had to keep a strict register of all the ingredients and how much was allotted for each meal. Precision and honesty were crucial here because pilfering food was extremely tempting for anyone in this job. Even the crumbs were counted, my mother said. Here was another world, far removed from the prisoners' miserable diet of only four hundred grams of bread a day (less than the weight of a block of Canadian butter, or one hefty beet), watery soup, a rare morsel of meat. Any prisoner caught stealing food, even digging up a potato, would be punished with jail time. But the officers had excellent food, including two hundred grams of bread just for dinner, and luxuries like chocolate and wine. The commandant made sure my mother ate as well as the officers, and allowed her to pass food to my father too. But even this generosity came with its perils. One winter night she was carrying soup from the dining room to her quarters, trying to make her way through knee-deep snow, when suddenly a wolf appeared. She described this moment of panic—what could she do to escape being mauled but throw the hot soup in the wolf's face and run?

My mother's friendship with the commandant's wife was a blessing to them both. I try to picture this young woman with two children, struggling to have a life in the midst of the Soviet gulag. I think she came from a family of Kulaks who had been deported by Stalin years before. What kind of lives did they lead, in this prison camp, so far from civilization?

Did they have books, or music, or any kind of amusements? How could she educate her children? I'm sure my mother must have been a godsend to her—a worldly, bright, educated woman who spoke her language and could lift her spirits and those of the children, in the bleakness of their deprivation. And my mother benefited for all the same reasons, and even more, in that the generosity she received could be passed on to my father. For example, he didn't have any warm trousers, only thin pants, while working out in the taiga, in -60° Celsius temperatures. My mother turned to the commandant and said, "My husband needs warm pants." He ordered a pair of quilted pants for him immediately. "Do you think we're in the tropics?" my mother overheard him yell to an underling. He made sure that he had warm boots too. Called *pimy*, they were a Siberian version of felted wool footwear that extended to the knee. The wool was so tightly felted that the stocking-boots were essentially waterproof. They could be worn all day out in the snow and your feet remained warm and dry. They'd be hung on a rail above the stove to dry out overnight, and worked like a dream.

But there was no escaping the reality of the Soviet gulag, with its horrendous living conditions—backbreaking work outdoors in -60° Celsius winters, quarters so bug infested in summer that sleeping outdoors was preferable to being eaten alive, no running water, no toilets, just rows of outdoor latrines, no privacy, extreme isolation—while being worked as slaves for crimes against the Soviet state, with no sentence and no release date. Perhaps it was here that my father first articulated his lifelong motto when faced with challenges: it could be worse.

Throughout their first year in Siberia, what news of home did my parents have? Did they have access to any news, given their isolation? I'm sure that much of each waking day was spent wondering about what was happening back home. My mother reported that once they received a package from my father's family; it was mostly food that they had sent. I remember mention of honey. I don't believe that my mother received any news from her family back in Kostopol. How were they faring? She had no idea that her mother Yelena was writing desperate letters to Stalin, imploring him to release her daughter and son-in-law, because they were deported by mistake. How my mother endured this separation and the absence of news is beyond my comprehension. She must have suffered with worry day and night, and would have given anything to at least let her family know that she and her husband were alive and relatively well.

Shortly after my parents marked their first year in the gulag, on June 22, 1941, Hitler surprised Stalin with a declaration of war. This was Operation Barbarossa—an all-out lightning invasion of the huge territory the Russians had claimed in September 1939. The Nazi intention was to push the Soviets all the way back to Moscow and create their greatly enlarged Reich. In just a matter of days, the Nazis routed the Soviets and overran the former Polish territories. Within a few weeks they were in control of what had been eastern Poland, and what is now Lithuania, Latvia, Estonia, Belarus, Ukraine, and Romania. It was in these territories where millions of Jews lived—the largest concentration of Jews in all of Europe—in villages and towns, like Kostopol, as well as in the bigger cities like Vilna, Rovne, Lvov, Czernowitz. With the Nazis in control, the greatest Jewish disaster since the Roman exile from Jerusalem two thousand years before began to unfold in a fury. I wonder how much my parents, cut off by thousands of kilometres, were aware of what was happening, and how they managed to live with their constant fear and dread. It seems to me that knowing and not knowing were equally fraught. There was no comfort anywhere.

My mother said that with the Russians unexpectedly at war, their lives in the gulag changed dramatically. A curfew was instituted for five o'clock. Restrictions were placed on their movements. My mother now worked out in the taiga along with my father, stacking wood that had been cut. Their status as prisoners also changed. Given that they were Polish citizens, and the Russians overnight became allied with the Polish government in exile, at war with Germany, they were no longer considered political prisoners, and they had to be released. It must have been a stunning reversal to realize that one day you were a prisoner of Stalin, and the next you were his ally. Although their status changed, their release was not so simple. My parents remained in the gulag for another year and a half before they were finally set free. Sometime early in 1943, the commandant sat my mother down and announced, "You are being sent to Uzbekistan."

Why Uzbekistan? It was a long way from the fighting, protected by distance and geography. The Russians put them back on the same trains that had transported them to the gulag, but this time they were free people, being delivered to relative safety. They weren't alone; their fellow prisoners were also released. It's hard for me to imagine the Soviets caring for their slave labourers, many of whom must have been sick, exhausted, spent—hardly useful labour for the war effort, and costly in terms of food that was already scarce. What's more, when the Germans attacked Russia in June of 1941, the Soviets instituted a gigantic evacuation policy for its citizens who lived in danger of the German advance. Although not specifically targeted for evacuation, many Jews were thus able to escape the Nazi claws that stretched eastward.[6] It was this Russian evacuation policy that produced the majority of Jewish survivors of the Second World War. I always find it surprising that the Soviets chose to be so generous, given the brutality that was often central to their governance, but I am indeed grateful; I wouldn't even be alive to tell this story if they had been otherwise.

I don't know exactly how long my parents' journey took, nor what route they travelled, but it was a huge distance. As I write, my map of the former USSR lies unfurled upon my desk, but the full map, three feet by four feet, does not entirely fit. Two folds of it—the far eastern, Pacific portions—hang over the edge. It boggles my mind to picture my parents travelling from the Siberian taiga to the hot desert of the Fergana Valley. Just to traverse the immense region of Kazakhstan, to get to Uzbekistan, must have taken a week or two. My mother said that at some point in their long journey, they had to cross the Volga River in a boat. In my ignorance of the geography, I cannot figure out how they could have crossed the Volga on their way from Siberia to Uzbekistan. It is an enormous river, the largest in Europe, flowing from Moscow through central Russia down to the Caspian Sea, but it is nowhere near the trajectory I think they would have travelled. Perhaps they crossed a tributary, or another river, or perhaps they had to make a tremendous detour, given that the war was raging, and the priority for the rail lines had to be the war effort. I don't even know what rail lines existed at that time. It's very likely that there were no direct routes. I also must remind myself that my parents had no access to maps, or to any news, except word of mouth. They were completely unfamiliar with this part of the planet, tumbling across a continent, grateful to be alive. Soon they would encounter the Pamir Mountains, which my mother described as dominating the Fergana landscape in the distance. These mountains mark the beginning of the region sometimes called "the roof of the world." Beyond the Pamirs, the Himalayas begin. Across Uzbekistan's southern border lies Afghanistan. They were half a world away from home.

At some time on this journey, my mother met a young Russian soldier on his way back to the front. As they rolled along on the train, conversing in Russian, she told him that they were going to Fergana. Even though they were ultimately heading in different directions, for a short while their paths had crossed.

"My parents live in Fergana," he exclaimed, "and they would be overjoyed to receive word from me that I'm alive and well."

"Of course, we'd be happy to deliver news of you to your parents," my mother offered. (I'm sure she wished more than anything that she could have done the same for her own family.)

He wrote his family's address—it was on Vtoraia Ulitsa (Second Street)—on a tiny piece of paper and suggested that his parents would most likely help them find a place to stay in Fergana. It is so surprising to me that my mother would remember the address more than fifty years later. She had a remarkable memory, and I suppose that encounters like these left their indelible mark. Here was another improbable instance of what can only be described as my mother's charmed life. What are the chances of striking up a conversation with a young soldier on a train, who was heading to another destination, yet was able to give the gift of friendship and shelter to a couple of penniless Jewish refugees? Once again, my mother's treasure chest of languages, and her natural friendliness and warmth, opened the door to the next chapter of my parents' survival.

7

Surprise in Amsterdam

2014

AFTER OUR VISIT TO POLAND, Amsterdam felt like a different world. We managed to find our way out of the airport and down to the centre of the city, where Robbie had booked a small apartment for our brief stay. Marike, our bubbly young host, showed us into her artsy place and we felt immediately comfortable. Just perusing her bookshelves let me know that we were on the same literary wavelength. But we hadn't come to Amsterdam to be tourists, much as we would have enjoyed that. Amsterdam was almost an afterthought.

I had wanted to spend some time with my cousin Barbara, whom I hadn't seen in at least twenty years, but Barbara was not quite as eager to see me when I approached her about a visit. Her biggest fear was that her mother Sonia could need her, and she might have to fly to Israel unexpectedly. She was so noncommittal when we spoke that I didn't think it would work out. Barbara had become somewhat of a recluse in recent years, and I knew that she suffered from ill health, but as our flight home was routed through Amsterdam, we decided to take our chances and spend a couple of days there in any case. Fortunately, our timing worked.

Robbie and I thought it best to simply walk over to Barbara's place, which was about a half hour away by foot. The thought of having to negotiate public transport was too daunting. We were travel weary and emotion weary, still digesting what we'd experienced in Poland. But walking the streets of Amsterdam meant we had to have our wits about us, our eyes on the road, and not be lost in conversation. We quickly figured out that the bricked sidewalk extensions were strictly for bicycles, as Robbie pulled me out of the way of a speeding cyclist who could have knocked me dead.

I was trying to fill Robbie in on what I knew of my cousin Barbara, whom I always thought of as my very own Polish cousin, since she'd lived the first decade of her life there. She'd spent her adolescence in Israel, and after her stint in the army, made her way to Amsterdam for art school and never left. The first time we'd met was in Israel, in 1966, when we were still teenagers. She was two years older than me and already serious that being an artist was her only way of dealing with the world. The next time was almost a decade later, when I visited her in Amsterdam, in 1975. At that time, I was twenty-five years old and living my dream year as an American *artiste* in Paris, doing improvisational dance and theatre.

Barbara had become a sculptor who, at the time of our first meeting in Amsterdam, was living in a cramped garret of a place, in between boyfriends. She was pretty gorgeous, with wild, layered black hair, flawless skin, grey-green eyes and white teeth that flashed brilliantly when she smiled. She was sinewy and sexy, but almost too thin. I was impressed with her command of Dutch—it must have been her fourth language, but we Kramer girls had the language gene. I remember going around the city with Barbara, ogling its tall brick buildings that curved and narrowed as they rose in sharp contrast to the whimsical houseboats that crowded the many canals. She used her given name, Barbara, in Amsterdam, although her parents called her Basia, and Batia had been her name in Israel. Like all of us cousins, we'd been named after our dead relatives, and our names were adjusted to fit more comfortably in the countries we landed in. Barbara was an only child, born in Breslau (Wrocław) in 1947, because her parents, committed communists that they were, chose to stay in Poland and work on rebuilding it after the devastation. My mother could never understand how her baby sister could choose this life in a country soaked with Jewish blood, often spilled by Poles themselves, who were happy to get rid of the Jewish parasites in their midst. So when another convulsion of Polish antisemitism erupted in the late fifties, Sonia and Juzek regretfully packed up their lives in Warsaw, and with their daughter emigrated to Israel, a country they came to love and cherish. Sonia and Juzek, that is. Barbara was ten years old and had a harder time adjusting. I'm guessing she felt more at home in Europe, so she chose Amsterdam.

Back then, on my first visit, Barbara and I rode bicycles, went to museums, hung out in the parks, took a canal boat ride; I still have a picture of us in high spirits on the boat. I have wonderful memories of the Rijksmuseum and looking at gigantic Rembrandts, and smaller portraits of eighteenth-century gentlemen in black velvet jackets and white shirts with lacy collars and cuffs. I thought they looked so contemporary, and imagined how much fun it would be to meet one of those men. I even glued a few postcard portraits into my memory book of that time, and it sits on my bookshelf to this day. Of course we admired the Vermeers and Van Goghs, and made our pilgrimage to Anne Frank's house of hiding, but I have so little recollection of that place. Somehow, I see buttery yellow walls, wood floors, but I have no sense of the constricted anxiety and fright that those walls contained.

Now, forty years later, my husband and I rang Barbara's doorbell and were greeted by a woman with salt and pepper

hair, her lively eyes deeper set, her cheekbones more prom-
inent on her angular face. Her beauty was still evident, but
it was obvious that she had lived a difficult life. When we
hugged on her doorstep, I hoped I managed to conceal my
distress at seeing how pain had carved itself so deeply into
her body.

We entered her ground-floor apartment, which was dark
and airless, and passed through a hallway filled with paint
cans and other art supplies, to enter her humble kitchen.
The back door opened onto a small, mostly untended garden,
filled with spring bulbs and shaggy shrubs.

"The worst for me is not being able to care for my garden
anymore," Barbara told us. "It was my biggest joy."

In this green refuge, dotted with tulips and crocuses, we
sat in rickety old chairs and began to talk.

What did we speak about? I wanted more than anything to talk about our experiences with our mothers, and
to exchange notes about what they told us about their lives.
I had a faint hope that Barbara might help me track down
Basia's lost poems. I hungered for anything she could add
to what we knew about Basia. Shortly before our trip, I had
asked our oldest cousin, Ilana, and was shocked when she
replied that she knew nothing about Basia. The same was
true for Rachel, her younger sister. All that Pola had told
them was that Basia was very pretty. That's all. This complete absence of story surrounding Basia saddened me more
than I could express.

Barbara and I agreed that our mothers tried to shield us
from their traumas and withheld much from us as we were
growing up. It stunned me to realize how much of the past
they had kept behind tightly sealed doors that they feared
opening and exposing us to.

"But your mother did tell you lots," Robbie interjected.
"And certainly in her older years, she spoke often about her
childhood and her family life."

"I know I'm the one in our family who asked the most, and I tried to record whatever I could," I added, "but she hardly ever spoke about Basia."

"And don't forget our mothers' age difference," Barbara said. "My mother was the youngest, so she didn't really spend that much time with her twin sisters, who left home when she was still very young. I don't have much to add about Basia because I simply don't know."

We reflected on our own childhoods, observing how our mothers lived their lives. Of course they were focused on the here and now—they worked hard to make a living, to be good wives and mothers, to cook and clean and do laundry. Perhaps they tried to find a friend or two, if time permitted, and they did all the things that must be done in life, with the constant background hum of worrying about their children. These were their antidotes to too much contemplation and remembrance of the terrible past. We all knew instinctively not to ask too many questions, not to bring on tears or the faraway looks that meant that no matter how we tried, we could never console, we could never relieve the pain that singed their souls. Their pilot lights were *Yizkor* candles, forever burning with mourning and remembrance. Our mothers, although appearing to be on this side of life, each had a foot already planted on the other side, and we could never make them whole.

Before we knew it, evening had come, and it was time to think about dinner. The three of us walked to a North African restaurant that Marike had recommended—a poor choice, as it turned out, but I didn't care. Here we were, members of a far-flung family, dispersed like seeds blown in a raging storm, yet brought together for the briefest of time. I was happy just being family, feeling connected and whole before taking flight again.

The next morning, over our breakfast coffee, Robbie suggested that Barbara and I spend some time alone together while he went off to do some exploring. "I'm sure you'll get deeper into your exchanges without an outsider present, even an interested outsider like me."

"And I'm sure you'll enjoy the vibrant city," I replied, "as long as you watch out for the cyclists on the sidewalks."

"I wish we'd planned to be here longer."

"Me too, sweetheart."

Now I knew the route and walked briskly toward my cousin's place, stopping at a little concession stand to buy her a potted hyacinth for her garden. It was purpley-blue, on its way to full blossom, and its intense perfume lifted my spirits the rest of the way to Barbara's door.

We settled in her kitchen while she prepared some bread and coconut topping to have with our coffee.

"You know, my mother suffered the most unhappiness," Barbara started. "She was the fifth daughter born into the family, when four were already too many, and our grandmother didn't get any consolation in finally giving birth to a son. My mother grew up feeling unwanted, and hungered not only for enough to eat, but enough love to sustain her."

"I can imagine that life wasn't easy for her, especially since the family fortunes were so bleak after she was born," I said.

"You can see it in her eyes in the family photograph from Pohorelowka," Barbara exclaimed.

"What family photograph from Pohorelowka?" I replied.

"You know, the one with our grandparents and the five daughters," Barbara continued.

"No, I don't know anything about that photograph. Do you have it? Can you show me?"

Barbara asked that I be patient while she disappeared into one of her closed rooms and searched. A few minutes later she emerged with her picture album and presented the photograph.

My hands shook. How was it possible that I'd lived my whole life in complete ignorance of this photo—a typical, somewhat formal family photo taken in the late 1920s? How serendipitous that I'd come to Amsterdam, more as an after-thought than an intention when I planned my research trip to Poland, because my eccentric, sad, beautiful cousin was so noncommittal about being here should we come, given that her mother could die at any time, and she would have to fly to Israel at a moment's notice. But here we were, in her cluttered kitchen, wiping our eyes as we spoke of our childhoods.

I was amazed to see an intact family, to see my mother, about ten years old, and recognize my daughter's uncanny resemblance to her grandmother. I'd never seen my mother as a child. On the other side of the image, like a bookend, was Basia. The twins were dressed identically, in dark dresses with white collars, tied with flowing ribbons, a sprig of tiny flowers tucked into each of the knots, but their hairstyles were different—Sabina had long dark braids, while Basia's hair was shorter, with soft curls. Her eyes, even at age ten, had a great intensity. This was now the third picture of her that I'd seen, and in each, the white space is visible from below her irises. Sanpaku eyes, they're called, and there's an eerie superstition attached to this term: that for one with such eyes, life will be short, or that their death will be violent. Barbara expressed to me the distress she feels when looking at the only formal portrait we have of Basia, who was about fifteen when it was taken. The pain and weight of Basia's terrible fate is so palpable to her in this portrait. It's different for me: I see Basia's beauty, her enigmatic mystery. I was thrilled to see my grandmother, with her striking, chiselled features, looking like her father, Mordechai, whose portrait sits on our entrance hall desk. The only photos I'd seen of my grandmother were from an earlier era. Now I could picture Yelena as a "modern" woman, her hair bobbed, wearing a simple linen suit, country-elegant. She was so young when she married, fifteen or sixteen, against her parents' wishes—her Isaak not good enough, not rich enough, not religious enough for her more established and more observant parents, according to Barbara. She looks worn out in the photo, exhausted, and far older than what would be her thirties. Next to her is Isaak, looking even more aged and forlorn, the weight of the world pressing on his narrow shoulders; between them sits Sonia, a wild-eyed child of about three. Pola stands behind her parents, while Manya is in front. There's a wildness in everyone's gaze. Perhaps the photographer was too demanding, insisting on a perfect composition, and gave the girls too many orders. Maybe the weather was changing, and he wanted to capture the image before the light dimmed. It's easy, in retrospect, to read anger, anxiety, and hopelessness in their expressions. Did they sense the coming catastrophe as a storm blowing in?

I was reminded of Susan Sontag, who once wrote that photographs give people an imaginary possession of a past that is unreal, but in drinking in this photograph, with all its detail, I felt the opposite.[1] It was, finally, a real past that I gathered, the past of my family, still intact, living in a complete world, with leafy trees, wooden chairs in the grass, a rail fence, fields in the distance, tired parents and defiant children dressed in their best clothes, posing for posterity.

What struck me most of all was the mystery of this photo's existence. Why had Sonia never shown it to my mother, or let her know that she had it? Barbara had assumed that I had seen this picture; she assumed that all her aunts and cousins had. I don't think of my family as the kind that keeps secrets from one another; on the contrary, the Kramer sisters were always intimate with each other, despite the geographic distance between them, so why the lack of communication and sharing of the one fragment of evidence of life before the cataclysm? After I'd regained my composure, I steadied myself with my camera and took a picture of the photo.

We continued talking into the afternoon, catching up on our current lives, but mostly we spoke about what happened to our family during the war, and after. Back and forth, we lobbed our little shuttlecock of family history from her side to mine—until the ringing of the doorbell startled us. So deeply were we immersed in the past that I'd forgotten that Robbie was coming to pick me up. We had agreed that we had to have one visit to an Amsterdam landmark, and it would be to the beautiful seventeenth-century Portuguese synagogue. It had been on my list for a long time, and Robbie was just as interested.

"Looks like you two have been busy," he noted. "I gather you've covered a lot of ground." He scanned our puffy eyes and red noses, took in the wreckage of Barbara's table, our empty cups and plates littered with bread crusts and crumpled tissues. He leaned down to the fragrant purple centrepiece, inhaling deeply.

"You're not going to believe this surprise Barbara showed me," I said as I slid the family portrait into his view. "Pohorelowka, maybe 1927," I added.

My articulate husband was at a loss for words. He sat down, fingers outstretched, as he cradled the paper with a delicacy hard to describe.

RETURNING HOME AFTER A LONG journey is always difficult. But this time I felt not just the discomfort of sitting upright for hours, cooped up in a metal can, unable to sleep. Added to this was the pressing expanse of all the experiences that jostled for space in my mind. Flashes of people, fragments of conversations, images of places all blurred behind my eyes as I tried to make sense of the emotions that kept churning within. Most of my mental agitation was about how to make sense of Poland. I couldn't articulate anything with even a semblance of coherence. It was as though all my energy and brainpower were localized in my gut; even my speech was diverted to the effort of emotional digestion. All the while I was still thrilling over the photo discovery at Barbara's, and

I couldn't wait to get home to my computer to upload it and send it to my sisters, cousins, and children. As I leaned into my neck pillow, trying to rest my head, I was struck by the irony of having put so much effort into searching for family documents in Warsaw and coming up almost empty, when my most spectacular find was in my cousin's possession in Amsterdam, and I nearly didn't get there.

As soon as we finally and gratefully walked through our front door and I was able to unpack my camera, I uploaded the photo and sent it to everyone in my immediate family. No one had seen it before, and all marvelled over it, puzzled that we'd never known of its existence. My sisters couldn't stop saying "Wow." Oren, Ilana's son, was convinced that it captured all their anxiety and premonition of the hell they would soon enter. Rachel's husband, Victor, inserted names into the photo and sent his doctored version to all. Even Manya's daughter Janina, who usually kept herself very aloof, emailed me to express her shock and appreciation. Everyone was gobsmacked. The next day, after dragging myself out of bed, I made a paper copy of the photo, found an old frame, and stood it on my desk so I could visit with the family when I sat down to think and record some of my thoughts.

IT WAS EARLY MAY IN Victoria, and the flowering cherry and plum trees were in full glory. Our front garden rhododendrons were ablaze in every shade of pink. Lilies of the valley spread like a carpet over the bulging roots of our hundred-year-old linden tree. The lilacs were about to bloom. Robbie was out back, examining his vegetable garden, dismayed at how late he was for planting his beloved fat white boy beans. It was already too late for the favas.

Stepping out into the soft, perfumed air on my way to the grocery store, I felt lightheaded with happiness. I'm sure the warm sun on my back as I walked down Cook Street added to my state of being. Suddenly, I was struck with this radical thought: Why couldn't I choose how to think about Poland, even if it meant going against most everything I'd learned? Why couldn't I revise my notion and accept that Poland is a place that I can love as well as despise and fear? Why must it be either/or? Was it possible to live in the uncomfortable in-between, where both realities coexist?

I'd lived my life in a black hole of absence, of never having the experience of grandparents, of feeling rooted and at home with extended family. And this was not because of a tsunami, an earthquake, forest fire or plague. It was because of tribal hatred. I'd grown up with the knowledge that Poland was a country so filled with it that it didn't take much more than striking a match before neighbours would burn Jews alive in their barns. I'd had a lifetime of damnation, prohibition, tears and silence about Poland in my immediate family. It was compounded by irrefutable evidence from the larger Jewish family, and the historians, writers, filmmakers, artists, academics, researchers, museum curators, journalists, March of the Living veterans, and friends who'd gone back and returned with their stories to firmly situate me in the camp of condemnation.

But I had just had my own living experience of Poland, in which I was graciously welcomed by Poles whom I admired and respected, and I had been introduced to the beauty of the culture, which I had never imagined experiencing. I was smitten. There were Poles discovering their Jewish identity, Poles dedicated to honouring Jewish memory, and Jews from the great Jewish diaspora returning to Poland, to live and work. Jewish history was being celebrated, housed in old synagogues, or recreated in new museums. Jewish cemeteries were being preserved and reclaimed. The end of communism in Poland in 1989 had opened the country to self-examination, especially of its wartime history—a pursuit that had been frozen for forty-five years. We felt the discourse everywhere we went. Yes, there was still antisemitism in Poland, but it was far from the dominant melody, as I had feared it would be. Certainly not in the milieus we found ourselves in, in Lodz, Krakow, and Warsaw. The impression I had was that Poland was a country taking steps to own up to its past, as painful as it was.

Coming back laden with my shopping bags of groceries, I'd stocked up on some of the discounted Polish products that our tiny local supermarket kept packed in shopping carts at the bottom of their aisles because they didn't have space on their shelves. They didn't really fit in at all. It was a treat to have very good Polish pickles in brine, boxed buckwheat kasha, and delicious plum compote bottled in big glass jars. Looking at the labels, trying to pronounce the Polish as I was putting the food into the cupboard, I said to myself: *Here I am, living the in-between of my love–hate relationship with Poland.* As I allowed my radical notions to come out into the fresh air to play, Robbie came in from the garden, his jeans streaked with dirt from his planting. I guess it was the look of surprise on his face that stopped me. I'd been dancing around the kitchen as I was tidying, madly leaping from thought to thought.

8

Fergana

1943

S TEPPING OFF THE TRAIN, MY parents must have rubbed their eyes in disbelief. Fergana was a beautiful city. Its sandstone buildings shimmered in desert light. Wide avenues were shaded by oak, poplar, and plane trees, watered by narrow canals that ran alongside. As they entered this city in the Central Asian valley of the Silk Road, it must have felt as far away and foreign to them as the moon would have been. Compared to the gulag, it was like a dusty, forgotten corner of a biblical garden. Perhaps they noticed, as they got deeper into the city, that its initial appearance was somewhat deceptive. Fergana was not an ancient city at all, but a relatively modern one. It was mostly built in the late nineteenth century as a garrison town, after its capture by the Russian empire, and incorporated into the Soviet Union after the revolution.

People spoke Russian there, so my parents had no trouble finding the street the young soldier had written down for them.[1] Just as predicted, his parents were thrilled to receive word from their son, and welcomed my parents with great warmth. They invited them to spend the night, and the next day, over a simple breakfast of bread and cheese, they learned a bit more about this city where they had landed. "As you can see, we don't have the means to invite you to live with us," the soldier's parents said, "but we have some friends who could offer better accommodations." The friends were a childless couple who had good jobs and were well off, by Uzbek standards. They had a cow, a garden, and enough land for a one-room shed. They offered my parents the shed.

Their first night was nearly fatal. They had lit a coal fire in the stove, but unfamiliar with its idiosyncrasies, they went to bed believing that all was well. As they slept, the stove produced noxious fumes, and if not for their alert hosts who dragged them outside, they would have died of carbon monoxide poisoning. It took them a few days to recover.

Soon my father was working, fixing and maintaining the ovens in a bakery. I have no idea what he earned, perhaps daily bread, but one job wasn't enough to survive. He worked at whatever additional jobs he could find, sometimes fixing tractors—a skill he'd perfected in the gulag. But it was not so easy for my mother to earn anything. She offered her help with childcare, with nursing the elderly, with sewing clothes—whatever she could do. Despite its beauty, Fergana was a city filled with poverty, especially during the war when supplies of everything were hard to come by—even paper was a precious commodity. Hundreds of thousands of people, Jews and non-Jews, had fled or were deported to Uzbekistan (and Kazakhstan) when the German–Russian war began, and everyone struggled to survive in a region and climate that could barely support its native population. People were accustomed to hardship, but the enormous influx of refugees, in addition to the hundreds of thousands of Russian evacuees from its western cities, made starvation, disease, and death far too frequent an outcome for those displaced.[2] Polish Jews landed in a very different culture, far from the ingrained hatred of Jews that characterized Eastern Europe. No doubt the Soviets had their own forms of antisemitism, which carried over from centuries of czarist rule. The Soviet government did very little to assist the Jewish refugees, but at least it wasn't bent upon their annihilation. Their Great Patriotic War against the Germans was so enormous that all the resources the Soviets possessed were needed to defeat their enemy. Although the figures are impossible to verify, approximately sixteen and a half million people in the Soviet Union were evacuated and displaced during this war. Nearly thirty million, civilians and military, were killed. I cannot conceive of this number of people, except to imagine that it's almost the entire population of Canada.

What do I know about my parents' experiences in Fergana? A few childhood stories. I remember best how they described the fruit. Grapes shaped like ladies' fingers. Pomegranates. My father taught us the best way to eat them. First, squeeze it all over, like kneading a baseball, until it was all wrinkly but intact, then cut a tiny hole through the skin, put your lips to it, and suck. To this day, no juice tastes better to me.

I learned about illness and deprivation, too. It was here that my mother was bitten by a mosquito and got malaria, which was endemic in Uzbekistan. The fevers and chills she had were so severe she didn't expect to survive them. I'm not sure if she had access to quinine or any treatment. I know that she suffered the aftereffects of malaria for a long time, but I never witnessed any bouts later in her life. In her official interview with the Holocaust Documentation Center in Miami, she described another medical nightmare, when she was stung by a scorpion. As horrible as it was, she told the story with humour. Typically, to stop the venom from spreading, you apply a bandage so tightly to the area affected that it's almost like a tourniquet, she explained. But my mother was bitten in the neck. There was no way to deal with the venom except to apply some arum powder mixed with honey—the traditional medicinal treatment. Again, I may be dreaming that this was offered to her. She suffered terrible pain, but mercifully it passed, and she lived.

I know it was a time of great tumult. My parents were strangers in a distant land, recovering from the slavery they'd experienced in the gulag. They were now free people, but freedom meant struggling to survive along with everyone else. All the while, as they clung to each other for consolation and support, they felt very much alone, separated from their families and fearing the worst. I'm sure that the news of home they heard from landsmen (people from the same region) they met, or the newspapers they read, must have chilled them to the bone. I don't know if they encountered anyone specifically from their hometowns who had managed to escape, but the likelihood is great. From accounts that I've read, there had been reunions so improbable that they seemed closer to miracles than real-life possibilities.[3]

I try to imagine what they felt when the war finally ended in May 1945. They would have been in Fergana about two years by then. I don't believe that their day-to-day lives would have changed. To be honest, I can barely fathom their mental state other than anxiety and exhaustion. What means did they have to celebrate, and how could they celebrate until they knew the fate of their families? And how could they find out?

Soon they learned of an office in Moscow, most likely the International Red Cross, which was dedicated to finding people in the aftermath. Given the displacements of millions, and the chaos that characterized the end of the war, I'm sure the office was deluged with requests by survivors desperate to find family, and desperately hoping that family had, against all odds, survived. The Soviets had set up an office in Buguruslan, in the Ural Mountains, because it was far from the front.[4] I don't know how long it took for mail to travel all the way to Moscow and back to Buguruslan, but it was through this office that my mother and her sisters found each other. Pola, Manya, and Sonia were alive and living in Siberia. I can sense the jubilation they all felt upon news of their survival. The irony of discovering that the sisters were living not so far from where my parents had been enslaved in the gulag was surely part of their astonishment. But where were Basia and Pesach, and what happened to their parents, their extended family?

It was through letters that my mother learned what had happened. She'd already spent over a year in the gulag when the Germans had surprised the Russians with all-out war on June 22, 1941. At that time Manya, the middle sister, was a student at the university in Rovne. The Russians needed all the manpower they could get, so they acted fast to evacuate all the universities and even allowed the students to bring their families with them. That's how the three sisters travelled together. Amid all the frenzy of their departure, Isaak, their father, sat them down and instructed them to always stay together and to look after one another, no matter what happened. I can hardly conceive of how hard it must have been for my grandparents to say goodbye to their three younger daughters. While my mother was weighing bread in the commandant's dining room in Siberia, her father was standing at the platform, holding Basia's baby boy while waving goodbye to his younger daughters as their train pulled out of the station. This news sent shockwaves through my mother's body. She had no idea that her twin sister had given birth to a son. It had been a difficult birth, and because she was still very sick, she couldn't leave with her sisters. That's why Isaak and Yelena stayed behind—to look after her and the baby. Pesach, like all able-bodied men, had been drafted into the Russian army to fight the Germans.

The sisters' train ride from Kostopol was terrifying. They couldn't hold back their screams as German bombs exploded along their route. They were fleeing east, heading far away from the front, beyond Ukraine, to where the Russians thought they'd be safest—they were going to Stalingrad. Pola, the eldest of the three at age twenty, was soon working in a munitions factory that made cannon shells for the Russian army. Unlike Sabina, Pola was more reserved than her older sister, taller and plainer in looks, but she took charge of everything in her quiet, competent way. How eighteen-year-old Manya, auburn-haired, petite and refined, continued her studies in philology and history at the university baffles me. Sonia, willowy but tough, though not quite fifteen, did whatever she could to survive. Each looking out for the other, the three managed to survive together in Stalingrad, living mostly on sunflower seeds, for the better part of a year.

In the summer of 1942, while my mother was stacking logs with my father in Itatka, the whole city of Stalingrad was preparing to defend itself against the German attack they knew was coming. Manya was out digging trenches with all the university and high school students who'd been enlisted to create defences for the city, while Pola was desperately trying to find her. She was being evacuated to Siberia, along with the other factory workers, and there was no time to lose. The factory boss had reluctantly agreed to include Pola's sisters in the evacuation, but where were they? Sonia ran from street to street, looking for Manya, and when she finally found her, Manya didn't believe they would be evacuated, and wouldn't stop digging. Sonia had to drag her away.

I am mesmerized by these details. Just thinking about them in Stalingrad, knowing that the battle and siege of this city was one of the longest and bloodiest in the history of warfare, gives me the shivers. It lasted over five months, with close to two million casualties (both military and civilian); the city was completely starved and reduced to rubble before the Germans were finally turned back toward Berlin. It was the turning point in the war. The Germans never recovered. As I reflect, picturing my aunts clamouring onto their packed train to Siberia, the day before the battle of Stalingrad began,

I hear the echoes of the old woman on my parents' deportation train to the gulag, suggesting that maybe it was *bashert*.

The sisters' destination was Yurga, not far from Tomsk, where a munitions factory was built. In Yurga, Pola continued working in the factory, but did other jobs as well. She was a teacher, a mathematician, and a knitter, determined to look after her younger sisters by whatever means possible. She worked long into the night making things so she could exchange them for food. Sonia was not eligible for food stamps, which were reserved for workers, so she was constantly hungry. Manya, who by this time had a teaching certificate, taught history in a high school. (I can hardly think that there were high schools at this time in this godforsaken part of the Russian world, but this is my ignorance speaking.)

By 1943, when my parents had been freed from the gulag and shipped across a massive chunk of the Eurasian continent to Uzbekistan, Pola and Manya met their husbands. Kuba and Michal, Polish citizens, had been drafted into the Russian army, but somehow their whole division was sent to Siberia to work in a munitions factory. It was the same factory where Pola worked. The men had heard that there were Jewish women at the factory, so of course they were interested in meeting them. At that time, everyone knew that life was conditional, and you couldn't count on having a future. Their courtships were very brief. Pola married Kuba, and Manya married Michal shortly after they met. By this time, Sonia was a flamboyant and strikingly beautiful seventeen-year-old. She too was engaged, but called it off, knowing it wouldn't work out. True to their father's instruction, the sisters remained together and looked after each other throughout their entire time in the Soviet Union.

As much of a relief as it was for my mother to learn about her sisters' survival, more than anything she needed to find out what happened to her parents, and her twin sister Basia, and everyone left behind in Kostopol. To the letters and postings she sent out to the International Red Cross, there was a response from a close family friend in the village of Pohorelowka. He, his wife, and son Kondrat had remained friends with the Kramers long after they'd left the village and moved back to Kostopol after their mill had burned down. Perhaps they were close because they too were from a persecuted minority—they were Subbotniks. Since they worshipped the Sabbath on Saturday, and followed the rules of the Torah, or Old Testament, they were as close to being Jews as Christians could get. I suspect that the similarities of their religious practices were another reason for the families to feel a kinship. I wish I knew their surname so I could find out more about this family that risked their lives to help the Kramers in Kostopol.

This is what my mother learned. Within days after Pola, Manya, and Sonia stepped onto the train heading toward Stalingrad, the Nazis had overrun the whole region of Volhyn in late June 1941. While Russia scrambled to defend itself from the onslaught, Pesach, along with all men who could walk, had been drafted to fight with the Soviets. Miraculously surviving the short but devastating battle that had taken so many lives, he somehow managed to return to Kostopol, which was in the hands of the Nazis by the first of July. All hell had broken loose. I never really understood this cliché, but as I write I feel in my gut how apt it is in describing the unmooring of morality that occurred. Whatever restraints that normally hold back human savagery were completely ripped away. Whether it was Polish or Ukrainian men who stopped Pesach on his way home, we don't know. On the rutted street of the poor Jewish section of town, they made him point out exactly where he lived. Banging on the door of his home, they forced Basia, gripping their baby son, along with her mother Yelena and her father Isaac, to stand outside and watch as they hacked Pesach Fishman to death on the street. The brutality was so enormous that Basia and Yelena became widows together on that day. Isaak's heart shattered; he died that evening of a heart attack. I have no eloquence, cannot find words to express the anguish I feel just writing this, but I can't escape my task. There is no redemption except to say their names and acknowledge that indeed, this is what they had to endure. I picture my aunt Basia and my grandmother Yelena, frantic with grief and fear beyond reckoning, knowing in the deepest parts of themselves that they were no longer considered humans by their neighbours, and that torture and slaughter were their lot. Even the dignity of burying their men was denied them.

The first official Nazi *Aktion* began in August 1941.[5] With the assistance of local Ukrainians, approximately five hundred Jewish men of influence in the community were singled out and brought to a forest outside Kostopol, where they were shot into a pit that had been prepared for them. The Germans requisitioned local men, women, and children and forced them to do the digging, tamp down the bodies, and fill the mass graves with lime and earth to cover their atrocities. The wives and families, the community that remained, were told that the men had been sent to a work camp. The next two months were eerily silent as conditions for the Jews worsened daily. In October, the families were informed that they would be joining their men. During the chaos of rounding up one thousand four hundred Jews of Kostopol for mass killing, my baby cousin Mordechai was pulled out of Basia's arms and buried alive. Bullets were reserved for the adults. How Basia could continue living after this torture is beyond my ken.

The Jewish ghetto was erected a few days later. It was here that Basia and Yelena suffered their last days on earth. These days lasted almost a year. Kondrat's family trudged the twenty-seven kilometres by foot from Pohorelowka, risking their lives to bring them food from the village so they wouldn't starve. While my mother was weighing every gram of meat served in the commandant's dining room in Itatka, her mother and twin sister were living on two hundred grams of bread a day.

The last of Kostopol's Jews were murdered in Kostopol forest on August 25, 1942. Five thousand Jews in all, from neighbouring towns as well, were brought to the forest where huge pits had been dug. After they'd been forced to undress, they were lined up in rows, facing the pit, mounting with bodies of their friends and family, and shot in the back of the head or neck. Among them were Basia Kramer Fishman and Yelena Bebczuk Kramer, and the entire extended Bebczuk and Kramer families. The earth trembled for three days after as those still alive slowly suffocated beneath the weight of their dead.

My parents were numb with shock and grief. They knew the same story had repeated throughout all of Yiddishland, but the full extent of the murder of the Jews of Europe was beyond their awareness. My father learned that his mother, sister, and extended family suffered the same fate in Stolin, but somehow his brother Aaron, and his cousin Yossel managed to survive. He could not truly imagine the extent of the brutality. When his mind ventured there, he descended into a pit so dark that his only choice was to become as silent as his dead. My mother rarely told the particulars of this horror, but I've known it as long as I've had consciousness, in one form or another. How could she speak of this to her children—that human beings have the capacity to reduce other human beings to garbage, to torture and kill and feel nothing of the pain? From the moment of learning the truth, sorrow raged into my mother's bones and lived in her marrow for the rest of her long life. If only she had been there, she repeated to herself, she could have saved her sister. She would have carried her on her back, and her baby too, she was so strong.

Because my father could never speak about his murdered family, I know so very little about them, to my enduring regret. No matter how often I think about *that which happened*,[6] and by this point in my life I can do so mostly without tears, I still cannot comprehend it and don't understand how it is possible to comprehend. If not for news and experiences of good deeds and acts of compassion, especially at the worst of times, I would truly be in despair.

THE CALENDAR WAS MOVING TOWARD 1946, and my parents and my aunts were still stranded in a foreign land. How could they possibly go home, as there was no home to return to, and no permission yet to leave the Soviet Union in any case? There was no freedom of movement; Stalin ruled with an iron fist. On the diplomatic and bureaucratic levels, they were Polish citizens and had a right to be repatriated to Poland, but the map of Europe was once again being redrawn by the Allies. Kostopol would no longer be in Poland, but would join Ukraine in the Soviet Union. To compensate Poland for the loss of its eastern borderlands, the German regions of Silesia and Pomerania, on Poland's western border, would fall under Polish dominion. It's one thing to draw lines on a paper map, but the miserable reality of human populations forcibly removed from their homes is devastating. Hundreds of thousands of people were on the move—Poles from the east expelled to Silesia, Germans in Silesia pushed back to East Germany—while tribal hatred and uncontrollable revenge ruled the day. The aftermath of the Second World War, with all its killing, pillaging, raping, and theft, was shockingly brutal.[7] Much as I'm sure my parents wanted to be freed to finally resume their lives, their biggest challenge was to reimagine life after their unfathomable catastrophe. Where could they go? Their homes were ruins. Their families murdered. Their communities eradicated. They knew that they would not be welcomed back if they would try to return. All this convulsing agony, while they were stuck in Fergana for almost a year after the war in Europe ended.

Finally, in the spring of 1946, they, along with their Polish compatriots, were told that they would be transported back to Poland. Their life was again in upheaval, tempered by the excitement that my mother would finally be able to reunite with her sisters, as would my father with his brother. They had nothing to pack. My mother described her one dress. It was polka dot, with a hole in every dot. My father made her shoes from tire treads. Once again they boarded a train, very similar to the cattle car they rode in to Siberia six long years before. Now they felt aged, desiccated, far older than their years. By this time, my mother was twenty-nine, my father thirty-two. They would spend a couple of gruelling weeks in transit. As I examine the map, I wonder the route they took. Perhaps they went by way of Stalingrad. Somewhere past Ukraine they re-entered Poland, boarded another train, and continued west. When the Soviets finally moved to repatriate their Polish residents, they did so with a speed and efficiency not possible during the war.

From Siberia, Pola, Manya, and Sonia, with their now-expanded family, were heading off as well. Pola and Kuba had a two-year-old daughter, Ilana. Manya and Michal were expecting their first child. On April 27, 1946, after crossing the border into Poland, the three sisters registered with the Central Committee of Polish Jews (CKŻP), which was tasked with helping Jews, including refugees from the Soviet Union, to reunite with surviving family. From Uzbekistan and from Siberia, the sisters travelled great distances, counting the days until they would embrace. Their destination was Breslau—the once-German but now Polish city of Wrocław.

9

Searching for Basia

2014

I N MY STUDY SURROUNDED BY a pile of books, I'm trying to write a poem. I look out the windows beyond my computer screen, to the linden that's bursting into leaf, all the promise of newborn life in the shimmery shake of the branches. They get smaller and more delicate the closer they reach toward the glass, so close I could lean out and touch them. It's such a huge old tree; it towers over our old house, which is a very tall 1890 Victorian. It's the tallest most beautiful linden in all of Victoria. Sometimes I feel my mind lift away from my body, like a bird seeking to perch on a high branch, all the better to scout for an image to set me off. I try to command my fingers to start typing, to put something on the page, to kill the surface, as the artist instructed me years ago when I asked how he started his collages. Make a mark, grab a line, I tell myself. Perhaps a sensation remembered from Warsaw—the musty odour emanating from the orphanage in Praga, or the sight of a friendly mouse face sculpted into the concrete embellishment of the doorway to the Jewish school dormitory. Perhaps the look of the art deco covers of

Płomyk on the computer screen in Anna's office at the Jewish Historical Institute, after I'd asked her for a glimpse of them. How enticing they were. Can I describe the desire to climb into those pages, clamber over the words that I couldn't make sense of, and travel back in time?

I can't get the story of Basia's book about Moscow out of my mind, and how surprised I was to hear about it at my mother's reawakening. I'm trying to imagine her motives in writing her book, and how far she got that year she lived with Bat'ko Ivano. Until the day my mother told the story, I had never given much thought to Basia's interests, as my mother had rarely spoken of her. I knew instinctively not to probe or ask too many questions because it was too painful for her. Who were the writers that inspired Basia's literary imagination—was she keen on Tolstoy? Dostoyevsky? Mandelstam? Akhmatova? Perhaps she wasn't even interested in literature, per se, but in architecture, or history, politics, or religion. The sad truth is that I know virtually nothing about my aunt Basia.

I wonder if there is any real chance of finding her poems. Just to read a few words that originated in her mind, to give me a glimpse of her inner self, a tiny emanation of her humanity, is what matters most to me. I long for a transmission of her that survived beyond her terribly short and tortured life, something that carries forth from the horrible pit where her earthly remains lay hidden and unmarked, eradicated from history. If I can't know her, at least let me know a few of her thoughts.

Gazing at the photo of young Basia, posing with her parents and sisters beneath a couple of leafy trees in their village home, I ask myself how poetry happened for her. I always think of her as having a serious, almost brooding intellect, as someone who thought deeply about the world and her place in it. She was only fourteen when her poems were published, but fourteen meant far more maturity than what it meant in my youth, and what it means now. She lived in such unsettled, violent times, when the world was lurching toward the bloodiest apocalypse ever known. Where did Basia stand, how did she define herself as a budding writer? I believe that she was a Zionist in her heart. It might seem strange to consider a fourteen-year-old captivated by a political movement, but hers was a different world. How could she not recognize that there was no future for herself in Europe? When I ask myself what subjects she could have entertained in her poems, beyond Zion, I list mother tongue, womanhood, end of childhood, the future. I know that I am wildly unrealistic to think that I will ever find out what fired her imagination. What I am sure about is that she felt the roiling turmoil that surrounded her, that she lived in increasingly dire economic circumstances, and it all combined with her exquisite sensitivity and intellectual engagement to propel her to pick up her pen and let flow the drama of her thoughts. It started with poetry, when she was just fourteen.

I DON'T RECALL WHEN I first was introduced to poetry, but it certainly was not as a young child; of those years I have virtually no memory. What I do remember of my early years is that I felt different from those around me, and that I had a desire to pass as a "normal" child. I tread carefully, quietly, not wishing to be noticed, with a heart full of apprehension. My parents never read to me because English was so foreign to them, and Yiddish too distant for me; there was no comfort to be found in beautiful words and sentences, although my mother did sing to me in Yiddish.

I sit and recollect my adolescence and those long-ago high school days, when I had my unexpected initiation into the world of poetry through Hebrew poems and songs about the scent of roses in the evening. I loved the alchemy of words put together in ways that caused a ripple through my body and stopped my breath for an instant; in the suspension of that moment, it made me feel something almost holy. Poetry created an altered state of being, a recognition that a different reality also existed if I opened myself to it. Most of the time I walked around blind to the present, like most humans, but poetry had magic when it worked, so I gave myself permission to try to write poems too. It was playtime, dreamtime, puzzle time, and became my great escape. I was a loner in high school, always on the margins of popularity, and because I was never sure I wanted to be closer to the centre, I learned to find some comfort where I was and sought company with more mature university students who came to study in Boston, the "Athens of America." When it was my turn to study in Boston, it was Auden's "Musée des Beaux Arts" in freshman English class at Tufts that bowled me over with its stunning impact. I was hit by the power of poetry.

Many years later, as a young mother, I was still pulled by poetry's forces. I remember the summer day in Quebec's Eastern Townships. My three children were about six and seven years old; my sons were playing in the tall grass that surrounded the funky clapboard farmhouse I'd rented, while their older sister was minding them. I pulled out a notebook and put pen to paper, lines on a page. Bluebottles buzzed, startling me with their colour. The sun embraced me, and the warm earth was a bed of comfort. The voices of my children in the near distance reassured me they were fine, while the laundry snapped in the wind on the line strung from the porch above. It all came together and created a pure state of authentic happiness. My pen glided along, and line after line, I filled the page. This was the moment when poetry returned to me.

I'M BACK TO THE BLANK screen in my study, trying to write. What good does a poem do in this world anyway, and how can poets afford to sit in their studies writing poetry? Most poets don't make their living through writing. What makes them think that a poem can put bread on the table? Artists need a community around them; they need permission to write something as silly and ephemeral as a poem. I am the luckiest of women and wouldn't be here without Robbie's encouragement.

One day, not long after we had met, I surprised him with a poem:

> *Take the way we met. What fiction*
> *were we creating*
> *floating in that salty pool?*
> *You told me about the whale that slid*
> *right under your boat in the kelp bed.*
> *I remember how we couldn't let go.*
> *How we awoke with hand cleaved to hand,*
> *like your tongue to the roof of your mouth*
> *on the day you were born ...*

He was caught off guard. His usual fluency and wit abandoned him for what felt like a long time. Of course I was hoping for his approval, not just as my beloved, but as a professional writer at the height of his craft. He wasn't a poet, but a journalist who'd studied classical poetry seriously. He'd written his master's thesis about Milton's *Paradise Lost*. I was just feeling my way around poetry in the dark.

"Sweetheart," he called me, as the paper rustled ever so lightly in his hand, "I'm impressed." He leaned in, drawing me closer and said, "More poetry. This is what I wish for you. More poetry, and more art. I'll do whatever I can to bring them into your life. I promise."

I let out a deep breath. "You have no idea how much this means to me," I blurted, or something like that. Every cell in my body glowed. What comes back to me is the feeling of encouragement and validation that I'd never received about my writing before.

"And what about you? What do you wish for, that I can give to you?"

"I'll have to think about it," Robbie said, after a pause. "But it will most likely involve fish."

It took me a long time to start the poetic journey. I still marvel that Basia was published at fourteen. I'd always heard that Poland was a land crazed with poetry—it was a national passion—so it's not such a stretch to picture the Kramer sisters caught up in it. In the period of their youth, between the two world wars, there were many journals and magazines dedicated to poetry, and even children's poetry. The story my mother told is that Basia received a letter from a publisher saying, *The crown of the poet belongs on your head*. I can imagine the thrill of receiving those words, and at such a young age.

My first published poem appeared in 2002, when I was fifty-three years old.[1] Robbie and I had moved to Victoria six years before. It was a long-awaited homecoming for him, and with this move I was finally liberated from a full-time job. True to his promise, I immersed myself in poetry and painting in my free time, and felt the exhilaration of unshackling my creativity. I signed up for workshops and classes and met wonderful teachers; they opened their homes and cleared their dining room tables, spreading out a feast of poetry knowledge to partake in. It felt like the gift of a second adolescence. It was during this time that I started to write the stories of my family history in poetry. "Searching for Wallenberg" told the story of my involvement with a passionate Russian scientist who was committed to finding the truth of Raoul Wallenberg's disappearance after his arrest by the Soviets in Budapest, in 1945. He'd always been a hero of mine, and Vera Parnes, whom I'd met in Montreal after she'd left Moscow for Canada in the 1990s, became my heroine. The poem was an absurdist's tale, written as an exercise in adopting a particular voice. As I wrote it in what felt like a fugue state (the best conditions for "gift poems" that seem to drop into your mind virtually formed, with no gestation), my mother's gulag stories entwined with Vera's stories and what I knew of the prison-like conditions of Russian life:

> *My name is Vera. I work for Raoul.*
> *He disappeared after Budapest and*
> *my job is to find him.*
> *In the gulag you'll find no wild game but*
> *many have lost teeth biting into*
> *a wolf. When there is no cutlery*
> *such things are possible. Why, one night*
> *as I hurried from commissary to hut*
> *through knee-deep snow*
> *I was forced to throw hot soup*
> *in a wolf's face ...*

BEFORE EVEN GOING TO POLAND, my initial effort to find Basia's poems (with Kasia doing the search in the Polish national archives in Warsaw) turned out to be a bust. Since my hopes had been raised the moment that Alan Rutkowski, my friend from the synagogue, informed me about the children's magazine *Płomyk*, Kasia had looked through all the issues of 1930 and 1931, even 1932, but came up empty. No one with any knowledge of Polish children's literature had ever heard of *Płomyk Alfa*, which was the journal that Sonia had insisted upon, during the Kramer sisters' reunion in Israel in 2000. So I decided to ask Kasia to return to the journal my mother had claimed was the one, the Polish daily, *Nasz Przegląd*. Given that it was a newspaper, it rarely published poems, but it did have a weekly supplement, *Mały Przegląd*, with children's writings from all over Poland. Kasia scoured each issue, but the poems were signed with pseudonyms, or nicknames, no family names or addresses. (If only the children had been encouraged to sign their full names.) I'd even asked her to go further afield, after I'd heard from a Polish academic in Krakow who suggested I look into *Chwila*, a journal published out of Lvov, which was not so far away from Kostopol.

In my own research, I'd come across Anda Eker, a poet five years older than Basia, who was often published in *Chwila*, and I imagined that their sensibilities would have matched. A prodigy herself, her first poem was published when she was only thirteen. Just knowing this, I imagined that their paths could have crossed, or if not their paths, then their words. When I discovered Eker's poem "About a Certain Little House,"[2] I couldn't help but picture the Pohorelowka childhood of the Kramer sisters:

> *It would be nice to be a child again*
> *And live in an old-fashioned house,*
> *In a tiny house with a motley garden*
> *And take leave of my old sadness.*
> *In a tiny house with a gate and fence,*
> *Without worries and yearning*
> *It would be nice to be little again,*
> *As if nothing had yet happened,*
> *As if life held*
> *No sorrows, loneliness, or grief*
> *As if what had happened*
> *Had been just a bitter dream,*
> *As if what had happened*
> *Had been a scary fairy tale.*

It reminded me that my mother's childhood, and that of her sisters, though challenged by poverty and antisemitism, was still relatively normal compared to the shock and trauma of inheriting genocide, which was my generation's experience. Reading this poem transported me back to the little girl I was, emotionally battered and terrified that evil lurked behind every tree and hedge on the seemingly peaceful streets of Boston's Jewish district of Dorchester, where I first came to consciousness. It brought to mind a few lines of my own:

> *I grew up with fear,*
> *as familiar to me as my own bed,*
> *as the sound of my parents breathing*
> *in the next room ...*[3]

After Kasia's repeated searches, and communications with Polish and Jewish academics, I began to lose heart that I'd ever find Basia's poems. So I asked myself once more: Could I imagine them? I needed background knowledge. I began to dig into Polish poetry, to get a feel for the poetic landscape of Basia's young life. Ever since learning about the great Polish poet Tuwim, while standing in front of his mother's grave in the Lodz Jewish cemetery, my curiosity was ignited. While visiting Krakow, our knowledgeable guide introduced me to the Skamander group,[4] avant-garde poets of the twenties and thirties, including Tuwim, who had strongly influenced Polish poetics; among them were Jewish poets who wrestled with their unique position of being outsiders/insiders in those tumultuous interwar years. Apart from Szymborska, Miłosz, Zagajewski, I had hardly read Polish poets. Through my reading I began to understand that Polish Jewish writers were caught in a terrible bind.

When Sabina and Basia were coming of age, the notion of Jewish art in Polish was gaining credence among the intelligentsia, but not everyone applauded. There were those Polish nationalists who viewed Jews writing in the Polish language as a travesty, or cultural appropriation at best. I can well imagine the tensions boiling up and how difficult it was for Jews to assert their place in Polish society. Jews were essentially foreigners, guests who'd outworn the invitation to visit long before. Within this existential discomfort, some Jewish writers were bold enough to publicly express their angst in Polish, declaring their Jewish identities and manifesting their connection with Jewish culture in the land their ancestors had dwelled in for a millennium. It was hazardous territory to inhabit. As European hatred of Jews brewed in an ever-hotter cauldron, the idea of going back to the land of Jewish origin, and even engaging in the positive work of draining swamps and planting vineyards in Palestine, was understandably attractive. This is what drove Sabina and Basia, Olek and Pesach to their training "kibbutz" in Kostopol. Perhaps this yearning is what Basia wrote about.

MY EFFORTS TO FIND HER poems hadn't yielded the results that I'd hoped for. I'd just received an email from Kasia. She'd done another fruitless search of the journals I'd asked for, and it had been a struggle. "When I was going through the *Mały Przegląd* issues it was very painful," she wrote. "There was so much hope in those children. They wanted to be happy, and they had dreams. Some of them could have been great writers one day, but most of them were murdered, and their artistic effort is completely unknown." Kasia asked me to do her a favour. "If you let me, I would like to translate (I'm not a poet but will try to do my best) and send you some poems from the issues around the years when Basia was published. Please make a better poetry correction of my translation and put one poem in your book, just to pay tribute to Basia and to the other young poets who perished during the Second World War."

Reading the children's poems, I felt a terrible nostalgia rise up—a dangerous nostalgia. Even now it hurts too much, this intense longing for a conversation with Basia, for a meeting, a recognition that we've lived on the same planet, come from the same earth, share blood and bone. We share a love of poetry, but I shall never know her, not even as smudged ink on a page.

10

Reunion

1946

MY MOTHER AND FATHER WERE two drops in the huge wave of refugees sweeping across Europe in 1946. After the war ended they were stuck in Uzbekistan, waiting impatiently to be released, while the Allies—Britain, France, the United States, and the Soviet Union—were redrawing the map of the continent, jockeying for their best positions in the race to recreate a Europe that suited their geopolitical goals.[1] What to do with the millions of people who would be displaced seemed the least of their concerns.

I know very little about my parents' journey from Fergana back to Poland. My mother had no intention of returning to Kostopol, nor did my father imagine going back to Stolin, if they even had a choice. Kostopol was now in Ukraine, and Stolin was in Belarus—both Soviet republics of the USSR. All I know is that their destination was Breslau, the ancient, stately, once prosperous city in lower Silesia that was home to over 600,000 Germans (including 23,000 Jews) when the war began. My parents were heading to Breslau, along with countless other Jewish survivors, because it was the largest city in the region that Poland had designated for the repatriation of homeless refugees. My parents had no idea what kind of life they would find there, but it didn't matter so much to them at that point. What they knew, and what kept them going for three weeks in a better equipped cattle car, was that the Kramer sisters were there, and they would finally have their family reunion.

Pola, Manya, Sonia, and their families had arrived only a couple of months earlier, at the end of April 1946. It's a miracle that the sisters not only managed to survive the war, but had stuck together throughout, as they promised their parents they would. Together they were plucked from certain death the day before the siege of Stalingrad began, when Pola was evacuated from the munitions factory to work deep in the Russian interior, and she succeeded in bringing her sisters with her. They had survived five years of misery in Siberia.

My parents arrived in Breslau in late June. Due to the chaos caused by the redrawn national boundaries, what had been a German city for centuries was now Poland. Much of the city was in ruins, although the streets were cleared of most of the rubble a year after the official end of the war in Europe. Thousands of German people were still being expelled from their homes and driven west, back to the new, vanquished Germany, which was totally incapable of absorbing them. Although thousands had been evacuated by the Nazis just before the Russian siege of Breslau began, in the last con-vulsions of the war in 1945, the majority—mostly women, children, and the elderly—had nowhere to escape the bomb-ing and destruction that occurred. When the Russians finally prevailed and Breslau capitulated after two and half months of hell, the bloodletting, rape, and plunder were brutal. Amid this horror, Poland reclaimed its ancient city and anointed it with its former name, Wrocław.[2]

As my parents entered the city, they saw that the street signs in German were pulled down and replaced with signs in Polish. In the cacophony of public space, they heard

Polish, German, and the surprising sounds of Yiddish, too. Everything smelled of raw wounds and decay. Their world, broken apart in such a gigantic rupture, had accepted savagery as the new normal. No ethnic group or nation had escaped the torture of its people; revenge, hatred, and despair fired the actions of just about every human treading the scorched earth of Europe.

There were no organized welcome committees in Breslau that spring as refugees poured into the city seeking shelter and relief. "Where can we go to find our family?" my mother asked as their train pulled into Breslau station. By this time, my parents had figured out that the best source of information was another person in the same boat as them. Everyone had the same mission: to find news of any surviving family and tips about where news could be found.[3]

"I know there's a café in this city, not far from the White Stork synagogue," a fellow traveller advised, "a place where you can post your name and who you are looking for." So my parents headed to that café. It was relatively easy to find, as the White Stork was the only synagogue left standing in Breslau after the war. It was tucked behind a large courtyard, back from the street that was lined with cafés and shops, though they were hardly stocked with goods. It was a deceptive setting because they couldn't see the synagogue from the street, but they tried their luck and entered a café that seemed livelier than the rest. It took a few moments for their eyes to adjust to the grey light, dulled further by wafts of cigarette smoke. The din of conversations rose in their ears while they sorted the multiple languages they overheard. As they scanned the scene surrounding them, they noticed a window at the far end of the place that opened onto the courtyard. In the distance they made out the shape of the once elegant synagogue.

"The *Umschlagplatz* of Breslau," someone announced to them as they stared out. "It was here that the Jews were brought for shipment to Auschwitz."

My mother shuddered in silence. As she tried to regain some composure, she looked up at the wall facing her and saw it was covered in scraps of paper.

"You must be searching for someone," the patron continued. "Everyone is searching. So you've come to the right place. Go read the walls, my dear lady. You might be lucky."

Luck did not seem likely as my parents moved closer to the wall before them and began to scan the hundreds of notes scribbled in Polish and Yiddish. The first sighting of a *Kramer* caught my mother's breath. But it was not one of her Kramers, and given that it was such a common family name, she realized it was going to be an impossible task. An empty chair beckoned; she collapsed into it, propped her elbows on the table, and cradled her weary head, feeling an exhaustion so complete it frightened her. My father continued to read the walls methodically, moving around the café as she sat there, immobile.

"Sabina, come look," he called from the far corner. Hearing the tone in his voice, she felt as though a spring had released in her, lifting her from her seat. Everything around her blurred; the walls looked like they were pulsating, but it was her heart beating too fast. She steadied herself by leaning against the table, took a deep breath, and then made her way toward my father. Putting one arm around her, he pointed to the yellow scrap of paper taped on the wall. "Pola, Manya, and Sonia Kramer," he read, "20 Loschstrasse apt. 44."

HOW TO DESCRIBE MY MOTHER'S reunion with her sisters? Their voices opened with sounds they'd never made before, more keening than joyous; deeper, more primal than words. The press of their bodies so tight they could hardly breathe was a comfort; their faces now wet with tears they couldn't shed during those six long years of exile and grief.

Reunion

Squeezing each other's arms and shoulders, their fingers tingled in recognition of familiar contours of flesh and bone. Then, leaning back slightly, so their eyes could trace the features of their faces, they noted how much each of them had changed.

"But where is Manya?" my mother asked Pola and Sonia, conscious of her absent sister.

"She is in the hospital, but all is well," Pola said. "Michal is with her and their new daughter."

My mother described her happiness as a wildness rising up within her that she could not explain. Too much joy after too much sorrow was dangerous. She felt very faint. My mother closed her eyes for a few moments, and when she opened them, she saw the little girl, Pola's two-year-old, looking out from behind her mother's skirt. Crouching down to her dark-haired little niece, my mother lifted her into her arms. As her small body curled happily into hers, she had to will herself to stop from squeezing her too hard. New skin against her skin was the only pleasure she could wholeheartedly accept, and she wished with every scrap of her being for a child of her own. She tried to force herself to stop from thinking about Basia and Pesach and their little son Mordechai but it was impossible. They were just at the beginning of their lives together as a family, having a child of their own, wishing the best for his future and theirs; despite the grimness and horror that had closed in on them, they must have had some hope. How could they have faced each day otherwise? Memories of their unlikely love affair sprang to her mind, that long-ago summer in Kostopol, when Basia's initial disdain transformed into a passion she could hardly contain. But now, night and day, my mother saw their brutalized bodies lying in a horrible pit, and no matter how hard she tried to rewrite the story, or erase it from her mind's eye, she could not. More than ever, she felt herself half dead. With her twin sister, her other half, already dead, she struggled to go through the motions of being alive. She didn't understand how she was incapable of tears, as though everything was frozen in her; each molecule of her body slowed so much as to mock the rules of nature. Finally, in the embrace of her living sisters, she cried.

"Take me to Manya, take me to the hospital," my mother said, after she'd regained some composure. "We must go at once."

When the sisters entered the ward of the old brick building, only parts of it still intact, they found Manya in one of the metal cots, cradling her infant daughter Janina, with her husband Michal by her side. It was June 20, 1946.

—

MY PARENTS DIDN'T REMAIN IN Breslau for very long. During the short time they were there, they and their expanded family were completely preoccupied with the most pressing questions: Where could they call home, and how could they get there? Staying in Poland was unthinkable. After all they'd been through, the few survivors who'd emerged from the Nazi death camps, or their hiding places in cellars, attics, barns, or forests, or those who'd returned from the Soviet Union, like my parents, were not welcomed home. Far from it. Jews were still being murdered in Poland.[4] After all the killing, during such a horrendous war, Jews were still pariahs as far as many locals were concerned; even though ninety percent of Poland's three and a half million Jews had been murdered, many Poles were not sympathetic to the ones who survived. "You're still alive?" was a common expression of greeting to Jews who had returned to their hometowns and villages. The Kielce pogrom, where more than forty Jews were murdered in the most notorious act of postwar hatred, happened just a few weeks after my parents arrived in Breslau. News of this atrocity was the death knell of any future for Jewish survivors in Poland, although a surprising number of Jews defied this outcome and chose to remain. Sonia, my mother's youngest sister, was one.

On the train returning to Poland from Siberia, Sonia had met Juzek, and they fell madly in love in the classic strike of lightning and thunder. A handsome, intensely vital man, he was a dedicated communist, and despite all that had happened to the Jews of Poland, he wanted to stay in the land of his birth and join in the rebuilding. Sonia, who had embraced socialist ideology as a teenager, did not need her arm twisted. She was willing to join him. My mother couldn't understand this. For my parents, and their other surviving siblings, staying in Poland was impossible.

IN THE SWIRL OF POSTWAR turmoil, my parents tuned in to the underground networks to plot their escape. They knew of Brichah, the clandestine group dedicated to helping Jews make their way out of Poland.[5] Although Poland had re-established a government, it was the Soviets who controlled the borders and dictated how the Polish government operated. The Iron Curtain had dropped as soon as the war had ended, if not before. Perhaps the Soviets wanted to enable Jewish departure from Europe at this critical time. That may have been why the new border between Poland and Czechoslovakia was relatively easy to cross. Brichah operatives helped Jews obtain forged documents so they could cross with greater ease. Between July and December of 1946, approximately 150,000 Jews fled from Poland, many taking the route through Czechoslovakia. My parents were two of this number. Pola, Kuba and Ilana, Manya, Michal and Janina were another six. As far as I know, they travelled separately; my parents left Breslau in the fall. They'd hopped onto trucks in the night, their dubious papers folded in their pockets, fooling border guards to let them pass, and journeyed south to Bratislava. From there, they crossed the Austrian border and headed to Vienna, only sixty kilometres away.

More luck was in store in Vienna. One of Sonia's girl-friends from Kostopol had miraculously survived the war in Nazi-occupied Poland. Hana Nussenblatt had been active in the tiny underground resistance during the war, and was now working with Brichah.[6] She greeted my parents in Vienna, found them some beds to sleep in during their short time there, and got them to Salzburg, where they crossed from Austria into US-occupied Germany.

The only thing I know about my parents' brief time in Vienna was that they visited the old Jewish cemetery to pay homage at Herzl's grave. The father of Zionism, his vision for a Jewish state was born in the late nineteenth century, when he realized that the roots of European antisemitism were so deep it would be impossible to eradicate them. He believed that there was no future for Jews in Europe no matter how much they assimilated in their host nations—they would always be considered a separate, foreign nation—so he began working with tremendous dedication for a Jewish state to be recreated, ideally in the aboriginal homeland. The growth of Zionism as a Jewish movement in Europe was explosive, particularly in the latter interwar years, when antisemitism was peaking and there was no escape for European Jews. Herzl tragically died young, but he was revered by Jews as a modern-day Moses, and never more so than in the fragile days of Jewish life resuming in the ruins of Europe in 1946.

In Vienna, my mother and father stood in the old Jewish cemetery, dwarfed by a tombstone twice their height. It was late November, and for the first time, my parents were dressed in warm clothing—no longer in the rags they'd worn for so long. As they embraced this rare moment of tranquility, they stood with eyes closed, heads bowed, and thought about where they were going.

Now warm and comfortable in a fine wool coat, my father, I imagine, reflected on everything that had happened to him since his deportation. His years of slavery, chilled to freezing in the Siberian taiga. Then the heat of Fergana, where he nearly suffocated in the fumes of an Uzbek hut. He knew he was as wanted in his ancestral home as a cockroach the exterminators failed to gas. The end of war had not yet brought an end to Jewish suffering. The British were blocking all ships to Palestine, homeless Jews be damned. He thought about their dream of liberation—to finally step foot in Eretz Yisroel, and start their lives again. But Palestine was a hornet's nest of warring parties—the Arabs outraged at the thought of a Jewish homeland in the land they considered theirs, while the Jews clamoured for justice and safety in a state of their own. The British, deaf to Jewish claims, knew they were incapable of defusing the escalating violence in Palestine and were counting the days until they could extricate themselves from their Mandate.[7] So even if they managed to get to Palestine, my father asked himself, what would they have, how would they live? Suffering and hardship were definitely in store.

This could have been the moment when my father began to question their plans. Once he dreamed of Zion as much as my mother did, but now he wasn't so sure. War there seemed inevitable, and my father couldn't stomach the idea of more deprivation and death. How could he express these fears to my mother? They had endured so much together, each one holding the other when it didn't seem possible that they could withstand any more pain. She still had her heart set on Eretz Yisroel, and so did Pola and Kuba, Manya and Michal. She had never wavered from this dream, and now more than ever it beckoned her. Talking with Hana and the other survivors they had travelled with solidified her desire. Hana was ablaze with the urgency to escape Europe and get to Palestine no matter what. After all she'd witnessed in the killing fields of home she had become a fearless warrior, daring the powers in control to try to stop her.

As my parents contemplated their future, standing at Herzl's grave in Vienna, a city they never imagined they'd visit, I'm sure they were struck by the irony of it all. The surprise of finding a field of Jewish graves that had remained intact, despite all the destruction of Jewish life, must have resonated deeply. Here they had come to contemplate their future, while overwhelmed with all they had lost. They had no idea how much longer they would have to live in limbo, and even worse, they wondered if they could live in comfort and peace ever again. Here, only the dead lay undisturbed.

MY PARENTS, ALONG WITH HANA and a small group of Jewish survivors, made their way to Salzburg, high in the mountains of Austria, on the border with Germany. How strange it was for them to have Germany as their destination for this in-between time of their lives. But it was US-occupied Germany, and despite all the headaches of housing, feeding, and looking after thousands upon thousands of displaced persons, it was a task the American army took on. They didn't have much choice, given the reality on the ground. Soon the responsibility was passed to the United Nations Relief and Rehabilitation Administration (UNRRA), and other organizations whose missions were to aid. I wonder how it felt for my parents to find themselves in Germany, the country that had nearly succeeded in eradicating their tribe. Even hearing German spoken had startled them in Vienna; in those moments, their instinct was to recoil, but they couldn't hold their hands over their ears forever. In reality, my father had spent no time under Nazi rule, and my mother had only spent three months in Nazi-occupied Warsaw; they never had the full experience of living under Nazi brutality. Conversations with the German officer in her apartment in Ząbki reverberated in my mother's memory. She heard the echo of their footsteps as he escorted her across the bridge in Warsaw, and she knew that he had saved her life. Nothing less. But how

could she tell this story of a German officer who helped her
when it was so different from all the other stories whirling
around her? She felt alone with her experience. Her worst
villains were the Polish and Ukrainian neighbours who killed
her family. How could they have lived together in the same
village and town, shared the air and water, the fields of grain
and the forests surrounding, where they hunted wild ber-
ries and mushrooms? They'd buried their dead in the same
pungent earth. Was the hatred always there, but contained
through the niceties of civilized behaviour? What was it that
could turn neighbours into murderous beasts? How was it
possible to trust ever again? She hated how black and bitter
her heart had grown, as though it had been dunked in acid
and left to corrode. She couldn't rid herself of the poison no
matter how much she scrubbed.

I'm not sure how the Americans decided who would
go where. Hundreds of thousands of people needed to be
sheltered somewhere. Fortunately, it became clear to the
American authorities as early as September 1945 that Jews
should be sheltered separately, and not mixed with people
who had been their oppressors and exterminators. All I know
is that my parents were processed as Jewish displaced persons
in Landsberg, Germany, in late December 1946. They were
handed over to the International Refugee Organization (IRO)
and the Hebrew Immigrant Aid Society (HIAS), and sent
to the town of Schwäbisch Hall. There they were joined by
Pola and Manya and their families. Each family was assigned
a small apartment in a dwelling that had been emptied of its
German residents; the sisters lived a few houses down from
each other. For the first time in seven years, my parents were
surrounded by family and had an address: Kocherfeld 393.

Sabina Kramer, *circa* 1932.

Olek Milman, *circa* 1936.

Sabina and Basia Kramer, Warsaw (Praga), Poland, *circa* 1937.

above Bridge over the Vistula Connecting Warsaw with Praga, 1934.
Photo by Willem van de Poll. NATIONAL ARCHIVES, NETHERLANDS

opposite, top Palac Zeliszew.[1]

opposite, bottom Jewish bronze figures purchased in Warsaw, 2014.
PHOTO BY AUTHOR

right Olek Milman (standing), Itatka,
Siberian gulag, *circa* 1941.

opposite, left Barbara and Isa, Amsterdam, 1975.

Kramer family (Basia, Yelena, Pola, Sonia, Isaak, Manya, Sabina) in Pohorelowka, *circa* 1927.

Olek and Sabina Milman at
Herzl's grave in Vienna, 1946.

opposite, top Olek Milman teaching at ORT
school, Schwäbisch Hall.

opposite, bottom Cousins Rivka Kutz and Sabina
Kramer, *circa* 1932, Pohorelowka.

below Olek and Sabina Milman in Schwäbisch Hall, 1947.

opposite, top Elea, Jonah, Mica, and Isa arrive in Poliske, August 2016.

opposite, bottom Isa, Mica, Elea, and Jonah stand beneath the chestnut trees in Poliske, 2016.

above Sabina, Manya, Janina, Schwäbisch Hall, 1948.

opposite, top Sabina, Olek, Estera, and Isa depart Germany, May 1950.

opposite, bottom Sabina holding Chava Tzipora (Mayim), Boston, 1951.

above Back row, from left: Isaak Bebczuk, Fejge Bebczuk,
Moshe Bebczuk, with family in Kostopol, circa 1920s.

above Sabina in the Negev, Israel, 1964.

below The Kramer sisters in Haifa, Israel, 1964.

11

Mother Tongue

2015

I NEVER IMAGINED THAT KRZYSZTOF MAJER from Lodz would be sitting in the synagogue of Victoria with his fiancée when I delivered the talk about my journey to Poland and search for family history. Almost a year had passed since the conference in Lodz that had brought us to Poland. Friends and colleagues kept asking about my progress, and the Jewish Federation in Victoria was eager to hear how I was advancing in the work they had generously funded. After our visits to Krakow and Warsaw, and Amsterdam, with my cousin Barbara, I immersed myself in Polish Jewish history and poetics.

Many of my days were spent in conversations with friends, often about the meaning and language of home. I knew that my mother's family spoke Polish and Russian but not Yiddish at home, which was far from typical. According to my friend Goldie—whose mother, Chava Rosenfarb, had survived the Lodz ghetto and Auschwitz, and came to be regarded as one of the greatest postwar Yiddish writers—speaking Yiddish at home was what the majority of Jewish families did in Poland before the war. Writing in Yiddish, and not Polish, was even a political act, a response to the hateful antisemitism so current in the Poland of the interwar years. Goldie reminded me that Rokhl Korn, a major Jewish poet who'd made her mark before the war, abandoned Polish to write exclusively in Yiddish precisely because of Polish antisemitism. My mother's family, then, did not fit the profile of mainstream Jewish home life—perhaps because they lived in a provincial town, and even smaller village, where in order to survive they had to communicate in the local languages. A poor yet ambitious family, their greatest assets were their intelligence and education. If they were to make a living in their society, fluency in Polish was absolutely critical. Russian was equally important during the Kramer sisters' childhoods, so it was not such a leap for my mother to attend a Russian *gymnazium* in Rovne.

I tried to envision the literary landscape of the Kramer household—all the languages they spoke, and the books they read. I went further afield and approached scholars with my queries. "What books would have been on the shelves of the Kramer household?" I asked, describing the family situation in the interwar years. My mother often told of how friends in Kostopol would say that if you wanted a good book to read, go to the Kramerovkes. Books were their greatest wealth.[1]

"Your family sounds like they were Polonized Jews, distancing themselves from the tight reins of Judaism and leaning toward immersion in Polish culture," one academic replied.

"But they completely identified as Jews," I huffed back. "Just because they spoke Polish at home didn't negate their deep attachment to their roots."

When I described this exchange to Goldie, she said, "Well, why were they not Polonized?" As we continued speaking, we realized the breadth of the spectrum of Jewish experience in Poland. "But I have to admit," Goldie added at the end of this conversation, "that when my father wrote love letters to my mother, he wrote them in Polish. He thought it was a more romantic language than Yiddish."

All the while, I was still chewing on my experiences in Poland. No doubt my reflections were greatly informed by the conversations and encounters I'd had there. I recalled how in Warsaw, Kasia had waxed on about Tuwim, a poet of great stature in Poland, despite his Jewish roots; he had a broad scope in that he wrote many kinds of poems, including children's verse, which she was already introducing to her young son. My mother had not taught us Polish, but when my children were babies I asked her to tell me what she would have sung in Polish, and she taught me "Jedzie, Jedzie Pan" (whose nearest English equivalent would be "Ladies and Babies How Ride They" or "Yankee Doodle Dandy"). When I sang it to Kasia, as we walked the streets of Warsaw's Praga district, she was clearly surprised by my emergent Polish. But I only knew the first verse. The second and third verses were all about Jews. Why hadn't my mother taught me the best verses, Kasia wondered, with all the fun of dropping the child between your knees at the final moment? Somehow fun and Polish never seemed a possible combination in my childhood experience. In fact, I was surprised that my mother taught me any of it. Good as her word, Kasia emailed me her version after we'd returned home:

> *Jedzie, jedzie pan, pan*
> *[Here comes the lord, lord]*
> *na koniku sam, sam*
> *[riding on his horsey]*
> *A za panem chłop, chłop*
> *[Then rides the serf, serf]*
> *na koniku, hop! hop!*
> *[on his horsey, hup! hup!]*
> *A za chłopem Żyd, Żyd*
> *[Then comes the Jew, Jew]*

na koniku hyc! hyc!
[on his horsey, trot! trot!]
A za Żydem Żydóweczki
[then the Jewettes come a-clutter]
pogubiły pakuneczki
[all their little bundles scattered]
A my wszyscy BĘC!
[and we all fall DOWN!]

I kept wondering why Tuwim would write this, as I believed he was the author of this nursery rhyme. Krzysztof Majer straightened out my misconception before I could embarrass myself with a riff about the tormented Jewish soul as it manifested in the children's verse of a national poet. What impressed me most—beyond Krzysztof's unexpected efforts, and the seriousness of his approach to language, wherein each word has an essence, defined by sound, meaning and context—was that the lyrics Krzysztof knew were so different from those Kasia had sent me:

> The rhythm and the repetitions of one-syllable words in the song were essential to the translation, so that it could actually be sung in English. Also, it's important that this is a sort of social (indeed, feudal) arrangement in miniature, which is why I say "serf" instead of "peasant" (luckily, it's also one syllable). But what's interesting is that in the version that I know the final lines are different. No Jewettes make an appearance; rather, it is "a za chłopem jedzie Żyd, a za Żydem nikt już, nikt" ("after the serf rides the Jew, and after the Jew nobody, nobody at all"), indicating even more clearly his position in society ... In any case: I tried to capture the rhythm, the simplicity, the repetitions and the roughness of the language.

After the Jew nobody, nobody at all. I confess how much it stung to read this. I could feel my mother's fingers slammed on the Warsaw tram. No wonder she only taught me the first verse, and only at my urging. This exchange had occurred months before, but it hustled its way to centre stage as I banged around trying to organize the clutter of my conflicted emotions into some kind of coherence. It felt unreal when Krzysztof let me know that he'd be coming to British Columbia, with his fiancée Paulina Ambroży, and their dates coincided with my scheduled talk about my research and experiences in Poland.

I had finally read Katka Reszke's *Return of the Jew*, a book I'd first encountered in Krakow.[2] She'd sought out and interviewed fifty people who, like herself, only discovered their Jewish origins in young adulthood. I was really intrigued by the narratives of these third-generation post-Holocaust Jews in Poland and how they constructed their identities. I tried to imagine myself discovering that I was a Jew, having spent my childhood in ignorance, in a country and nation where being a Jew was often considered a great catastrophe. All of her subjects had been baptized and raised as Catholics, and their language was Polish, as was their culture. In most cases, their parents didn't know that they themselves were Jews, or they'd kept it secret. These young people were truly Polish Jews, but most were not recognized as such by Jewish officialdom, which insists that one must be born of a Jewish mother. Whether they chose to officially convert to Judaism was not really the point—some did and some didn't, depending on their feelings about God and religion. For most, their Jewishness was about tribe, about the blood in their veins; claiming their identities as Jews was their mission, essential for the revival of Jewish life in Poland. They were the authentic essence, their heartbeats the timbrel drumming the news that Jewish life had not entirely disappeared. It was present and vital.

I was reminded of Mount St. Helens, after the volcano. The shock of renewed life rising so quickly from the lava ash that had obliterated hundreds of thousands of acres. The audacious tenacity of flora and fauna. I pictured the great poet Stanley Kunitz, observing the noisy crickets in his Provincetown garden as he wondered what was the engine that drove life. *Desire, desire, desire*, he insisted, and his answer is such powerful solace.[3]

Katka Reszke and her friends inspired me. Here in North America, it's easy to choose one's identity, even as a Jew; to be or not to be one is not a complicated question, given the ease and freedom we have. So different from Poland, where to be a Jew is an enormous choice, a badge of honour.

Part of my previous understanding of the place of Jews in contemporary Poland was sealed by a 1986 issue of *National Geographic*, which I'd kept on my bookshelf for decades.[4] "Remnants: The Last Jews of Poland" told the story of those few who remained—elderly, poor, isolated, living in ill health in miserable hovels—so few they could hardly pull a *minyan* together for prayers wherever they lived. Many had abandoned their religion, in any case; some had converted and married Poles, while others denounced their children for doing so, even when there were no Jews to marry. Each had their reason for remaining in Poland after the war and the antisemitic purges of the 1950s and 1960s.

"Today the remaining Jews number perhaps five thousand, nearly all of them old, scattered like withered straw across the Polish plain," the piece by Niezabitowska and Tomaszewski began, with photographs recording the last of the once formidable tribe. At the time of its publication in 1986, I could hardly bear to read the text. I pictured my parents in these pages, had they stayed, and all their *grineh* (greenhorn) friends that I'd grown up with; I imagined Sonia and Juzek, toothless, grateful to be eating matzos by an ancient stove.

In truth, the photos made me feel sick. I kept the magazine tucked away on my bookshelf because I can't bring myself to throw things away. It bothered me that Polish Jews were the subject of study as a nearly extinct tribe, that this article was an examination of the shrivelled remains of a once mighty civilization that had repeatedly overcome annihilation so improbably, over millennia, that it defied imagination.

Back then, my understanding of these Jews was limited. I still believed that Jews who stayed behind in Poland were aberrations, that their choice to remain demonstrated character flaws or wilful delusions that their lives would improve, just as the Poland they knew and loved before the war would become livable again. I honestly had no room in my consciousness to consider that some of these remaining Jews, for whatever reasons, did not have the means to leave Poland, when they had had the chance but were later trapped, or that they had justifiable reasons to stay. Some had really wanted to remain.

When I reread the text, I was surprised by my reaction. Yes, the sadness was still a dark cyst lodged in my heart, but I felt a new understanding, certainly coloured by my experiences of contemporary Poland and the people who had made them so rich and meaningful. The authors of the piece—a husband-and-wife team, photographer and journalist—spent years seeking out Jews, asking, with enormous respect and sympathy, to enter their lives. The stories they recorded were similar to the narratives that Katka Reszke recounted, but of earlier generations—mine, and my parents'. Three years after this article appeared, Polish history was rewritten, with Solidarity's successful overthrow of communism. Free at last, after forty years of repression, during which the Communist government insisted on its skewed telling of the history of the war. After the outright suppression of the truth about the Jewish annihilation, Poland could finally exhale and do the hard work of remembering—and so could the remaining Jews as they picked up the threadbare rags of the tribe and chose to live again as Jews in their home country. Niezabitowska and Tomaszewski were pioneers in their efforts, and they recorded a budding Jewish renaissance. True, most of it was still underground, but Jewish life had survived.

Not long after we returned from Poland, Katka Reszke had a Jewish wedding in Wrocław, at the White Stork Synagogue. The whole city was invited. I watched it on YouTube, in a moment of true cognitive and emotional dissonance. I imagined their feelings of pride and excitement, the joy of being able to be who they were, and the significance of expressing that publicly, inclusively. When was the last time a Jewish wedding was such a cause of celebration in Wrocław?

MY SYNAGOGUE LECTURE, ILLUSTRATED WITH slides and augmented with music, began with the story of my quest to find Basia's poems. Somewhere in the text and the images I was still wrestling with my own attitude toward Poland. I'd grown up and spent my life thinking of Poland as a place of hatred and pain—not a place of any virtue. But I had found virtue in Poland, despite all the "lucky Jew" figurines holding a grosz coin between their hands, despite the remnants of burned synagogues and decayed cemeteries overgrown with ivy. For example, there was Milena Wicepolska, dedicated to cleaning up the forty-four-hectare Jewish cemetery in Lodz, section by section. And Barbara Stojowska, walking and talking us through Jewish Kazimierz in Krakow, with her impressive knowledge and sensitivity. There was Barbara Kirshenblatt-Gimblett, chief curator at the POLIN Museum, with her infectious enthusiasm for gathering the rich history of Polish Jewry (including her own) in all its magnificence and tragedy. I was startled every time I recollected my encounter with Damian in the Warsaw Uprising Museum, while the emotional connections with Kasia in Warsaw all combined to stretch the fibres of my heart, revealing chambers I didn't know existed.

As I pondered over my presentation, I received, as if on cue, the gift of Don McKay's inspired essay "Field Notes on Betweenity," in which he decries the necessity of having to constantly think in an "either/or" world, and makes a strong case to include "both/and" as part of our experience.[5] Why did I need to choose between condemning Poland for its antisemitism and my love for the Poles that I was getting to know? In my bones, I was ready to experience both. Reading Don's essay, I was transported back to the imaginary dark-room where I conjured up my first real images of Poland, metaphorically watching them emerge on the milky paper floating in trays. My brain was forming new pathways. I was realizing that it had been wrong to lump an entire people into one category, disregarding the fact that a people is composed of individuals. I had to remember and acknowledge that there are good people doing good things always, even in places at the heart of darkness.

So I introduced the individuals that had made my journey so astonishing: Kasia, and her request that I do her the favour of including a poem by a young Jewish poet who perished; she asked that I do this in remembrance of Basia because it mattered so much to Kasia's soul. There was Milena, with her dedication to respecting Jewish memory in Poland, plot by plot. And there was Damian, who believed that my mother, and I too, were part of the fabric of Poland. These are the stories I spoke of in the synagogue of Victoria, as my friends Krzysztof and Paulina sat in the audience, their faces beaming with what I can only call grace. I was so grateful for all the friends I had made over the past year.

I was about to meet one more.

Tomasz Różycki was a visiting Polish poet, invited by the University of Victoria for a week of readings and lectures. It was a great opportunity to be initiated into contemporary

Polish poetry and poetics, and knowing of my project, the organizers arranged for me to meet with him privately. In anticipation, I'd picked up a copy of his latest book, *Colonies* (translated by Mira Rosenthal); I discovered that our families' origins were only about two hundred kilometres apart, so I felt a direct kinship with a landsman.

"I wish I could speak to you in Polish," I began, "but I'm afraid that I only know a few swear words and a nursery rhyme. My parents saved Polish as their private language."

"I'm working on my English. It's not very good. But I can comment on this beautiful February weather. It's fantastic. Back home it is very cold still."

"Welcome to the Canadian Riviera. If they can't go to Florida or Mexico, Canadians come here for the winter. We're very lucky to call this place home. My husband is a rarity—his great-grandparents settled in Victoria, so he's fourth generation. Most people are newcomers, like me. When we were thinking of moving here from Montreal, he told me stories of how beautiful it was here, but I had to see for myself before making such a big move. When he told me that we wouldn't need screens for our windows because there are no mosquitoes here, I said, 'Okay, just buy the tickets.'"

Tomasz's grin completely disarmed me. I tried to restrain my desire to blurt out my story, and I struggled to damp down my enthusiasm to compare notes on our attachments to history and on how we deal with the concept of home after its vanishing. His family had been exiled from their home immediately after the war, among the masses of Poles forced to move from the Ukrainian side of Poland to the German side, in the former Silesia. But I immediately sensed his willingness to listen, to hold that ball of tangled wool and join me in pulling the threads, picking apart the emotional knots that bind us to a place that exists only in our imagination, or in the shadows of consciousness. The early afternoon sun bore down upon us, bleaching colours to the palest hues so that everything appeared almost black and white. I saw twinkly blue eyes, a salt-and-pepper beard, a shirt collar dark as the night sky.

"I've been searching for my aunt's poems, published in Polish around 1930, when she was only fourteen," I said. I mentally groped for a quick description of my project, my elevator pitch, a thirty-second condensation of the most important story I was seeking, but brevity is not my strong suit. Tomasz soaked up the sun as I gushed. I relaxed a little.

"I still have not found them, even though there have been moments of real hope," I continued. "So I asked myself: If I can't find my aunt's poems, could I imagine them? Can I find a way to appreciate her life and times, and enter this faraway place?"

Tomasz leaned forward, elbows resting on the table, hands clasped together. I felt his engagement in the hollow formed by his thumbs—a small, inviting well.

We met again a couple of days later, when the morning sun highlighted everything. We walked along the boardwalk of the Inner Harbour, past the float homes of Fisherman's Wharf, the arbutus smooth of bark and about to bloom, under a postcard blue sky. A circular rain garden was punctuated by deep red canes, bare of leaf; the whole scene throbbed with spring, as if the entire world was about to give birth.

"Last night's reading was so emotional for me," I began, picking up the thread of our last conversation. "The minute I heard your voice, reading in Polish, my tears surprised me. Just to hear Polish, so familiar and at the same time completely incomprehensible. It's the story of my life, encapsulated. I held the paper with the Polish words and followed through the thicket of consonants as best I could. Then we had the English experience. I underlined a few precious recognitions, but mostly bobbed along as wave after wave carried me."

"I'm in a state of transformation, Tomasz," I continued. "Since our experience of Poland a year ago, I realize that I'm becoming a different person. It's because I feel like I've fallen in love, and it is dangerous, and I don't know how to be.

Forgive me if I express my intimate thoughts to you, perhaps it's too much, and inappropriate, since we are strangers after all. Just tell me and I'll shut up."

"No, please, I want to hear, it's not too much at all," he insisted. His tall frame close behind me, he leaned his head toward me as we walked the narrow path single file, then side by side, as the path widened.

"Well, you see, I never heard a good word about Poland when I was growing up. It was the place of all the killing, the loss of all human goodness, made worse when one's own neighbours were complicit. But it was also the place where my family lived for centuries. I have no idea how long, maybe a thousand years. How do you dismiss that history?"

"So you have to know this place," Tomasz added, "even when you can never have it back, not even the memory of it. And that's why I try to write it down, to capture something, knowing that it's really impossible. But I do it anyway, actually losing whatever it is, in the act of writing. The reality is that you can never have it."

"Exactly. But we are compelled to do it. Something stronger than us insists. To just express this loss, this yearning, is all we can hope for, to touch another with our being. It is so hard to live this experience, trapped inside our heads, so isolated, so human."

We sat on the bench by the rain garden, listening to the soft, gentle patter on native grass.

"*Tikkun*—this beautiful Jewish concept of repair. Have you heard of it?" I asked. Tomasz shook his head. "This is our task on earth, to heal what's broken, to make it a little better. It's the most we can hope for."

We talked and talked. Compared notes on how we began writing poetry. He studied French philology, never studied poetry formally. Just began to write one day, lyrics for his band; he played no instrument, so he had to do something to contribute. His father had a great memory for poems and would often recite from the classics—Adam Mickiewicz's ballads, the music of the language so appealing. All these bits conspired to bring him to poetry.

"Do you think it's crazy for me to even think of trying to imagine Basia's poems? I have days when I ask myself if I can write a poem at all."

"Not at all. You must not be afraid to try. All I can do is urge you to try."

"I realized not long ago that even if I were to experience the miracle of finding her poems, I wouldn't be able to understand them fully because we don't even share a language. And just thinking this thought filled me with such sadness. Maybe that's why I was in tears when I heard you read last night."

I rooted around in my big black bag and pulled out the page where I'd copied Anda Eker's poem. "Do you know this poet?" I asked. "She was from Lvov. I came across her when reading about Polish Jewish poetry in the interwar years, and she was a child prodigy, too. I keep imagining her as a writer that Basia would have admired. They could easily have been friends."

From my bag I next brought out Miłosz's anthology of poems, *A Book of Luminous Things*, and we read Anna Kamieńska's hauntingly beautiful "A Prayer That Will Be Answered."[6] "When I read 'Scorched Maps,'" I said, "I couldn't help but be reminded of this poem because of crying out one's love with a head buried in the grass, and the bumblebees." But Tomasz didn't know this poem by Kamieńska.

"Do you think there's such a thing as a cultural unconscious?" I wondered aloud as I turned to "Scorched Maps"[7] to appreciate it once again:

> *I took a trip to Ukraine. It was June.*
> *I waded in the fields, all full of dust*
> *and pollen in the air. I searched, but those*
> *I loved had disappeared below the ground,*

deeper than decades of ants. I asked
about them everywhere, but grass and leaves
have been growing, bees swarming. So I lay down
face to the ground, and said this incantation—

you can come out, it's over. And the ground,
and moles and earthworms in it, shifted, shook,
kingdoms of ants came crawling, bees began
to fly from everywhere. I said come out,

I spoke directly to the ground and felt
the field grow vast and wild around my head.

"There are many layers to 'Scorched Maps,'" Tomasz explained. "I did go back to Ukraine, searching for what my family lost when they were forced into exile after the war. Actually, my grandmother wanted me to bring back the little statue of the Virgin Mary that was left at the old family house. It was in a village not far from Lvov. She drew a map for me, with all the landmarks to help me locate the place. I got off the train and tried to find places marked on the map, but there was nothing there. Not one helpful thing. I was sure that I was in the wrong town. But eventually one helpful person brought me where the home had stood. All that was there was a cellar. It looked like a tomb."

"I dedicated the poem to J.B., my French translator, who died a couple of years ago. You know, his family story is so similar to yours. His parents too were Jews deported to the gulag, then Kazakhstan. After the war they settled in France, where Kuba was born. It was something quite remarkable, his French, which had such Polish musicality. We knew we came from the same place. It was our place, and it is lost to us."

"I can't believe I came here," Tomasz continued, "to the very edge of the Pacific, as far west from Europe as we can go, only to find people from the same part of the world that I come from. It's just fantastic. So many people I've met here, and I never imagined it."

"'The whole world is a very narrow bridge,' said Reb Nachman of Breslov," I told him.

———

THE NEXT DAY, I HAD one of those early morning awakenings when the hopelessness of going back to sleep stirred me to get out of bed. It was 6:00 AM, after I'd already spent a few hours tossing about. In my groggy state I went downstairs and grabbed a pen and scrap of paper—the scrappier the better, my thinking went, so I wouldn't be invested in anything so important and frightening as a clean blank page. I scribbled lines, scratched out and wrote over my scratches (just like the old days, before I had a computer), and slowly, a little poem began to emerge—my first Basia poem. "Basia, at Fourteen":

> *How many tiny flowers make one lilac sprig?*
> *How many stars in the night sky have names?*
> *How many yet to be seen?*
> *They disappear with morning sun*
> *too soon*
> *but in darkness or in light*
> *tucked in their beds they remain.*
> *My house is full of sleep, but I*
> *cannot. If I must believe in God,*
> *pin a lilac at my breast.*
> *When troubles search for me,*
> *plunder my dreams*
> *I will float in the starry night*
> *carried by earth's dark perfume*

12

Displaced Persons

1947

I T WAS NOT LOST ON my parents that they were surrounded by family, living in a medieval German town with some basic facilities that survived destruction, rather than in former army barracks or makeshift tent cities in muddy camps, alone and desolate, which was the fate of tens of thousands of survivors. The sight of intact couples and families was actually shocking to some of their neighbours. Many Jewish survivors who had narrowly escaped death in the concentration camps, or were hiding in the most desperate of conditions, struggled to resume life in devastating loneliness. Most had lost their entire families. Jews who had spent the war years in the Soviet Union, either as prisoners and slaves as my parents had, or as refugees or evacuees who had fled to the farther reaches of Siberia and Central Asia to escape the war zones, like my mother's sisters had, were considered the lucky ones who'd spent the war in relative paradise. Sure, life during these brutal years was full of hardship, but they weren't hunted, betrayed, or killed for measly rewards, forced into ghettos, worked and starved to death, or herded onto trains for gassing and extermination. The list of horror is so long and terrifying that I can hardly stand to write it. In this hierarchy of suffering, which was explicit and understood in every Jewish displaced persons camp, my parents and their siblings could hardly step foot onto the bottom rung of this ladder.[1]

My parents set up life in the small apartment assigned to them. Strangers were thrust together in tight living spaces; each individual, couple, or family was given space in a building that had previously been a home for a family. When shown their quarters, my father voiced what had by now become his favoured expression: "It could be worse." They were living in an actual dwelling, and no matter how cramped it was, it was more spacious and comfortable than the fifty-square-foot anteroom to the prisoners' barracks he'd shared with my mother in the gulag, or their rickety shack in Fergana. The buildings that housed them in Schwäbisch Hall were pock-marked with bullet holes, their stucco exteriors grim and decaying, but if one pressed an ear close, faint echoes of ordinary life that had been lived behind these walls for centuries could be heard. Even the threadbare half-curtains strung on a wire spoke with a particular eloquence about how necessary it was to reclaim even the tiniest bit of normalcy. Everyone knew they were living in other people's homes, but what choice did they have? Other people were living in their former homes. It was better to try to not think of home because it inevitably led to thoughts of the greatest loss of all, beyond the bricks and mortar: parents, siblings, extended families, entire communities. Falling into the blackest hole of grief and pain was a constant hazard for my parents and every Jew alive in Europe after the war. For those who had been far from Nazi-occupied territory, it was a shock to realize how nearly complete the annihilation of Jewish life in Europe had been.

Slowly, my parents found the daily rhythms in which to live. They'd rise with the sun, boil water for breakfast tea, and use what was left for washing up in a metal basin. They'd dress in clean, second-hand clothes, share a simple meal, and embark upon their day. Their lives were directed by the many relief organizations that were brought in by the US army, which couldn't possibly have managed the displaced person-hood of the 140,000 Jews in the US zone of Germany. The Joint Distribution Committee (JDC), the Hebrew Immigrant Aid Society (HIAS), under the auspices of the International Refugee Organization (IRO), were tasked with housing, feed-ing, and organizing the employment, education, and health of the stateless Jews while they waited to be released to a permanent home. For the majority of Jews, the yearning for a home stretched directly toward British Mandate Palestine, but for others, equally strong was the light that beckoned from Lady Liberty's torch in New York Harbor. After their initial relief at having succeeded in escaping from the blood-lands of their former homes, my parents realized that, given the dismal geopolitical realities, their exit from Europe and the beginning of their new lives was going to take time. How comfortable could they become with their new routines? How temporary was their situation? No one could say.

As they waited for news of their future, my father began to work as a teacher of mechanics in the ORT school that was established by this organization dedicated to rehabilitating and training people who had been so disadvantaged by his-tory. All his years of hard labour had given my father plenty of experience, and I remember him telling me how much he loved teaching. Being in the workshop, guiding young men in their trade was the one place in his life where he felt con-fident and useful.

Like many women, my mother did not have a job to go to, even though she had so many skills, including nursing. While my father taught at the ORT school, my mother would spend most days with her two little nieces who needed looking after. Pola was lucky to be given a job as a kindergarten teacher. Caring for her sisters' children was a good way for my mother to feel useful. During this time, my mother was driven by two dreams: to create a life with her sisters in Palestine, and to become a mother. As the sisters did their laundry, washing diapers by hand in a big metal tub, or when they'd share a cup of tea in the afternoon, their talk invariably turned to Zion.

"We will finally have a garden again, like we had in Pohorelowka," my mother would say. "Think of all the fruit and vegetables we'll have. Not just potatoes. It will be hot and we'll learn how to grow peaches. And we'll have orange trees and pomegranates and grapes."

Ever the realist, Pola would inevitably interject. "Sabina, we'll be lucky to live in a tent in the sand when we arrive. There's not enough housing, hardly enough food for all those already there. It's nice to imagine such a life, but I'm afraid to let myself. Look where we are, and look at the news in the paper. The British have rejected the plan to allow another five thousand Jews into Palestine. First they said no to two hundred thousand, then one hundred thousand. Even President Truman couldn't convince them. Now even five thousand are too many. As long as the British rule Palestine, the doors are closed to us. More than ever, we need a Jewish state so we can finally have a home."

Folding the clean diapers, my mother could only say that one day soon it would change—it *had* to change—and their dream would be fulfilled. Although she believed with all her heart that they would all live in Eretz Yisroel, my mother always described this period of her life as loaded with fear. Her worst fear was that she couldn't conceive. She'd been married for nearly ten years. At the age of thirty, she thought that she was already too old.

I can picture her incredulity when she discovered she was pregnant. It was in early spring, 1947. The worst of the cold weather had passed; trees were beginning to show the promise of buds, their brittle branches softened by rain and the pulse of sap coursing invisibly within. As my mother walked home from the clinic, she felt the sun warm her back with just enough heat to make her believe it was possible to feel warmth again. Her body tingled. When my father came home that evening, she was unsure of how to tell him. My parents were always very prim around their children, and they rarely showed us their intimate, loving selves. They didn't hug or kiss or even hold hands in our presence, but of course things were different between them when they were alone. Perhaps my mother simply blurted out her news when she set eyes upon him. Or maybe she waited until they tucked into bed, and in the press and warmth of their bodies in repose, she whispered their good news.

I'm reminded of the photograph that a distant cousin in Israel presented to me a few years ago, when we met for the first time. She had removed it from her mother's photo album and slid it before me, asking if I knew this couple. There were my parents, in a grassy, leafy place. My mother was seated; my father stood behind her, leaning down to press his cheek against hers, his left hand resting on her shoulder. They were dressed formally—he's in a jacket and tie, she's in a fashionable dress, topped by a simple coat with a shawl collar. Her braided hair is pinned up in a crown. His face is full of affection, his posture playful; there's a feeling of happiness emanating from him that I'd never seen before—he is not his usual, formal self. I could see they were a couple in transformation. The new life they'd created lifted them both from everyday sorrow, and their joy throbbed in the cheek-to-cheek closeness they offered up to the camera. This picture must have been very important to my mother because she sent the only copy to her dearest cousin Rivka, with whom she'd grown up in Pohorelowka. I knew the day this photo was taken, as I'd seen others where they're dressed in the same clothes, in the same setting, but never had I seen this one that showed my parents' loving happiness. This is what she chose to share with Rivka.

When my sister Estera was born in December 1947, my mother joined the mass of Jewish women who created the largest baby boom in the world at this time. Soon Pola would be pregnant again. Back in Wrocław, Sonia and Juzek rejoiced in the birth of their daughter, Barbara. After Estera's birth, my mother was even more grateful to have her two sisters close—they were experienced mothers who knew better how to cope with all the demands of a newborn. In the fog of her new state, between feedings, colic, and hardly any sleep, my mother couldn't stop thinking of Basia. She wondered how Basia had coped with her baby son, when she was so ill after the birth and her world descended into a darkness without end. How could she not think about her twin sister? It wasn't right, in her mind, to not think of her, but when she did bring her close, in her mind's eye, she could only weep for her pain. As she held her living child, more precious than she could ever describe, she shuddered in horror as she imagined her ripped from her arms, tossed in a pit and buried alive. More than ever, my mother longed for her own mother. It had been seven years since she had sobbed in her arms as they bid farewell at Kostopol station. Two years afterward she too would be dead. Her brilliant mother, who was always reading, even when making pancakes at the stove, was only forty-two years old when she was murdered. It surprised her that this memory of her mother standing in their meagre kitchen, a book in one hand, a spoon in the other, would rise up so often, unbidden. Then the reality that her child would never know a living grandparent seared her with grief, in wave after wave.

MY PARENTS HAD SPENT THEIR first year in Schwäbisch Hall in limbo, and with the coming of the new year they were now a family, but no closer to knowing when and where they would be released from Europe. Central to their dilemma was their need to establish their identities on paper, which they had been attempting to do since arriving in Germany. My father had a few documents from his former life that my mother had grabbed when she packed up for their deportation to Siberia, but her own papers—a birth certificate, passport, school records—were all lost during the war. She had nothing to prove who she was.

Wrapped up in this challenge to claim their identities was the need to explain their wartime experiences. Where and how had they survived the war? What seemed like straightforward questions was in reality a dangerous conundrum, given the circumstances on the ground. Announcing to the American authorities that they had spent the war years in the Soviet Union was not a good game plan because the Cold War had already begun. And even if it hadn't begun, communism was an enemy concept, anathema to everything that American democracy represented. Being tainted by association, even if they were not willing participants, was a real problem. My parents had to prove they were Polish citizens before the war, not citizens of the USSR, because Soviet citizens, even if they were Jews, were not considered stateless refugees.

Although Stalin was well known for his antisemitism, Jews were not murdered in the USSR after the war because they were Jews, so they could be deported back there. On the other hand, Polish Jews were being murdered in Poland, and especially after the Kielce pogrom they were acknowledged to be "stateless" persons, and truly had no home to return to. Western European Jews did return to their home countries of France, Belgium, and the Netherlands, for example, but they were in the minority; the majority of Jewish survivors were from what was Poland in 1939, and three-quarters of these Jews had been refugees or deportees who'd spent the war in the Soviet Union. Some chose to immigrate to Canada, or Australia, or Mexico, or South American countries like Argentina, Paraguay, or Uruguay, because they were sponsored by families already resident there, or the doors of these countries were opened to them. But most of the Jews in the US zone of Germany were hoping to go to Palestine or the United States—the two destinations least ready to receive them.

IN THE SUMMER OF 1947, my father's brother Aaron came to visit Schwäbisch Hall from another displaced persons camp where he was resident. How he had survived the war is a complete mystery to me; I know that he had lost his wife and child. My father never spoke of these things to me, or to anyone. I do know that Aaron came with news: their two aunts in Boston, their father's sisters who had landed there in the great surge of Jewish immigration around 1910, wanted to sponsor him to come to the United States. His next statement was a bombshell: These same aunts were offering to sponsor my parents too.

For my mother, Aaron's news was devastating. Now she understood better why my father had been evasive when they spoke of their future. He'd been talking with his friends, as men huddled together to discuss news and politics, in their after-hour gathering places. Everyone was frustrated and frightened about the logjam of refugees trying to get into Palestine. The men couldn't stop arguing about the recent incident of the *Exodus*—the ship that had been turned back from Haifa by the British. They couldn't believe that the fate of Jews was to be killed because of their determination to finally step foot in the Jewish homeland. That the British government had ultimately forced all four thousand of its desperate passengers back to Germany sickened public opinion about its treatment of Jewish refugees. After the *Exodus*, Jews who attempted to reach Palestine illegally were sent to detention camps in Cyprus, which were hardly better than prison camps, surrounded by barbed wire. Exasperation and anger were reaching a boiling point as the situation seemed insoluble. The British, who'd been trying to work out a solution between the Arabs and Jews since 1939, knew they had to withdraw from their mandate to govern what was now ungovernable Palestine. By February 1947, they passed the problem to the United Nations, which needed the wisdom of Solomon to come up with a plan that would be acceptable to both claimants of the tiny strip of land that held such foundational importance to each. So as my father sat with his friends in the DP (displaced persons) camp of Schwäbisch Hall, waiting for news from the United Nations Special Commission on Palestine, his mind was awhirl as he thought of his future. And now his brother had brought him another choice: America.

"I want us to keep our options open," my father urged my mother, when they stole a private moment. "Of course I know your desire, but can you at least think about the possibility of going to the United States? The opportunities we could have, and our child could have?"

"But what about my family?" my mother cried. "Are you asking me to give up my sisters? I had to do that once already, to go with you to Siberia. If I had stayed, who knows, I could have saved Basia. I would have carried her on my back to make our escape. I would never have left her. You know how strong I was."

"Yes, you chose to go with me, and it turned out that it saved your life," my father shouted. "You have no idea what would have happened if you had stayed behind."

His breathing slowly quieted as they sat facing each other in a long, uncomfortable silence. My mother was frightened. Just opening the door to imagining the possibility of living apart from her sisters made her shiver. She couldn't bear the thought of it.

So my father came up with a plan. He knew that he had to hide the fact of his years spent as a prisoner in Siberia because the Americans would never consider him for a visa. He would have to fabricate an alternative story of how and where he spent the war. I know this because I discovered his fiction in the box of papers and photos that I'd brought to the fishing camp in Cluxewe. Tucked in the small, black marbled composition notebook were all kinds of official documents, as well as some slips of yellowed paper, handwritten in Yiddish. It was so exciting to uncover this cache—original evidence from this important period of my parents' lives. I tried deciphering the Yiddish script—I didn't recognize the handwriting—and immediately realized that it was my father's account of what had happened during the war. Reading Yiddish is extremely difficult for me because I never formally learned the language, so I remember the pride I felt in making out the first line:

The outbreak of the Polish-German war found me in Stolin where I was visiting. And my wife remained in Warsaw.

I was amazed that I would finally have my father's own words, describing his war. It was as if he'd come back from the dead and would tell me his story. I trembled as I continued to read, but the next line caught me completely off guard:

and in the 11th month of 1939 my wife arrived in Stolin and we were together until the outbreak of the German-Russian war.

This was not what happened. He joined my mother, not the other way around. However, according to my father's report, they survived the war in Stolin. With the help of a Yiddish translator, the English version of my father's text made it clear that what he wrote was an invention. There was nothing in his report about my parents' deportation to Siberia, or their journey to Fergana. Instead, my father recorded details about the German onslaught in the summer of 1941, when they routed the Russians and assumed control of Stolin. He named the Ukrainian head of police, Commandant Urbanovich, and the German commandant, Wacker, and the leader of the Judenrat, a devout Jew from Lodz. He described the Stolin ghetto's three gates, fifteen wires three metres high, and what happened on September 9, 1942, when the ghetto was liquidated. How he and my mother survived he does not say. He included details of the gruesome killing of Commandant Urbanovich by the Red Army in 1943, when the Soviets drove out the Germans. In his account, my father remained in Stolin until May 1945, when he finally set off to find family back in Warsaw. He found no one, so he returned to Stolin, where he learned that an acquaintance had met his wife's sister in Wrocław, so my parents travelled there. And that's where he finished his account, in August 1946.

Reading it, I was shocked and deeply troubled because I couldn't understand why my father would fabricate such a thing. Only after delving more deeply into the history of Jewish displaced persons did I start to understand the necessity of such deception, which was not at all uncommon.[2] When my father decided to aim for the United States, he knew that he could not present himself as someone who had spent the war years in the Soviet Union. Exchanging stories with his buddies in Schwäbisch Hall, he learned of compatriots who were denied visas for that very reason. Since no one could verify his or my mother's whereabouts during the war, he constructed their story, including much detail that added to the veracity of his account. I had no idea how he came upon such details, like the height of the barbed wire fences of the ghetto. How could he possibly know that, if not by learning from eyewitnesses, that the German orders to the locals requisitioned to build ghetto walls were very precise? I came to understand that the brittle yellow scrap of paper I'd found was my father's rehearsal note, to memorize and present to the powers that would determine his family's future.

It may sound surprising that my mother agreed to this plan of action, but she did, reluctantly. They most likely made a pact that they would pursue both options—Palestine and the United States—and allow the future to unfold. Maybe current events, over which they had no control, would catapult them in the direction they were meant to go. Perhaps they would not get the visa to the United States, or if they did, it would be a long time coming. Maybe, as they waited, my father would have a change of heart.

13

Return

2016

"SO, WHEN ARE WE GOING?" Robbie asked as he sipped his morning coffee. My husband knew it was inevitable that we would have to return to Poland and visit my mother's hometown and village where she grew up, now in Ukraine. The big question was when. He'd been observing me working in my study over the last year. I'd been diligently struggling to translate Yiddish and Hebrew texts, writing hopeful emails to academics and strangers I'd found through the internet, and corresponding with family and friends, including my new Polish friends, all in pursuit of more details about my family and their experience of the war. I was still as eager as ever to find Basia's lost poems, although the trail grew increasingly cold. Robbie knew how serious I was about my project, which had by this time taken over my life.

"I was thinking of July," I ventured.

Friends of ours were getting married in Ireland, and we had an invitation to go. Since we'd be in the European neighbourhood, it made sense to include Poland and Ukraine in our travel plans. I could see mixed emotions crossing Robbie's face. He was thinking of the garden. Midsummer was the worst time to abandon his precious fruits and vegetables. Figs, the highlight of every summer, would be starting to ripen, and he had to defend them from the rapacious racoons.

"It looks like we don't have much of a choice, but the timing does not please me," he said.

"I know, sweetheart. I wish it could be another time, but what can we do?"

Robbie put down his seed catalogue, opened to the tomatoes. He always dreamed of tomatoes in early spring. It was his best antidote to the rainy days of February.

"I guess I'll just have to pass on the Ardwenas this year," he said in a voice barely audible.

Soon our plans began falling into place. An unexpected house exchange with a couple from Berlin came up through a friend; we could experience Berlin, especially how German society memorialized the war and the crimes against humanity that it perpetrated. We could get a feel for how the city knitted together, east and west, after the wall came down. Because we'd be in Germany, we could even travel south to the DP camps where my parents spent almost four years, and where my sister and I were born.

Krzysztof and Paulina were excited when we announced our return trip to Poland. Poznan, the city where they resided, was only a couple of hours by train from Berlin. Paulina's sister lived in Wrocław, and we could all travel together to spend a few days in the city I was eager to visit. Maybe I could even find the place where my mother reunited with her sisters. My new poet friend, Tomasz Różycki, hoped we'd come to Opole, not far from Wrocław, where his family was sent after their exile from Lvov. It would be summer, though, and he wasn't sure of his holiday dates. I wrote to Kasia to tell her to expect us in Warsaw. Besides our reunion with Kasia, we would be heading back to Warsaw to set off on our journey to Kostopil, where my mother was born, and Pohorelowka (now named Poliske), the village where she grew up. The Taube Foundation organized private heritage tours for people like me who wanted to visit the sites of their family origins. I'd met the director of the foundation when we were first in Warsaw, and she assured me that they could customize a trip for us, with a skilled guide and driver who was experienced with travel to Ukraine. It wasn't easy to get there, I was told, but it was doable.

Before we knew it, we were packing our bags. All our fancy wedding clothes went into a separate garment bag bound for Dublin while we carefully selected only enough that would fit into our carry-ons for three weeks on the road: Berlin, Poznan, Wrocław, Warsaw, and Rivne, the big city closest to Kostopil that actually had a few hotels. This time, our plans coincided with those of my niece, Mica. She and her family would be in Europe, so we arranged to hook up in Warsaw, and travel all together to Ukraine.

OUR GUIDE KUBA HAD WARNED me that crossing the border from Poland into Ukraine was very difficult. To say that relations between the two countries were always frosty is to put it mildly, and now, given the economic disparity since Poland joined the European Union, there was a tremendous amount of smuggling going on. Ukraine's recent uprising and war with Russia in the east had made matters much worse. "I hope we won't have to wait more than a few hours to cross," Kuba sighed. "My worst crossing took eleven hours, and I didn't think we were going to get across that day." We sat in his air-conditioned van, looking out at the chaos and boredom, not comprehending why nothing moved ahead in an orderly fashion. With no clear lines to queue into, it was impossible to gauge where we stood and whether we were advancing. We learned that we had to pass through two border controls—first to exit Poland, and second, to enter Ukraine. The guards directing us didn't seem to be concerned by the long waits. They looked as if they liked it that way. I couldn't help but think of my mother trying to cross the Russian-controlled border when the war began in 1939. It was winter then, and she was starving. I swallowed my snarky comments and counted my blessings. "It's our lucky day," Kuba exhaled when we finally got through. "Only three hours."

Once across the border, for at least five kilometres, we passed tractor-trailers parked on the side of the road waiting to cross into Poland. I stopped counting, as it sunk in with more shock than I expected how arduous it was to move goods and people in this conflicted part of the world. Kuba accelerated. We had many more kilometres to cover to reach Rivne, and we'd already been travelling for six hours since leaving Warsaw that morning. The road conditions were much poorer once we'd entered Ukraine. As Kuba drove expertly, we drank in the landscape; fields of grain, sunflowers, small towns, and scrubby woods blurred as we passed, while my original misgivings about our tour guide melted away with each passing kilometre.

Arranging this trip had turned out to be a huge challenge. Once the Taube Foundation in Warsaw had done the initial organizing, it was up to me to carry on directly, but communicating with Kuba had been frustrating. I knew I had to give him some slack, given that English was not his language, but my patience was stretched to the max as I waited, sometimes weeks, for every fundamental question to be answered—basic questions, like "How much will the tour cost?" or "Do you speak Ukrainian?" When he finally replied, he quoted me a small fortune for a three-day tour, breezily insisting that the Ukrainians would understand his Polish, no problem. I tried to supress my anxiety that our trip would be a disaster; I knew that more than anything we needed a good Ukrainian translator with us, but I had no idea how I could make that happen.

It was dusk when we finally drove into Rivne, the city closest to our destinations that had hotels. We were booked into the best Rivne had to offer, an imposing peach-coloured structure which faced a huge plaza bordered by monumental buildings of classical design. The old bones of an impressive city were still intact. Stepping into the hotel was a trip back to a time when grandiose ostentation was thought to be classy. The marble foyer was decorated with overstuffed chairs and sofas, the walls were hung with paintings of pastel landscapes set in gilt frames, and the whole scene was lit by enormous crystal chandeliers. Bunches of artificial flowers crammed into pedestalled vases dressed up the long corridors. When Mica and Joe chose to upgrade to a room that would accommodate all four of them, they got a suite the size of a small apartment, complete with an ornate office desk, a living room with brocade sofas and armoires filled with porcelain coffee sets, and two bedrooms, all for a ridiculously small price. As soon as Robbie and I settled into our more modest room, I could finally call Nataliia—a young historian who taught at the university in Rivne—as I had promised. A flutter travelled down my spine as I thought of how she came into our story. I couldn't wait to meet her.

I was working on a chapter, searching for details about Kostopol during the war, when fortune smiled upon me. Perusing the US Holocaust Memorial Museum's website, I found Jared McBride, a fellow in their research institute. It was the title of his project that attracted me: "Killing Neighbors: The Undoing of Multi-Ethnic Western Ukraine in World War II."[1] Before I knew it, we were facing each other on our computer screens. Jared's research was centred in Rivne. He'd even been to Kostopil and had met staff at the regional museum there. His Ukrainian colleagues, historians and archivists, were deeply interested in studying and writing the history that had been distorted and supressed for three-quarters of a century. He would ask his colleagues to search the archives for any information about my family that may be on record. He was returning to Rivne shortly after we spoke, and he would approach Nataliia, the young historian, to see if she could accompany us on our visits and act as our translator. She was the only person he could think of who spoke enough English to do the job. There was even one last seat available in Kuba's van.

Beautiful Nataliia. Good as her word, she came to meet us at our hotel, her pale blue eyes aglow with excitement. She had been in touch with a schoolteacher named Oksana who wanted to help us. Oksana taught middle school in Poliske, my mother's childhood village. She was particularly interested in history and had a blog—that was how I found her, with the help of a Ukrainian historian from the University of Victoria. Serhy Yekelchyk had suggested that many schools had little museums in them that told local histories, and perhaps the school in Poliske would also have one. So we wrote Oksana a letter, briefly introducing myself and my mother's family, and my quest to learn more about their life in this village for the book I was writing. I included the page from the Business Directory of 1926 that listed my grandfather as a mill owner, as well as the Kramer family photograph that had been taken somewhere in the village. When she received my little surprise package, with my expressed desire to visit the village in the summer, Oksana was keen to get involved, but I didn't know that then. When she finally replied to me, she said that she wanted to have some information to share with me before she wrote back, and that's why it took so long to hear from her.

"Oksana is eager for your arrival," Nataliia announced after she said goodbye to her on her cellphone. "She wishes you a good night's rest in preparation for tomorrow." We were sitting in a café next to our hotel, and it was closing time. We were going to Poliske the next morning.

THE CLOSER WE GOT TO Poliske, the worse the roads became—from paved highway to cobblestoned track. But not the kind of cobblestones you'd imagine. These were not smooth stones, rounded by wear, but sharp rocks that could easily slash your tires. We puzzled over why these would be used as roadway because it didn't make any sense. A heavy layer of sand had been laid down along the road's wide shoulders as an alternative surface to drive upon. We advanced very slowly and carefully while Nataliia checked in with Oksana at every crossroads because there was virtually no signage. Past more fields of sunflowers, Orthodox churches with gleaming onion domes, and tall silver crosses festooned with crepe streamers that seemed to populate every juncture of the road, it took us close to two hours to cover the forty-kilometre distance. Finally, standing out against the backdrop of green fields and farmhouses, a simple signpost announced Poliske. In my mind, this was the mythical village of Pohorelowka where my grandfather owned the flour mill, which he'd purchased in the early 1920s. It was here where my mother had spent her childhood, from around age five to fifteen. She never was very clear about the dates, but when my mother talked about those years, it was with a surprising fondness.

As I got ready for our return, I had no idea how much of the village itself was still intact. I recalled when Robbie and I had sat in Anna Przybyszewska Drozd's office in Warsaw, two years before, and she asked me the same question, not at all confident that she could find it on the map. But find it she did, and she let us know that the village was now called Poliske. Zooming in on it with Google Earth, she brought us right to a farmer's field, complete with horse and wooden cart filled with hay. And now we were actually clambering out of Kuba's van and standing by the sign we couldn't read, announcing our arrival.

Soon we were in front of the school where a group of people stood waiting for us. An attractive woman in a sleeveless black summer dress stepped forward, her short blond hair bobbing as she chatted excitedly with Nataliia. She looked to be in her forties, solid and comfortable in her appearance and her years. Oksana reached out to me, stretching her arm toward mine, a huge smile lighting up her face. "Welcome, welcome," she repeated, and introduced us to the teachers who were part of the welcoming committee. They were all in festive summer dresses and good sandals, happily babbling their words of welcome, gesturing to us as we excitedly gestured back. "Come in, come in," Oksana continued in Ukrainian, as she guided us along the walkway to the entrance of the large, concrete modernist building, definitely dating from Soviet times. Past the spacious foyer hosting shelves of potted plants, we entered the auditorium-gymnasium, which was filled with light from generous high windows. A few chairs had been set up for us to sit comfortably in front of the projection screen so we could watch the PowerPoint presentation that Oksana had prepared. She handed me a print version that she'd had translated into English, the cover page decorated in two strips of native embroidery pattern, like curtain panels framing the window of the story we were about to enter. It was the history of the village, complete with quotes by local poets. The name *Pohorylivka* derives from the word "burned," we learned. It was a place where, in the distant past, peasant farmers had often been driven from their homes— homes that were repeatedly burned down by an aristocracy that didn't want them there. "They fled to the forest to hide, then returned to rebuild their destroyed homes." It was a grim history we were taught, though Oksana delivered the gentle version. The Poles were occupiers in modern times, from 1920 until September 1939, and then the Russians, the Germans, and the Russians again, until Gorbachev and the end of the Soviet Union. Finally, Ukraine became an independent country in 1991. But Oksana's focus was not geopolitics at all. She wanted to inform us about the history of the mills that had existed here. After all, that's one of the reasons we were there—as descendants of Isaak Kramer, a mill owner. In slide after slide, Oksana elaborated and Nataliia did her best to translate as we struggled to follow. Needless to say, we were not expecting such a pedagogical introduction to the village history. She finished by letting us know that today there are no more mills in this village of about five hundred households; they'd all been destroyed by the Soviets. Even the Sergiyivka River had been diverted by Russian engineers back in 1958.

"Now come and let us show you our little museum," Oksana said after we'd finished the formal lesson. Sure enough, just off the school's foyer was a large room filled with antique objects of everyday life in the farming village—a long wooden cart draped with embroidered linens, shelves stocked with ceramic pitchers and bowls, a bench lined with wooden kitchen tools, butter churns and irons, barrels and jugs, implements for spinning and weaving cloth. The walls were covered with pictures of the village past and of more recent times. As I got closer to look at a poster display about religious life, I noticed a list of names and dates. Yes, it was the history of the village clergy. I asked if there was any remembrance of Subbotniks living in the village. They were an anomaly, a tiny minority thought to be descendants of Russian serfs, who shared much religious identity with Jews, perhaps even more than with Christians. I was hoping to discover Kondrat's family name, or any recollection of them living here. They were close friends of the Kramers, who'd risked so much to help Basia and Yelena survive in the ghetto of Kostopol. Kondrat, a schoolmate of Sonia, had kept in touch with her and her sisters for many years after they'd moved to Israel.

Nataliia turned to me, shaking her head. No one had heard of Subbotniks living here.

"Have any of you heard of Bat'ko Ivano?" I asked next.

They looked at each other, puzzled by my question. Why would I be asking about a priest from yesteryear?

"Well, he was a friend of the Kramers," I began, as Nataliia translated. "It seems there was a scandal over his marriage, and an affair," I continued, hesitating as the buzzing in the room suddenly quieted. All eyes were now upon me. "My mother told me his story shortly before she died," I tried to explain, as I added more details about what I knew of him. "In a way, her story of Bat'ko Ivano and how he tutored my mother's twin sister motivated me to write this memoir."

One of the teachers who was now scrutinizing the list beckoned me to come close. She pointed to a name, a third of the way down: Іван Міконюк (Ivan Mikonyuk). 1923–1925. The only Ivan on the long list. I couldn't quite believe my eyes. The dates were of the right era. So here was the first bit of evidence corroborating my mother's story. I wondered what she would have thought. Could she have imagined that her daughter, granddaughter, and great-grandchildren were there in her childhood village, talking about the erudite priest who loved the Kramers so much he took in and tutored a young Jewish girl named Basia?

After the shaded interior of the school, the afternoon sunlight dazzled us. We piled into our van and were guided to a farmer's field. Six girls, dressed in red and white embroidered skirts and blouses, stood barefoot in a grassy field as we climbed out. They advanced slowly toward us in pairs, carrying fresh baked buns, and as they approached they sang us a welcome song. They formed a circle when they reached us, each girl quickly picking up a wreath of wildflowers and greenery that had been put in place for them, and looking like woodland nymphs, they began a circle dance. Larissa, one of the teachers, poured cold drinks at the little table set up on colourful hand-woven rugs nearby. It was a scene that startled us out of our everyday reality. It felt like we were in a movie, as

if a production company had prepared the set, created the cos-
tumes, and written the dialogue. Oksana had promised that
she'd arrange for village children to meet Mica's children, and
the girls who greeted us with the gift of their cultural tradi-
tions included her daughters and Larissa's. Nataliia translated
the words of the songs and the welcome words that followed.
Robbie, along with Joe, was busy taking as many photos as
he could, but he had the presence of mind to suggest that I
should say a few words in response.

"My mother grew up in this village and always spoke of it
with fondness," I began haltingly. "She loved the fields and
the vegetables they grew in their garden, and the apples and
pears they picked from their trees. She loved hunting for wild
strawberries and mushrooms in the nearby woods. It was
here that her father owned a flour mill for ten years. She told
me that her family, one of only three Jewish families in this
village, was accepted here, and many of the villagers were
their friends. 'What we had, we shared with our neighbours.
When times were bad, after the mill burned down, our neighbours took care of us. We were loved,' was how she put it.

"All my life I've dreamed of this village," I continued,
as I struggled to speak through my tears, "and I can hardly
believe that today I am actually here, with some of my closest
family, and to be so beautifully welcomed astonishes me. I
don't know how to thank you enough."

The juice Larissa poured was just what we needed as the
sun beat down upon us on that unforgettable August day, while
the buns, filled with wild blackberries and poppy seeds, were
absolutely delicious. As we enjoyed our refreshments, Oksana
explained that here was the site of one of the earliest mills, but
they knew for certain that it was not our family's mill. "We've
identified two possible sites where your mill could have been,
and now we will go and visit these sites." But not quite yet. As
she spoke, we watched as a villager drove his horse and cart
ever closer to where we stood. At first I thought he'd lost his

way, before realizing that he'd come to get us all aboard to take us for a hayride so we could have a taste of old-fashioned farm life. The village children scrambled up, followed by Mica, Elea, and Jonah, Oksana and Larissa, while I did my best with my creaky knees. After this short escapade, we got into our vehicles—Oksana with her husband, Larissa with hers—and we drove to the first mill site.

What I remember most of this part of our experience in Poliske is that I expected to see a river that could power a steam mill. Our first stop was close to what one would call a creek, but that would be a generous term for what appeared to be a trickle of water in a culvert off a dirt road. Just up from this spot, of which not a shred of a foundation for a structure remained, stood an abandoned house, amid a cluster of houses, barns, and haystacks. "This could have been your family's house," Oksana said, "but there is no way of knowing for sure. Come, let's go in and you can have a look at a village house from your mother's era."

It was a whitewashed wooden box, with a pitched corrugated metal roof, its small windows and door painted a bright cerulean blue. We had to bend to enter through the low doorway, stepping onto a dirt floor. In what must have been the kitchen, a horizontal rectangular opening was scooped into the concrete wall above a grate for wood or coal that was built in close to the floor. Oksana informed us that this was the cooking stove. On the other side of this wall was the rest of the house—one long room, a seven-foot ceiling, dirt floor, and a small window at either end. An ancient wooden bed was shoved into the corner that backed onto the kitchen. This had to be the warmest spot in the house, with a ledge above what looked to be a fireplace. We wondered if it was the *pripetchik*, the fabled stove that my mother talked about, and Yiddish songwriters celebrated, where children would lie upon to snuggle for warmth. It was difficult to say how long the place had been abandoned. There was some wiring on the walls, which surely dated to after our family's departure from the village. The slats of the mattress-less bed were splattered in bird poop, but remnants of lace curtains hung from the windows. Piles of dusty debris had been swept into corners. We moved around this tiny house, each of us trying to stretch our imaginations and populate it with our Kramers. I was shocked by the poverty of it all and couldn't imagine a family of seven living in such a place. My mother's happy childhood here did not match my vision at all. I recalled how my cousin Barbara had spoken of her mother Sonia's misery in their village home, which seemed far more consistent with this reality.

I wondered if anyone in the village remembered the other Jewish family that I knew of. They were my mother's relatives, who owned a little grocery store. Nadezhda, the older village woman in a beautifully embroidered traditional dress, who had greeted us in the field with the girls, remembered Shaia Kuc's (the Polish spelling of "Kutz") store and offered to take us to the site where it had stood. Shaia's daughter Rivka was my mother's cousin, the beloved cousin who had survived and gone to Israel. It was to Rivka that she had sent the photo of her early pregnant self, my father's cheek lovingly nestled against hers. It was Rivka's daughter who had slid this photo before me, asking if I knew this couple, when we met on the beach in Jaffa. Yona knew nothing about her mother's life before the war, and now I was about to visit her grandfather's store, her mother's first home. Nadezhda led us to a garden plot, beside which stood a creaky wooden house, its whitewash nearly gone. It looked remarkably similar to the abandoned house we'd visited.

But this was not Shaia's house, nor his store, we were told.

"Where is it, then?" we asked as we picked our way through a wild garden of gourds and mammoth zucchini, mostly hidden by their giant leaves. We were standing in the plot where the store once stood.

Oksana instructed us to follow her car to our next destination, the other possible site of our family mill. She and her husband led the way as we drove a few kilometres, looking out at the village farms. The houses appeared very similar to the one we'd just visited—whitewashed, blue trim, pitched corrugated metal roofs—with a scattering of barns, haystacks, wooden carts, and horses. The fields were mostly flat, a rippling here and there; trees and scrub lined the road, with split log fences in the distance. Ahead of us, Oksana's car stopped at the edge of a field where a small crowd of children and a few older people were waiting. An especially ancient woman, whose wizened face looked to me like a female version of Pope John Paul II, caught my attention. Given her age, I wondered if she had living memory of the Kramer family, but Oksana shook her head when I asked. There was a thrum in the air as we were introduced; the children's excitement told me they had something important to share with us.

"The children are here because they worked on this project with me at school," Oksana explained as Nataliia worked hard to translate her words. "We examined the photograph of your mother and her family and tried to find the place in the village where they had posed. The trees in the background of the photo captivated us, and from the leaves we could identify them as chestnut trees. So we decided to go on a search for two chestnut trees growing together, which are not so common here. I even hired the school bus so the children could join in the search for the trees. About twenty of us drove around the entire village and discovered that there is only one place where there are twin chestnut trees. And this place happens to be close to where a mill once stood. That's why we have brought you here."

I was flabbergasted. I'd never even thought to look at the leaves of the trees, and I wouldn't have recognized them had I looked. My focus was always on the people in the picture, especially my mother and Basia as ten-year-old girls. I vaguely noted the fields in the distance, bordered by a rail fence. The children's imaginations were greater than mine. I was so startled to realize the impact of my letter to Oksana, and how my query had become a history lesson for the children of the village. Now the children were excited to lead us to the stream, which was once a river, decked out with a wooden footbridge that carried across into farther fields. Again, the exact site of a mill was impossible to determine, as nothing of a foundation remained to be seen. But the atmosphere of this location seemed very similar to what I saw in the family photograph.

I felt so light-footed crossing the little bridge, almost as if I were walking on air. We stepped single file, a line of people from far away and from next door, old and young, connected by a story and a picture that miraculously surfaced because of a conversation between two women whose mothers were sisters. Because history had ripped us from our roots and dispersed us like seeds, my cousin and I were strangers who lived oceans and continents apart. But our mothers grew up right here, intimate with these fertile fields and this small river where they most likely splashed on hot August days. It's difficult to express the emotions that charged all of us that afternoon, but it felt like history coming alive and full circle as we were making it, and we felt its significance; it shone from our faces.

We crossed back and were led down the road toward the chestnut trees. An elderly woman welcomed us into her backyard, and there they were: two enormous trees that really did stand out from any other trees we'd seen in the village. If these were indeed the two chestnuts in my family's picture, they would be at least one hundred years old, and they appeared to be from their height alone—they were so tall that their lowest branches grew at least a metre above the head of a full-grown human. "Come, stand by the trees," Oksana urged us. "We want to take a picture of the family returned here."

IT WAS NOW LATE IN the afternoon, and we were completely exhausted from our emotional day. As we stood by our van, I reached out to thank Oksana and the other villagers for the overwhelming welcome they'd given us, and I suggested that we should head back to Rivne so we could have a late lunch and a rest. But before we left, there was only one more place I wanted to visit: the Orthodox church. My mother had spoken of the church where the Kramer family was invited to village weddings and christenings, and how she loved the chanting of hymns. "I know all their songs," she would tell me with something akin to pride.

Oksana turned to Larissa with a look of alarm on her face—not because we wished to visit the church, there was no problem there, but we couldn't leave yet because they had something more planned for us. "Please, follow our car," she instructed. "It's a few kilometres away."

We climbed into Kuba's van, exhaling our fatigue, and drove slowly as the road became a narrow dirt track, the trees lining it growing denser as we entered a birch forest. As we drove farther into the wild, we wondered aloud, with a tiny bit of anxiety, about where we could be heading. "Don't worry," Nataliia soothed. "It will be a surprise."

Finally, after what seemed like ten kilometres but more likely just five, we entered a clearing where Oksana's husband waved from their car for us to pull over. In front of us was a festive gazebo, painted turquoise-green and yellow. To our right was a brick barbeque; the tantalizing smell of meat grilling gave us a rush of pleasure as we stepped out of the van. A few women and men scurried around, busy unpacking dishes and tending the fire. We approached the gazebo, which was relatively small, its walls only waist high, the middle open to the air and views of birch and pine trees, while the yellow roof gave shelter from sun or rain. Looking in, I could see a long table that took up the entire interior space, with only enough room for benches along three sides. Colourful rag rugs covered the seats, while the table, decked with a crisp linen cloth, was set with plates and glasses for our big party.

The feast of beautiful food spread across every available inch of table space made us go "aah" in unison. There were salads and fish, decorated with a lattice of mayonnaise, meats and cheeses, mushrooms pickled and others served in a soup, stuffed cabbages, pancakes rolled with sweet cheese, kebabs with tangy dressing, fresh baked bread and buns, watermelon and fruit plates—and this is a partial list. We were ushered into this sanctuary, along with a few more of the people we'd spent the day with, as Oksana's husband stood at the opening and held up a two-litre pop bottle filled with homemade vodka. We couldn't begin our feast without a heartfelt toast. We all stood up, raising our shot glasses, as he began speaking. Nataliia, exhausted by now, translated his well wishes for our health and friendship that must continue as long as we lived. And so began one of the most memorable occasions of my life. As was the custom, we went around the table and, between mouthfuls, each of us was urged to stand and deliver another toast, which we did with increasing fluency and abandon: to our families, to the kindling of new friendships, to education, to honouring our past, to freedom from persecution, to people getting to know one another and celebrating our common humanity, to the best food and the best handicrafts, to the old mills and the rivers still flowing, to the people we'd loved and lost, to the songs of the forest, to life, to life, *l'Chaim*, and to the humble potato that formed the potent drops we kept imbibing.

I limited my consumption of vodka, so full already with the intoxication of the day, and I admired Kuba for the great willpower he exercised to abstain. In the midst of our revelry, a car drove up with the daughters who had greeted us in the field earlier that morning. They'd changed into their jeans and T-shirts and brought the dance music, plus a fancy frosted cake for dessert. Mica had asked what dancing the polka was like here, and before we knew it, Nataliia and Oksana's husband were holding hands and swinging around in perfect step to the giddy music. There was no resisting the invitation to join in. We linked arms with our hosts and danced with breathless laughter to music that sounded very familiar to our ears. The boom-box brought forth the unmistakable notes of "Hava Nagila," the definitive song of joy danced at every Jewish wedding and festivity. We shouted out our recognition at once, singing the Hebrew words while our hosts looked at us in astonishment. I thought they were playing this tune to honour our visit, but they had no idea that their much-loved music was Jewish. To think that here in this tiny Ukrainian village there still remained joyful Jewish essence, but it was unknown to our hosts until our meeting! It was here in this forest, where we ate and drank and had a love-in dancing the *Hora* that we all realized the significance of our meeting. After so many decades of pain and erasure, we had come together across the narrow bridge to recognize each other as distant relations, connected not by genes but by history. As we caught our breath, after what felt like near delirium, Kuba said that of all the heritage tours he'd conducted, he'd never experienced a celebration like this one.

We exchanged gifts. Unsure about what we could offer, we Kramer descendants thought the best we could do was provide funds for the school to be used to teach history to the next generation. We handed Oksana our envelope, with a card that Elea and I composed, saying how much we believed the world could heal if we spend more days like this getting to know one another. Oksana presented me with an amber encrusted painting of an old-fashioned mill in a pine clearing, its wheel churning white water into the river that flowed upstream of it. On the back, she inscribed her message, a memento from the residents of Poliske, all their families and friends. It was a lousy pen she had, so she wrote it over and over, to make it legible, bearing down with the strength in her hand.

14

Exile

1948

M Y PARENTS, ALONG WITH ALL the Jewish refugees in Europe, heard the announcement in late November 1947. Because it was such a momentous event for Jews around the world, everyone who could was listening to the radio broadcast and holding their breath as country after country placed their votes. The United Nations was much smaller then, only fifty-six countries making up this body, with a two-thirds majority required for the resolution to pass. Thirty-three countries voted in favour, thirteen opposed, ten abstained, and one was absent. The resolution proposed that two states be created in Mandatory Palestine—one Jewish and one Arab—and even though the terms offered were far less than desirable, the Zionist movement accepted them. Finally, miraculously, after two thousand years of exile and the near-eradication of European Jewry, three tiny pockets of earth, mostly desert, were designated as home for the Jewish people.[1]

Was there dancing in the streets of Schwäbisch Hall, like there was in Tel Aviv, Jerusalem, and New York City, when the decisive vote was cast? My parents never spoke of that night; my cousin Ilana, who was not quite four, was there, but has no memory of it. Her parents never spoke of it, either. Maybe it was too close in time to the imminent birth of my sister Estera, less than two weeks later, or perhaps it was entwined with the memory of the painful events that would soon follow.

Six months later, in May 1948, when the British finally left Mandatory Palestine, Israel declared its independence. Offering friendship to its Arab neighbours, while knowing it would never be accepted, it braced itself for the worst. Since the vote at the UN, the furious Arab world had made it clear that Israel could not exist as a country and would have to be destroyed. As promised, Egypt, Syria, Transjordan, Lebanon, and Iraq immediately declared war and invaded the newborn state. The optics were incredibly bleak: Israel was vastly outnumbered and poorly armed; it didn't stand a chance of survival. Perhaps it was fear of a final Jewish annihilation that kept my parents, aunts, and uncles silent about this perilous time. They had close cousins, already resident in Palestine prior to the war, who were now fighting for their lives.

Much to the entire world's astonishment, after intensely difficult battles and reprisals that lasted roughly a year, Israel was not destroyed by the Arab armies but actually prevailed. When a final armistice was declared and accepted, around March 1949, a redrawn map of Israel was ready to begin accepting the stranded Jews of Europe—approximately 132,000 people. But immigration was not confined to surviving European Jewry. In retribution for Israel's victory, the Jewish populations of Iraq, Yemen, and Libya were soon expelled from their homes, while their property was confiscated. Other Arab countries followed suit. How could the newborn state absorb so many people in such a short time? I'm sure this was the primary question on my family's mind.

By early spring of 1949 my parents were still undecided about where their home would be. My mother's hopes for Israel were as strong as ever, although my father clearly leaned toward the United States. His two aunts in Boston were urging him to come, and his brother Aaron was already on his way. Having spent nearly three years in Schwäbisch Hall, my parents had made many adjustments. Parenthood had changed them, as it changes everyone who enters its hallowed gates. As they focused on the all-consuming needs of their child, who was just over a year old, the future smacked them in the face: it was time to leave Germany and choose a home. The government administering the DP camps wanted nothing more than to complete its job and shut the camps down for good. The people in their charge had become a little too comfortable as they lived in limbo, and some were already setting down roots. But the government back home in Washington was not so quick to issue visas to the 63,400 Jews waiting to receive them.

Pola and Kuba, Manya and Michal decided that they would fulfill their dream and, with their children, go to Israel as soon as their transport could be arranged. They were more than eager to finally leave Germany and make a home for themselves that had permanence. Pola and Kuba had considered going to New York, where Kuba's brother lived, but Pola was not swayed. "I never want to live in a *goyishe* (non-Jewish) state again," she insisted. "Only in a Jewish state."

My parents were faced with another complication that March of 1949: my mother was six months pregnant, with me. The authorities disapproved of transporting women on long, difficult journeys in late pregnancy. Too much could go wrong. Much as the urgency to close the DP camps drove the decisions that followed, there were these discomfiting considerations for pregnant women. So while my mother agonized about the prospect of separating from her sisters, she was disadvantaged by her condition. She couldn't press too hard about accompanying her sisters to Israel because the authorities wouldn't allow it so late in her pregnancy. My mother wanted desperately to live her dream of Israel with her surviving family, yet was unable to convince my father to make this choice. More than anything, my mother was fearful of losing her sisters again, this time to geographic distance. And she was angry with my father because of all the sacrifices she had made during the war. "I chose to go with you to Siberia—why can't you choose to come with me where my heart needs to go?" she pleaded with him. My father argued for a better life, more opportunity, and freedom from fear. He promised my mother the support from his family already established there. Yes, there was now a state of Israel, but the conflict appeared intractable, and life there would always be difficult as far as he could see. After everything they'd been through, he did not want that for his family.

In March 1949, Pola and Manya, along with their husbands and children, left Schwäbisch Hall for Marseilles, France—the first leg of their journey to Israel. It was not a smooth trip. They were obliged to remain in temporary quarters in Marseilles for some months until a ship was ready to transport them to Haifa. They finally arrived in the port city in the summer of 1949. Ilana, who was six years old by then, remembers their welcome as they descended the gangplank: they were greeted by a row of people, one of whom carried a pump that sprayed them with DDT to delouse them, after their long sojourn in Europe. They were brought to a tent city and lived rough for a few weeks, and then moved to a transit camp, where families were squished into canvas huts that had been impregnated with tar and whitewashed, to give them more permanence. Their quarters were so tight that they lived together with another family, with no partition (and no quarrels!) for an entire year.

For my mother, the shock of her sisters' departures was lacerating and salted the still-open wounds of the murders of her twin sister, her parents, and extended family. She was reliving the trauma of these unbearable losses, and there was no treatment, no pills, nothing that could save her. And while she was grieving, she and my father received notice from the camp authorities: their camp was closing soon, and they would be relocated to another camp in Heidenheim. From the relative comfort and familiarity of their lives in Schwäbisch Hall, now stripped bare of family, they were forced to move to a place that had once been a sub-unit of the Dachau concentration camp. Their temporary home would be in a former barracks. She was eight months pregnant and she would give birth in the hands of strangers. No family, no friends, no community. Her toddler, Estera, had only begun walking a few months before. My mother described this as the blackest period of her postwar life; she cried every day, while the creaking door played its repeating song of abandonment. I always had the feeling that in the fluid darkness, preparing to be born, I floated in her grief, and it was as familiar to me as the sound of her voice, underwater.

In Heidenheim we stayed only six weeks, impoverished in every way since separating from family. My mother hardly spoke of my birth and the first weeks of my life. All I know is that I was born around one o'clock in the afternoon, and that I was a big baby, over nine pounds. My parents' hopes for a son were dashed by my arrival. They named me Isa, because there is no feminine for Isaak, and my grandfather's name had not yet been passed to a newborn soul. They did not give me a middle name. I have no documentation of this time in our lives, no official papers or photos discovered in the box I'd brought up to Cluxewe. This first year of my life is a dark memory hole. The many photos of family life in Schwäbisch Hall had been taken by my uncle Michal, an amateur photographer, but he was now living in a transit camp in Haifa. There is only one photo of me as an infant, probably taken because of visa requirements. The look on my face is one of alarm.

But some records did exist in Germany. A researcher at the US Holocaust Memorial Museum in Washington discovered a trove documenting my parents' postwar experience.[2] I'd always believed that we lived in Heidenheim for close to a year, and it was from this camp that we left for America. The document that summarized all the places my parents lived since arriving in Germany rattled me as I absorbed what it said. After my parents were processed as refugees in Landsberg in 1946, they were immediately sent to Schwäbisch Hall, where they lived until May 13, 1949. That was the date they were forced to relocate to Heidenheim, just four weeks before my birth. Six weeks later, on August 1, we were moved to Wasseralfingen, another DP camp. This move lasted three and a half weeks. On August 26, 1949 we were moved back to Landsberg. Three moves in four months.

I'm staggered by the difficulty of it all, trying to imagine my mother, postpartum, having to cope with the upheaval, while caring for a newborn and a toddler. My sister Estera was exactly eighteen months old when I was born—our birthdays hovering close to each solstice, hers winter and mine summer. It must have been brutal to get through each day, and I honestly don't know how she did it. I don't like to think of my parents' misery, but I can't imagine that they inhabited a comfortable and loving emotional space during this stressful time. What my father did during this period is unclear to me. He had been teaching mechanics at the ORT vocational school in Schwäbisch Hall for much of the time they lived there, so perhaps he continued teaching in Landsberg, although I doubt it. The DP camps were winding down and preparing to close, so integrating new teachers and classes was not a priority. During all this time, the future was still uncertain for my parents. They had no idea that it would take another nine months for their papers to be processed and their visas issued for America. From August 26, 1949, until May 17, 1950, they lived in the camp where they had started out, three and a half years before. Full circle.

My mother always said that everything of import happened to her in May: her wedding in Warsaw in 1938, their deportation to the gulag from Kostopol in 1940, their move from Schwäbisch Hall to Heidenheim in 1949, and now, a year later, their departure from Europe to America. All their papers were finally in order. By this time, they had baggage to pack. With money provided by our Boston aunts, and the earnings from teaching at ORT, paid out at the time of departure, my parents made a few purchases. I don't know how they decided what to bring with them from Germany, but their choices were decidedly feminine. A Pfaff sewing machine housed in a handsome wood cabinet; a set of Rosenthal china, patterned in delicate dogwood blossoms, each piece leafed in gold. And an art deco silver candelabrum with three stems, hallmarked in Schwäbisch Gmünd, which my mother acquired soon after her arrival in Germany and used for her Shabbos candles every Friday night for the rest of her life. Of clothing and other belongings, nothing remains, except a hand-knit dress for Estera and a sweater for my mother. Clearly she loved these garments so much that she brought them with her to Boston and kept them for the rest of her life. There's one photograph of her wearing her sweater in Schwäbisch Hall, the upper bodice sporting an alpine pattern, the sleeves lined with a row of snowflakes from shoulder to wrist. She's outside with her sister Manya and little Janina, and a barely visible child in the baby carriage—my sister Estera. It looks to be late fall 1948, and my mother must have been pregnant with me. Because my mother only crocheted, I'm convinced that she didn't knit this sweater—a precious memento of her time with her sisters, and the happier period of her pregnancy with me.

On May 17, 1950, we were bound for Bremerhaven to board the *General Blatchford*, a retired navy transport ship on its final voyage across the Atlantic. I have no idea how my parents acquired the photograph taken of us on the train heading to Bremerhaven. Maybe it was a parting gift arranged by the Americans to have photographers on stand-by to shoot departures and provide forwarding addresses for mailing these pictures to the new world.

It was a dreadful crossing. Married or not, men and women were forced to sleep in separate quarters in the bowels of the ship, so my mother, suffering from debilitating seasickness, had to look after two seasick children on her own each night. The ship was never meant to transport civilians and was not outfitted with any comforts; it was about to be decommissioned after this last charitable effort. By the time they docked in Boston, fourteen days later, my mother was barely alive. On top of her physical wretchedness, each day at sea was a painful measure of the accumulating miles separating her from her sisters. The endlessly grey Atlantic Ocean heaved and submerged her spirit to a depth I can hardly fathom.

Apart from talking about her seasickness, my mother never spoke about our arrival in Boston. I'm sure that Tante Bessie and Tante Chaya-Rochel were counting the days and were there to greet us. They both lived in Dorchester, the heavily Jewish district of the city, and were well established there. Tante Chaya-Rochel was a petite woman, a long-time widow, childless, whose face always appears wizened and ancient in my childhood mind's eye. She took us to her spacious flat, a middle floor in a classic Boston triplex on Havelock Street. My earliest memories float in those rooms. Heavy drapes, dark furniture, a piano whose ivory keys enticed me, and a sunny kitchen filled with cabbages pickling in large glass jars.

The first weeks of American life were fraught for my mother. Estera's abiding memory is lying in bed with her, day after day, as she cried inconsolably. While my mother wept, my father went to work. He'd been offered a job in a factory in Boston's north end almost immediately upon arrival. While they waited for us to arrive, Tante Bessie and Tante Chaya-

Rochel had scraped together funds to purchase a triplex on Paxton Street so we could have an affordable apartment to rent. My memory of this top-floor flat is mostly of the wallpaper— creamy peony blossoms on a verdant background covered the bedroom walls. Outside, spikey hollyhocks stood in the small patch of green close to the stairs and porch. I love hollyhocks to this day, especially pale pink ones.

In Germany, our parents spoke to us in Yiddish, believing it was the best choice given the uncertainty of our ultimate destination, but my father had been diligently studying English. I treasure his copy of *Everyday Language Lessons*, where he penciled in Hebrew letters next to English vowels, to help with clarifying pronunciation. My mother, despite her incredible language skills, rebelled against English, branding it the most incomprehensible language on earth. It made no sense to her, these weird combinations of letters meant to represent sounds she could not produce. So she closed herself off from this language as her protest against America as a choice of home. But now that we were in America, they continued to speak to us in Yiddish while encouraging us to speak English so they could learn. One of my enduring regrets is that Yiddish is the language of my ears but not my tongue.

Tante Bessie doted on us. She was a tall, beautiful woman with refined features, always elegantly coiffed and dressed. She and Uncle Jimmy had three adult sons, each one with a glamorous wife. Although my father's American cousins were the same generation as my parents, their life experiences and cultural identities were so different that they could hardly understand one another. I gather that they spoke in English and Yiddish at their awkward first meeting. What could they talk about? Their years of slavery, deprivation, and the unspeakable murder of their families? Life in postwar Germany as homeless, stateless refugees? Their culture shock at the plenitude and luxuries of America? At that time, the Holocaust was so shameful a topic, even among Jews, that it was only addressed by silence. Groping for a comfortable subject of conversation, my mother's American cousins-in-law, who dismissed her as someone of lower intelligence because she didn't speak English, asked her if she liked to cook. "Oh yes," my mother answered, "I'm a very good cook. I speak to my pots in six languages."

My mother was an excellent cook, and having to cook for her family got her up in the morning and energized her days. She was a classic Jewish mother who always put her children's needs before her own, so she had no alternative but to choose life. Gradually, she came to appreciate the hustle and bustle of Blue Hill Avenue—the markets and delicatessens, the five-and-dime stores, butcher shops, and bakeries, where she rubbed shoulders with other newly arrived survivors as well as Jews resident in the neighbourhood for decades. The openness of civic life, with freedom to say whatever you pleased in public and in print, was startling to my parents. The American economy was pulsing fast in the early fifties, hungry for more workers. Would my mother be interested in earning some money herself, to add to the family coffers? She signed on to a part-time job at a shower curtain factory, bringing home fourteen dollars a week. Estera and I spent a lot more time at Tante Chaya-Rochel's.

Our first year in Boston was one of adjustment and a big surprise. My mother couldn't believe that she was pregnant again. Her last child, another daughter, Chava Tzipora (Mayim), was born in March 1951.

15

Kostopil

2016

I KNOW IT'S SUCH A CLICHÉ to speak about how I couldn't believe that I was actually walking the streets of Kostopil, but there I was, rubbing my eyes. By the time we had got back to our hotel in Rivne, driving the tortured roads through pitch dark, we fell into bed with an exhaustion hard to describe. We needed more than sleep to make room in our souls for all we'd experienced in Poliske. Although the distance to Kostopil was about the same as to Poliske, only twenty-five kilometres, the road was far better than the cobbled track we'd driven the day before. The ride to Kostopil was easy, but I was apprehensive.

Kostopil was no longer a small town, as it was in my mother's day, but a city of about 30,000 people. The number of times I'd thought about this place and imagined myself discovering it with my own eyes was impossible to calculate. I'd studied maps created by survivors that included the important local landmarks as well as the Jewish landmarks—the schools, synagogues, and cemeteries that predated the Shoah, and the worst landmarks from that evil time: the ghetto and the two killing fields where the Jews were murdered en masse. Going there would be my version of going to Auschwitz.

A petite middle-aged woman with bright strawberry-blond hair and a face shadowed by worry greeted us kindly as we entered the local museum. This was Alla, the museum's assistant director, and she was expecting us. She ushered us into the office, a large dusty room with creaky floors covered in faux-wood linoleum. It was a busy room, cluttered with furniture and piles of papers that overflowed onto available surfaces. I was carrying my mother's copy of *Sefer Kostopol*, the *Yizkor* book[1] that held the best clues about my family's life in this town. Neon pink stickies poked out from my bookmarked pages. My first surprise was watching Alla pick up her copy of this Hebrew book, opened to the hand-drawn map of Jewish landmarks. "We've had Jewish visitors here before," Alla explained through Nataliia, with whom we'd already bonded. I wondered how Alla could decipher any of it, but I forged ahead, anxiously expressing my list of places to visit that were most important to us. I wanted to get to the 3rd of May Street, not far from the railroad station, to try to find my great-uncle Meir Bebczuk's house. I also had the address of his brother Moshe's house, a recent, unexpected find. I wanted to make a pilgrimage to the ghetto, where Basia and my grandmother Yelena lived their last days, and of course we needed to pay our respects at the mass graves in the killing fields. I held a naïve hope that I might even find my great-grandfather's grave in the old Jewish cemetery, which had existed for centuries before the Shoah.

"We can start with a walk to the site of the old Jewish cemetery," Alla offered, "It's only a couple of blocks away from the museum."

We trod out of the museum together, all nine of us. Alla, Kuba, Nataliia, and three generations of Kramers—myself, Mica, and Elea and Jonah. Robbie and Joe completed our party. Within minutes we arrived at a small grassy park, bordered with children's playground stuff—swings and slides, seesaws, ropes and ladders connecting structures to climb and hide in. It all looked relatively new and not very much used.

"Where's the cemetery?" we asked Alla.

"This was the Jewish cemetery," she told us. "We were successful in blocking the city council from turning this into a shopping centre," she continued. "It was a difficult fight, but we convinced them that a park and children's playground would be more appropriate." She walked us toward the back of the park, where a statue of Lenin had stood for decades during the Soviet years. What remained was a rudimentary pedestal, in a shallow trough that might have contained a fountain. A few metres away we noted a shiny black granite memorial, topped with a large cross. "In remembrance of the Holodomor," Nataliia translated. "It's impossible to know exactly how many millions of Ukrainians were starved to death by Stalin in the 1930s."

"Yes, it was a horrific crime," I concurred, "unimaginable." But I didn't think the Holodomor happened here. "Wasn't this Poland at the time?" I asked.

"Our history is complicated," Alla offered. "As Ukrainians, we all suffered, and we remember this suffering. And we are in Ukraine now."

It was already clear that Jewish history did not even register here. Somewhere, beneath the jungle gym perhaps, the dust of the bones of my ancestors lay. There was no indication that this had ever been sacred ground, not even a little plaque telling the story of this tiny piece of earth. I wanted to lie down in that grass and weep. I came here to remember my dead, to find my great-grandfather's stone, but there was no sign, no acknowledgement of him ever even existing here. Why does it matter so much? *Why did the living house their dead before they housed themselves?* It's so fundamentally human, this need to say that life mattered, that we the living are here because of those who came before us; we feel compelled to honour this by tangible markers of remembrance. Who are we, then, and where have we come from, if not from the flesh of our forebears? Erasing our ancestors is such a violation of humanity; I knew in the deepest part of my being that rubbing out their names from history's ledger rubbed out my own human legacy.

"Is the ghetto far from here?" I asked Alla, feeling anger coursing through my body in a rushing stream. We walked to a part of the city that was crowded with vendors and small shops. Although it was high summer, the fruits and vegetables had the look of imminent decay. With people sitting on blankets spread on the sidewalk, the neighbourhood had a flea market air about it, decidedly not prosperous. People called out to us obvious strangers, trying to sell us their tattered goods. I usually love flea markets and junk stores, always fired up by the prospect of finding a hidden treasure in the midst of trash, but there was nothing appealing here. What I would have given to find the remains of an old synagogue, or a page from a Hebrew or Yiddish text; just the sight of a Mogen David framed in a window above the teeming street would have revived me. We were in the poor district of Kostopil, and somewhere here would have been the apartment where my mother and her family had lived. It was a Jewish neighbourhood once, and there had been two synagogues nearby. Alla pointed to the site where a nondescript shopping centre plastered in garish advertising stood in their place; across the street, a rotting Stalinist apartment block loomed large. Somewhere around here Pesach Fishman had been beaten to death by his neighbours, and Isaak Kramer had died of the shock. Somewhere around here my baby cousin Mordechai had been pulled from Basia's arms and buried alive. Somewhere close she and her mother had been imprisoned behind barbed wire for a year, kept alive by crumbs of bread brought to them from Pohorelowka by their friend Kondrat.

No one we saw cared about any of this, and how could they? What did they even know of it? Everyone was getting on with their lives, seemingly oblivious to what had happened here seventy-five years ago. As I struggled to breathe, my brain tossed up Auden's great poem about Bruegel's painting of Icarus plunging unnoticed into the sea,[2] and I remembered a few lines that never seem to lose their power: *About suffering they were never wrong, the old masters* ... I was reminded of how *the dogs go on with their doggy life,* while *even the dreadful martyrdom must run its course,* but it was little consolation as the reality of encountering such wilful forgetting sunk into my bones on the streets of Kostopil.

Our next destination was the 3rd of May Street. It wasn't called the 3rd of May Street anymore because that date was significant for Poland; it was May 1st Street since the Soviets took over. But the name change made no difference to the appearance of the street and the houses along it. It might as well have been the same street that my mother walked from the railroad station to her parents' home in December 1939, on the last leg of her epic three-month escape from Warsaw. With *Sefer Kostopol* in hand, we were hoping to identify Uncle Meir's house. I clutched it now like a bible.

Back home in Victoria I had spent hours, with the help of Dahlia Beck, my Israeli friend, struggling to translate passages in the book that held clues about my mother's family and their lives before and during the war. As I read in my halting Hebrew, any little bit of evidence was a blood-pounding find, signalling that I was getting closer. Like a forensic archaeologist, I imagined myself carefully sweeping the dust and sand inch by inch with a small brush. And just when I was ready to give up and move on, another tidbit revealed itself.

I scrutinized the pages with photographs, hoping I could recognize a face, a name, or a place that figured in the family story. One image stood out for me—a group of young men and women, five rows deep, posing in front of an old house, where only the roof was visible. It was a simple wooden house, embellished with a scroll border that looked like lace pinned above the hidden door. It was Uncle Meir's house, my mother's favourite uncle, who had rented out an apartment of four rooms on the 3rd of May Street. The text explained that Meir Bebczuk did this to enable the Betar group to set up a *hachshara*, or practice kibbutz. I scanned and scanned the tiny pixelated faces in the picture but recognized no one, not my mother or father, or Basia or Pesach Fishman, of whom nothing remains, not even a shadow. I felt in my bones that Pesach was in that group photo, but where? Everyone sat so still before the shutter was released, to capture that moment. I imagined that even the birds had stopped their fluttering.

And now we marched up and down May 1st Street, looking for a house that matched the grainy photograph. I was looking for the curly wood embellishment above a doorway. We saw lacy wood trim on doorways and vestibules, but nothing else was a perfect match. My mother always described Uncle Meir's house as being very large, but the houses we passed couldn't be described so, according to our inflated North American idea of house size. They were all small, squat, and homely, except for one. But the large, two-storey house had no resemblance to the house in the photograph. A woman came out, curious about this band of strangers peering intently at the architecture of her home. She stared at us with daggers in her eyes, and we knew it was time to move on. All the while I kept asking myself why I so desperately wanted to find this house, to simply stand in front of it and register that here, one summer day in 1933, Sabina met Olek, and his friend Pesach who fell for Basia. Here my mother spent loving time with her family, and here, at sixteen, she fell in love with my father. It was here where our future began. As we continued down May 1st Street to the railroad station, my heart pounded alarmingly. We stood on the deserted platform outside the handsome, nineteenth-century building, seemingly unchanged from the time of its construction, and I imagined my mother's arrival early one December morning in 1939, and then the scene of deportation, five months later. In the quiet, as I looked across the tracks, I noticed a couple of cattle cars innocently parked on the far rails. I pictured my young, fearful parents crying their goodbyes in the jostling throng before being shoved onto their cattle car to the gulag. As my mind tipped me into a dizzy swirl, Mica turned to me and said, "Isn't it here where our lives began?"

While reading *Sefer Kostopol* in preparation for this trip, I would take a break from my struggle by turning to the memorial pages to look at our family names. There were many Kramers, given how common the surname is, but only a few Bebczuks: my grandmother's brothers, Meir and Moshe, their spouses, Manya and Fejge, and their children. It surprised me to find these names faintly smudged with red, as if my mother's fingers had rubbed over the type so often that she left her mark; instead of a stone at the gravesite, there was her bleeding heart.

And now we were actually heading to the gravesite, close to the football field. This was one of those rare moments in my life when the boundaries between past and present collapsed, and I was caught in both dimensions of time. The site was so banal—a flat stretch of stubble adjacent to a sports field surrounded by bleachers. There was no separation, no partition, just grass, as though this mass grave were an extension of the playing field. One would have to advance to the far corner of the open field to reach the stone marker and read the carved inscription to even know what happened here. I expected the location to be far out of town, hidden away from sight. But it was here, in the open, on a site where people played soccer, and not very far from streets filled with houses where people lived. This is where you dig a large pit and commit mass murder? It didn't occur to me then that the murder of the Jews of Kostopol was no secret at all. It took many locals to make it happen, and many more, including children, who came to witness the spectacle.[3]

As we approached the small monument I felt a panic rise up in me. I was completely unprepared for this place and what it meant to me. We walked toward the dark rectangular slab, each one of us carrying our private thoughts, and I realized that I didn't even bring a stone to leave behind. I love this Jewish custom of leaving a memento to mark your visit. I had intended to bring something from my corner of the earth, a stone from British Columbia, from the edge of the Pacific Ocean, to this spot in the middle of the Eurasian continent. I wanted to say: *See how far I have come—halfway around the planet—to call out your names and remember your lives. You are not forgotten, and what happened to you will never be forgotten. Coming here is my tribute, my Kaddish.* There was so much more I wanted to say, but I stood there, mute and empty-handed. Even the Kaddish prayer that I have inscribed upon my heart flew out of my head, and I couldn't call it up to recite it. I'm embarrassed to say that I had to look it up electronically on Kuba's cell phone, but at least I could be sure that I chanted it correctly. I looked down to search for a stone in the vicinity of my feet, but there were none to pick up, not even a pebble. The only matter I found were pale little acorns that had fallen from volunteer saplings nearby. So I picked up a few of these living seeds, placed them on the monument to mark my visit, and put a sprig of them in my pocket to bring home. I stood there, inviting the tiniest bit of breeze to cool me, but there was no breeze on that sweltering August day. Finally, I started to sob.

After some minutes, I can't really say how long, I began preparing myself to move on. Not far from where I stood, in a shaded corner, I noticed a small white stucco structure that had the unmistakable look of public toilets. That's when I nearly collapsed. This had to be the place where Fejge Bebczuk had hid.

My mother always told me that Aunt Fejge had died twice. When the Jews of Kostopol were being shot into the pit by the football field, Fejge had miraculously dodged the bullets and survived. She managed to climb out of the pit and tried to hide somewhere, but she was soon caught, brought back to the pit, and killed again. The awfulness of this story defies my ability to write it. I can barely put it into words as I sit and type on this page.

But Meir Grinszpan wrote the story in poetry—a book-length poem, *Majn Sztetl Kostopol,* written in Yiddish in a DP camp in Germany in 1947.[4] I'd learned of this book when reading a paper about Jewish survivors who'd spent the war years in the Soviet Union, like my parents. I couldn't believe my luck to have discovered a book about my mother's home-town, and written in poetry no less. Only five copies were known to exist. The YIVO Institute in New York City had a copy, and I gratefully paid the library a small fee to receive a photocopied version. Like my parents, Grinszpan had spent some of the war years in Uzbekistan, but he returned to Kostopol immediately after the war in the vain hope that he'd find some of his family alive. Virtually every Jew was dead, and the few who had survived were barely living. One such woman, Fejge Milstein, soon became his confidante (and later, his second wife), and her eyewitness account forms the basis of Grinszpan's book.

I was more than eager to find even a scrap of text that might mention members of my family. I remember the evenings I pored over the text. With a glass of wine to fortify me, I haltingly read aloud the Polish transliteration of Yiddish, and tried my best to understand. I felt excitement, near joy, at recovering my ancient Yiddish, and satisfaction at piecing fragments of stories together, especially the corroboration of events from my other sources—*Sefer Kostopol* and Hana Bat-Ami's memoir, *Beyond Remembrance,* and of course, my mother's account. Through his book I learned of the richness of Jewish community life in Kostopol, a small provincial town of ten thousand people, a third of them Poles, a third Jews, and the rest Ukrainians. He explained that for the most part until the war began, there was harmony, and Jews were respected members of the community. Certainly many Jews struggled to make a living, and many lived in poverty, but there were business people too, Jews who owned lumber mills and flour mills, those who dealt in grain, cattle, and fowl. They were tradesmen, craftsmen, merchants, teachers, and professionals like doctors, lawyers, engineers, and pharmacists. Jewish Kostopol had a lively cultural life filled with a variety of schools, music, theatre, and literary, sports, and political groups. Yes, there was growing antisemitism in the 1930s, but once the war started, everything got worse; when the Germans arrived, they found residents willing to join them in mass murder. The terrible content of Grinszpan's memorial to the murdered Jews of Kostopol proceeds inexorably with gut-punching horror.

To my amazement, toward the end of his book, I came upon the stanzas where he described what happened to my great-aunt Fejge Bebczuk. He set up the scene almost cinematically. He's in conversation with the woman who would become his wife, whose name was also Fejge, as she tries to explain how she miraculously survived:

> She told me of many instances
> that were still concealed from my ken,
> how she managed, simply succeeded
> with enormous will, to win her battle with the devil
> One has to really understand, she said, and accept
> that more than once what occurred were true miracles
> "There's no other way to explain it,
> like the story about the two public toilets,
> where I hid a whole day, while the Germans
> swarmed like wasps, with their firearms
> equal to none.

Blocked from escape through the path to the river
where I feared I would drown, but thanks
to the 'klozetn' I remained safe.
In those moments, in that one second
when I parted from a Bebczuk, from Fejge,
in the time it took to hide in the field of rye
she was caught, killed by a shot"

It took me a while to fully comprehend these stanzas. I gathered that the two women were hiding together in the public toilets (*klozetn*) not far from the killing field adjacent to the football stadium. My mother's story was that her aunt Fejge had survived the mass murder at the pit and was frantically looking for shelter. Perhaps Fejge Milstein recognized her and beckoned her to hide in the toilets with her. To think that life or death moments could be so random, so immediate. It must have been incredible for Fejge Bebczuk to be so rescued, when she had just been spared the horrible death of everyone around her. But her luck didn't last long, because *in the time it took to hide in the field of rye / she was caught, killed by a shot*. My mother's version was that a local person found her and dragged her back to be killed again.

It is so ironic to me that I've chosen to write my mother's story in prose, not believing that I could do it successfully in poetry, but here was Meir Grinszpan's epic poem, which gripped me to the core. When he began to chant the story, it was as though he blew a trumpet blast. I was startled by his call to listen up. He's in Tashkent, he announced, on a train, filled with every kind of ragged passenger, of every age and condition, and they are all travelling home, with the greatest hunger to find those they've been cut off from for years. They'd heard the worst, they've suffered terrible deprivation, but they still have hope that against all odds their beloveds have survived. I rocked along the train of metre, eight syllabic beats, taking comfort in the rhyme and repetition; I was on board.

I was reminded of the act of writing poetry, the sheer challenge and pleasure of composing meaning within the strictures imposed. I pictured Meir Grinszpan and his new wife in their DP camp in Neu-Ulm, Bayern, Deutschland, in July 1947. I could see them, in circumstances so similar to my parents', waiting for papers, waiting to be released from Europe, waiting for their chance to get to Zion. While they waited, he poured his grief onto paper. It flowed from his pen and began to take form. He couldn't stop himself. It was the most important thing he could possibly do. It was his life's purpose to write an epic poem of his odyssey. He was the Jewish survivor-refugee "everyman," the Kostopol story his memorial book, filled with monstrosities that had to be recorded; he was writing a memory book in poetry, for the entire tribe, twenty years before *Sefer Kostopol* appeared in print.

As I stood at the site of the killing, I felt shock at seeing the public toilets that Grinszpan described. They were still there, as if nothing had happened. Again, it was the erasure of memory that left me incredulous. Maybe it was simply cowardice, but I couldn't bear the thought of venturing into the toilets. It frightened me too much to be confronted with the stench of it. I believed that the smell of the two women's fear had to have penetrated the molecules of the plaster walls and was still embedded there, mingled with the stink of human excrement.

Here, at the site of Fejge's tortured last moments on earth, I so needed to figuratively put flesh on her bones. I turned my back to the toilets and forced myself to rewind the tape from this killing scene, and see her alive and standing with her extended family. A wife, mother, daughter, aunt; a woman fully engaged in life, committed to her family, friends, and community. A human being who deserved to live out her days as all human beings deserve to live, with her personal triumphs and tragedies. I'm so grateful to Meir Grinszpan for helping me rescue Fejge Bebczuk from oblivion. And here am

I, her great-niece, almost one hundred years later, telling her
story for posterity.

—

OUR FINAL EXPERIENCE IN KOSTOPIL took us two kilometres out of town, to a quiet rural area. We got out of the van,
stepped down from the road, and walked single file along
a narrow path bordered by bleached grass that stretched
toward woodland. We were grateful that the museum director had arranged for us to be led by a local guide, a tall, silent
man; we appreciated his presence because it would have
been impossible to find our way on our own. I was completely
disoriented, so I cannot say which direction we headed, nor
can I name the forest we entered. It was an archetypal rustic
scene, complete with buzzing insects, occasional butterflies
clapping their wings as they landed on wildflower weeds, and
birds calling from above. After five minutes or so the path
veered left and we entered woods, the evergreen canopy a
welcome relief from the beating sun.

We were ten—eight adults, two children—marching
deeper into the forest, and as we marched I couldn't help but
imagine us transported back in time, to the summer of 1942.
I tried, as I often do, to put myself back in those times, but
couldn't manage to bring myself to the place where I knew that
I was marching to my death. My legs kept moving but my brain
was overloaded. Finally, we arrived at the clearing. Erected not
by townsfolk, but by relatives from far away (just like the memorial at the football field), the monument here was much larger. A
dark lozenge-shaped stone, it sat on a slightly elevated platform
surrounded by a turquoise wrought iron fence. I detested the
baskets of artificial flowers attached to the stone—such a tacky,
dishevelled tribute that offended more than my aesthetics.

I suppose I should have been heartened to finally see Stars
of David repeating around a railing painted the colour of spirit,

in the Jewish lexicon, but that is not at all how I felt. I was confused, trying to decipher the carving on the stone, matching the dates with what I knew of our family history, and it didn't make sense to me. Was this the site where Basia and Yelena were murdered, or was it in town, at the football field? Was it here that little Mordechai was buried alive? Each monument had the years 1941 and 1942 carved into it. In all, thirteen thousand Jews were murdered in the district of Kostopol—local Jews, and Jews brought from neighbouring towns.

The magnitude of the horror overwhelmed me as we stood in the green forest, trampling the grass that grew up from their remains. Where exactly was I supposed to mourn? I needed to guide my spirit, my thoughts, my love, my loss to a unique location where I could finally say *I have found you, and I am here with you*. It was the least I could do.

Standing there in the forest, which so resembled the forest of Poliske where we had feasted and danced the *Hora* the day before, I struggled to make sense of the extremes. Could I possibly engage my rational mind to comprehend it? I'd never had such a feeling of goodwill and genuine connection across a profound chasm as we'd experienced in Poliske. Kostopil felt like the polar opposite. And as I stood there, boiling in emotion, I had a vision of a golem towering over me, his huge head a mask with two faces. His front face was wildly joyful, while his face in back was all mouth, baring huge, jagged teeth. Yesterday I had so wished my mother could have been with us in Poliske, to meet the folks who'd prepared our encounter with goodness and where all of us experienced the rare, precious gift of *tikkun*. But here in Kostopil I was grateful that she was spared this return, knowing that it would be more than she could bear.

16

Finally

1964

M Y MOTHER SAT IN HER seat by the window, looking out at the parting clouds and fearing to register the reality of how far she was from earth. She didn't want to look down. It was her first time in an airplane, and she felt nothing but pride that this was not any airline, but El Al, the national airline of Israel. The stewardesses bustled around in their chic blue-and-white uniforms and spoke to her in Hebrew as they served her kosher food. She didn't even have to make a special request. She tried her best to understand them, her ears closely tuned to the sound of their words, knowing that soon she'd be hearing it all around her. She'd lost most of the Hebrew she had, after fourteen years of living in Boston and not using the language except for her prayers. It startled her to realize that it was easier to speak to the Israelis in English. Of course, the stewardesses assured her, whatever was more comfortable. Her comfort was their priority.

"I don't know how to be comfortable now, because I'm too excited," she blurted as they set down her tray, poured her some tea. "This is my first time in an airplane, and first time to Israel. I feel like I'm in a dream." She picked up the cup and drank with the sugar cube tucked between her teeth, Russian style. It was so considerate to be given sugar cubes. The sweet liquid calmed her nerves, helped her feel less guilt about leaving her girls, especially since her youngest would celebrate her birthday while she would be away. There was nothing she could do about her departure date, so her arrangements were made with anticipation and regret. How often life came this way. She resolved that she'd bring back an extra-special birthday gift from Israel. Looking out the window, she realized that she was flying over the Atlantic ocean, heading toward the Europe she never wanted to return to. The nausea of her crossing on the *General Blatchford* was now a distant memory. She shifted in her seat, pushed the button on her armrest, and felt herself recline.

Was it really all those years ago that my mother staggered off the boat, holding my sister's little hand, both of them barely able to walk? My father walked beside them, holding me in his arms, along with all their loose bags. My mother looked out at the jostling crowd at the pier, searching for people she'd never met. Never had she felt so alone, while she watched my father's excitement as he greeted his aunts. She wished that she could have felt something more than relief as she stepped foot on solid ground, in a country that grudgingly welcomed her. But she couldn't even understand the language people were speaking. Without language she was helpless, and she hated the feeling of being so reduced in her capacity to be human. Over the weeks that followed, she had no one to talk to, no one to confide in. In the beginning, most of the time she just cried. Even simple acts like buying a loaf of bread made her feel like an idiot because she didn't know how to ask. It took everything she had to look after my sister and me. And three months later, just after moving into our own apartment, my mother discovered that she was pregnant. Once again, she faced the prospect of giving birth alone, in a new country, with none of her sisters around for support. My mother was overwhelmed. Not even a year in America, and her Yankee daughter was born—an automatic citizen of the United States. But she took no consolation in having a third daughter, when she and my father both longed for a son. She could understand how her parents had felt at Sonia's birth. Five daughters. How had her mother ever managed five children with so little money and no help? But this thought woke up too many other thoughts, so she tucked it away, as she always tried to do.

She couldn't believe that her youngest was turning thirteen. Until now, she'd never left us for so long, but we were more than old enough to get along without her, and she would only be gone a couple of weeks. We were excited for her. My father reassured her that he would manage the business, a private nursing home, and look after us, so she should stop worrying. When was the last time she could leave all her responsibilities behind? Finally she was on her way to experience the country she'd longed for her entire life. Finally, she would immerse herself in the pleasure of her sisters' company, feel what their lives were like, and imagine what could have been.

She hadn't seen her youngest sister Sonia since Breslau, in 1946. Was it possible that it was almost twenty years? Now she would meet their daughter Barbara, who was born there after they'd all left Poland for Germany. How Sonia and Yusek could have chosen to remain in Poland was still a mystery to her, but at least they got out. She would stay with Pola and Kuba in Haifa, and spend time with their daughter Ilana, who was already studying at Hebrew University in Jerusalem. Their younger daughter Rachel, a baby when she said goodbye to them in Schwäbisch Hall, was almost sixteen. She tried to picture her, flipping the years like pages of an album, each page hinting at more maturity, but not revealing the steep changes that define a life. My mother wondered what her sisters would make of her. Manya would have given them lots of news, since she had moved back to Israel with Yanna (Janina) a short time before. It felt like yesterday when she'd opened Manya's aerogram telling her that Michal had died after his lung operation. Nine years already passed. "Bring Yanna and come to Boston," my mother had urged, and to her surprise, Manya listened and came. They stayed until Yanna finished high school, but Manya always intended to go back to Israel, where she felt most at home. Yanna didn't argue with her. Israel was where she wanted to study, and she'd just begun at Hebrew University.

My mother couldn't remember the last time she simply sat with nothing to do but reflect. Of course she knew that she had changed, even though she couldn't feel the extent of it. Could she really be forty-seven years old now, five years older than her mother's age when she was murdered? Thinking this thought made her gasp. The stewardesses walked up the aisles, handing out blankets and pillows and pulling down the blinds. Darkness ruled as she tried to settle into sleep, but sleep was impossible. She wore her rings, a comfort to touch them as she tried to relax. Her gold wedding band was a replacement because she had nothing from her life before the war. The filigreed antique diamond was new. She liked investing in jewellery now, loved the artistry crafted in precious stones. It was the one extravagance she allowed herself. She'd packed a few pieces for her sisters and nieces, along with finely tailored clothes that she could buy for next to nothing at Filene's Basement, the lower levels of a department store that sold off designer clothes as they were marked down the longer they remained unsold. She knew a silk blouse by Christian Dior or a skirt of the softest cashmere wool would be impossible to find in Israel.

She tried to sleep, but who could sleep sitting up, while more memories jostled for attention? Her thoughts drifted to her short-lived attempt to make a go of it with Sabina's

Dress Shop while they lived in Dorchester. She'd had enough of the shower curtain factory and thought her fashion savvy and skill with needle and thread would lure in customers, but she couldn't compete with Filene's Basement. Tante Bessie had warned her that it would be tough to succeed, but she had to give it a try. If she now lived in the land of opportunity, why not seize it, she figured. The risks felt small to her, compared to what she'd already lived and survived. Less than a year later, she packed up her Pfaff sewing machine and brought it home. Going back to nursing was a better choice—practical and down to earth, even though she had no papers to prove her training in Warsaw. The worst was passing the classes in English; working with patients was the easy part. She got her licence and her first official job at the Carney Hospital, a Catholic hospital run by nuns. The Sisters were kind to her, knowing all that'd she'd been through, although they hardly talked of it. Nobody spoke of it, then, not even Jews themselves—those who cared more about whether a box of cookies was kosher, or those who hardly knew what it meant to be a Jew. They had no idea what happens to a person who is starving. My mother adjusted her pillow, hoping to find some comfort.

She pictured the pleasure she would have as she opened her valises and gave her sisters their gifts. They hadn't done that since they were girls, and even then, hardly ever because they were so poor. She knew that, inevitably, they would talk of home, and much as she looked forward to their conversations, she feared them. They would talk of Basia, whom she missed with all her soul. She had no one she could talk with about Basia. Not even her sisters could understand what it meant to be a twin, and to live your life without her.

Sooner than she expected it was day again. A stewardess brought her a breakfast of bagels and lox, a salad of chopped tomatoes and cucumbers, and good hot coffee.

"Salad for breakfast?" she asked.

Finally

"Oh yes, this is how we eat in Israel," she was assured.

"Can you tell me how far away are we?" my mother asked.

"We're flying over Europe now—I think France," the stewardess answered. "Another few hours and we'll be landing in Lod."

Lod. Just the sound of the city's name made my mother perk up. So many places she wanted to see in Israel: Jerusalem, Tel Aviv, and of course Haifa, where her three sisters lived. She hoped to travel south to the Negev, the great rocky desert, and visit kibbutz Negba. Her cousin, Rosa Shadmi, was one of the founders. It hurt so much that Rosa had died three years before of a heart attack. She'd left Rovne for Palestine in 1935, and it broke my mother's heart that she would never see her again. At the very least she wanted to meet Avi, Rosa's son. He'd never known his father, who was killed four days after Avi was born, defending the kibbutz from the Egyptian invaders when Israel's independence was declared. At thirteen he was an orphan, but he insisted that Negba was his home and family, and there he would stay. And then there was her cousin Rivka, with whom she'd grown up in Pohorelowka. They exchanged letters now and then, but to see each other in the flesh, after twenty-five years? My mother's mind was full of memories that were rising faster and faster, like film coming undone from a projector's reel. Her heart must have beat very loud in its capsule while she felt the engines rumble as the plane began its descent.

I wonder if my mother bent down to kiss the earth upon arrival, as pious Jews did by custom. Not that my mother was particularly pious, but Israel was in many ways her fervent religion, so I could picture her prostrate when she finally stepped foot upon the tarmac at Lod. It meant that much to her. Pola was waiting with Kuba, their excitement palpable as they hugged and cried past the arrivals gate. It didn't matter that Pola and Kuba had visited Boston for the first time the year before, when they had lived this scene at a much higher emotional pitch. How could their reunions not be emotional?

Stepping out of the airport, the first thing my mother felt was the heat. Her red wool coat and long black gloves were far too warm for the March air. Riding up the coast in the big taxi with Pola and Kuba, windows rolled down and her short bouffant hair blowing wild, she could hardly converse. On her left, the turquoise Mediterranean lapped up against white sand and an occasional palm tree. It looked like she'd been airdropped into a postcard, more beautiful than she'd thought possible. To her right, all was bright spring, green fields dotted with red poppies, simple farm buildings scattered here and there. Definitely a rural landscape, not so different from the terrain of her childhood. She could picture herself in Uncle Meir's house in the practice kibbutz, dreaming of this earth as she baked bread, and now she was upon it, feasting her eyes as she dabbed away the tears. Approaching Haifa, the air shifted; she could smell the industrial fumes before catching sight of the giant metal drums dominating the shoreline. "Our refineries," Kuba announced, rolling up his window. "This is where I work."

Their apartment was in one of the small townships that skirted the city. Walking into their home, Rachel leaped forward and grabbed my mother in a giant bear hug. She leaned back to have a good look at her niece, whom she hadn't seen since infancy. Now she beheld a passionate girl on the verge of womanhood, with black curly hair, dark eyes, and an impish, gap-toothed smile. Joy and sadness swished together and overflowed. My mother hadn't felt such emotion since Breslau.

Looking around her, she took in the small space where they stood. Past the vestibule with its crammed library of floor-to-ceiling books, the kitchen consisted of a tiny stove, a sink, and a small table. Beyond was one all-purpose room: living room, dining room, bedroom. What served as a sofa by day became a bed at night. A toilet, sink, and shower in a space not much bigger than the airplane washroom completed their quarters.

"This is our palace," Pola exclaimed, holding her arms out to encompass it. "A few years ago we added another bedroom, but this is how the four of us lived before. After sharing a hut in the transit camp with the Shulman family for a whole year, it feels very spacious to us."

The look on my mother's face was not lost on Pola. The contrast in their living conditions couldn't be greater. As far as economics went, there was no comparison in the lifestyles of the Kramer sisters. My mother's elegant clothes, adorned with a string of pearls, were striking in comparison to Pola's simple cotton dress. Five years after arriving in Boston, my parents had managed to purchase their own home. It was a big old house that had seen better days, but it had three floors, with an apartment they rented out that helped pay the mortgage. They'd fixed up the attic for Manya and Yanna to live in when they came.

Within moments of my mother's arrival, Sonia and Juzek were at the door, accompanied by a beautiful young woman, their daughter Barbara (now called Batia). They lived within walking distance of Pola and Kuba, and the families often spent time together. Embracing her baby sister, my mother couldn't stop her tears. After eighteen years, she finally was holding her in her arms. Next, she reached out to Batia and invited her to come close. At last, and with no need for words, they clasped each other.

"Pola, I need to sit down," my mother said, her voice no louder than a whisper.

"Yes, of course, come, let's all go sit," Pola said, gesturing toward the sofa. "I'll get some cold drinks. Miriam and Yanna will be arriving in a moment. "

The cold water helped to calm her, although my mother's head was swimming. She tried to remember that Manya was called Miriam now. Of course she would use her Hebrew name.

"I'm in Israel," my mother exclaimed as she wiped her eyes, "with my three sisters. I still can hardly believe it. There's so much I want to see and do."

"There's so much we want to do with you," Rachel enthused. She put her arm around my mother's shoulder and pecked her on the cheek. "We have made many plans."

THE NEXT DAY, AS THEY were finishing breakfast, they were surprised by a knock on the door. Pola hadn't mentioned that anyone would be dropping by that morning. She opened the door, and there stood Hana Nussenblatt. It took a moment for my mother to recognize her. This was the woman who'd survived the war in Kostopol, who had been Sonia's childhood friend. Fearless Hana, who'd worked with Brichah. She'd met my parents in Vienna and looked after them, helped spirit them out of Austria all the way to Salzburg, where they crossed over to Germany. Hana had no time for displaced persons camps and years of waiting for papers; she was determined to get to Palestine as soon as she could. And that's exactly what she did, by way of Italy, arriving in Palestine in 1946. Now they stood facing each other, registering the tracks of their journeys on the maps of their faces.

"Come in, please," Pola invited, clearing space at the table and grabbing another cup for coffee.

Hana hadn't lost a drop of her vitality; if anything, she was more energized. Israel was young, and she was in the vanguard, still working hard to create a country that reflected her democratic ideals. Everyone in Israel had ideas of what made a suitable country, but these ideas often clashed. The religious versus the secular, the socialist kibbutzniks versus the free marketers, the Ashkenazim who'd arrived during the

Ottoman Empire days versus the Mizrachim, recent immi-grants from the Middle Eastern countries that had expelled them, and the European survivors who struggled to rejoin the living and find their place. It was noisy and messy and thoroughly exhilarating, Hana explained.

"You can't imagine what goes on here, Sabina, compared to our life in Kostopol, in Poland. Here we are, finally free to create our own home, our own country after two thousand years of exile."

My mother tried to maintain her composure. "And what about our old home?" she couldn't stop herself from asking. "Do you have any news?"

"You know that we're in touch with Kondrat, don't you?" Pola offered. "Sonia found his address while she was still in Poland, and they've been writing back and forth. Our bond with him and his family is strong, especially because of how they tried to help our mother and Basia when they were in the ghetto, starving. But we don't talk much about the past now. In one of her letters, Sonia told him how much she missed the blue cornflowers from the fields in Pohorelowka. Not long after, a package from Kondrat arrived in the mail. It was a shoebox, but very light in weight. When we shook it, we heard a shooshing, but couldn't imagine what was inside. He'd sent a box of dried flowers."

RACHEL INSISTED ON ACCOMPANYING MY mother to Negba. It was one of her favourite places in Israel, though she hardly had the opportunity to visit anymore. Now she would intro-duce Sabina to her much-loved cousin Avi, and give her a taste of kibbutz life. They would travel by bus and my mother would see the diverse landscape of this narrow slice of earth, from the fertile Sharon valley, past the Tel Aviv shoreline, and into the Negev desert. Young Avi was there to greet them as they stepped off the bus. He was sixteen now, tanned and tousle-haired, a redhead, dressed in khaki shorts and a T-shirt. My mother scanned his face, searching for resemblance to Rosa. She'd never met Avram, his father, so she had no sense of what he'd transmitted to his son. Avi extended his hand to my mother, and held hers firmly in his grip.

"Shalom, Sabina, and welcome to my home," he said. He grabbed Rachel in a huge hug, lifting her off the ground as he always did when they got together.

"I'll take you to the barn later, so you can say hello to your friends the cows," Avi promised, "but first, let's show Sabina our sites."

They advanced toward the three bronze figures that loomed large on the highpoint of the central square. "We might as well start here," Avi said, pointing. The graves of the military cemetery were spread below the monument. "It may be odd to start with my father's grave, but this is how I know him," Avi explained in Hebrew, with Rachel acting as inter-preter, going from her tentative English to her halting Yiddish, yet managing to convey the gist of Avi's rapid Hebrew.

"I love this monument because I can see here my father, the soldier and the farmer, and my mother, the nurse. They saved the kibbutz when no one could imagine it was possible. Come, I'll show you what they were up against." He led them toward the original compound, with its pockmarked water tower and wooden fence, nestled in low ground and entirely exposed. My mother tried to picture how this naked, vulner-able spot could be defended by a few men with rifles, against Egyptian army tanks. It seemed as miraculous as a biblical tale. "My father survived the battles but was killed when he stepped on a landmine when clearing up and gathering aban-doned weapons. He was on his way to meet me." They stood in silence as his words penetrated.

My mother was keen to tell Avi about her dear Rosa. Their fathers were brothers. Because Rosa's family lived in

Rovne, and hers lived in Pohorelowka and Kostopol, they didn't have many opportunities to spend time together, but the times they spent were memorable. Rosa was six years older.

"Rosa urged me to join Hashomer, and told me to stay away from Betar,[1] but we disagreed about our Zionist inclinations. She loved to tease me about it, and then she was gone to Palestine when I was only eighteen. How I envied her. It was hard for us to keep in touch after she'd left, and then the war broke out and we were in the gulag. We were lucky to survive."

Avi nodded. He knew the stories from Sabina's sisters. "Did you know that my mother volunteered with the British Army and worked as a nurse in the Medical Corps? She was stationed in Italy. After the war she came back to Negba and married my father."

They walked past the orchards, toward the expansive fields of tawny russet soil ready for spring planting. "Come, we're going to the civilian cemetery now. It's the green spot in the distance."

"You know, Sabina," Avi continued, "I grew up with a mother who gave me everything. We raised puppies and chicks, had an aquarium filled with fish, you name it. She encouraged my creativity and my talent for building things. She was just fantastic."

"I'm so lucky to have known her, Sabina," Rachel added. "She was so full of life. She had a young head—she didn't think like an old person."

"Everyone loved her," Avi continued. "She was the nurse for the kibbutz, and there was a tiny fridge in the dispensary to keep medicines. No one had fridges then. Now we're just starting to have them. Once, for my birthday, she brought me to the dispensary, on tip-toe, and she opened the fridge door and there was this beautiful cake filled with whipped cream—real whipped cream. Who had whipped cream then?

We had ration stamps for sugar and flour in those days. But my mother just made it happen."

They walked into the green pocket of shade as Avi led them toward Rosa's grave. Its simple headstone was carved with just her name and her years on earth.

"I suppose I should have put more," Avi said, "but what did I know? I was just thirteen when she died."

ON THE NIGHT BEFORE MY mother's departure, her sisters and their families all gathered for a farewell dinner. The time in Israel had passed so quickly that my mother could hardly register all that she'd seen and done. As much as she thrilled to the sights and the history that she'd spent a lifetime imagining, it was the people that she'd visited with that affected her the most. She'd seen family members who'd survived, like her Bebchuk cousins—Fejge and Moshe's sons. Her cousin Rivka Kutz, from Pohorelowka, who lived in Jaffa, and her two children. Friends from after the war who remembered her with warmth. Everyone was making a life for themselves. Some would have liked to exchange places with her, although most were happy to live in Israel and were prepared to lay down their lives if need be. It was not easy to live surrounded by enemies, no matter how just the claims.

But what she felt the most was how her sisters were living their lives as best they could, without her. Sonia could walk a few blocks and be with Pola; it took Miriam about ten minutes by car. Rachel, Ilana, Batia, and Yanna knew each other as cousins and shared one another's lives. Her own daughters were strangers. How she envied her sisters their closeness. What she wanted most—to share her life with her sisters— she could never have. History had written their stories, had ruptured their lives with a savagery that was impossible to weigh. She knew that her family was luckier than most. How many Jewish families could count the survival of all siblings, save one? They were anomalies. But she could never feel relief by thinking this thought.

As she lay in bed, hoping for sleep before her long journey home, her thoughts drew her into in the dark, familiar rooms of her mind, the rooms better left closed, but she couldn't stop herself from entering. She wondered where Basia would have chosen to live, had she survived. Would she too have come to Israel, or would she have chosen a life near hers, in America? And in the darkest corner of the darkest room lay little Mordechai. Who would he have become? What gifts could he have brought to this world? My mother knew she had to leave these black chambers where no light could ever penetrate, and go to a place where she could be released. Fate was fate, she repeated, and she couldn't change it no matter how much she tried. There was nothing she could do about it but accept.

17

A Chapter in Three Movements

2018

FROM MY TRAVELS, I'VE A collection of objects that I keep on my desk. Mostly small things: the acorns from Kost-opol, the miniature menorah dug from the rubble of Warsaw, and various stones I've gathered from the beaches of Vancouver Island because I love their shape or colour. I picked up a mottled one; it fit perfectly in my palm, like a worry bead not yet strung, and I enjoyed its cool smoothness. Since the news of Poland's new law against telling the histor-ical truth about what happened during the Holocaust, I've been catapulted back to where I started on this whole journey, emotionally speaking. The last time we were in Warsaw, not even two years before, Kasia had suggested that I could easily get Polish citizenship because I had my father's Polish army documents as proof, and I laughed about the irony of it all, saying that the only reason for me to do it would be poetic justice. But for a long moment I seriously thought about it, and that in itself astounded me.

Could I really conceive of the notion that Poland was my ancestral home? Or would it be Ukraine? Or even Belarus, where my father's family lived for generations? New borders had put my parents' origins in different countries, and in the aftermath of the war, and the vicious bloodletting that followed, thousands of locals were exiled because they belonged to the "other," non-dominant, tribe. Our experiences in Poland and Ukraine had been intense in different ways, and going there helped me appreciate that the history of each was entwined by tribal hatreds as strangulating as convolvulus vines in a garden. Yes, the morning glory blossoms were appealing, but they bloomed on cords so tightly twisting they destroyed the healthy growth of whatever lived near. I had always believed that my parents' ancestral home was Poland, but this was never the belief of the Ukrainians and Belarusians who considered themselves overpowered by Polish colonizers (or Russian colonizers, depending on location). Caught in the tendrils of these perilous, suffocating vines, clinging to life in the small crevices available to them, was my tribe, the Jewish nation, a foreign species blamed for all the ills surrounding them. So poisoned was this debasement that the German–Russian war created the conditions for genocide: over a vast territory filled with big cities and thousands of smaller towns and villages, 1.5 million people, including my grandparents, my aunts, uncles, and cousins, their friends and neighbours, virtually every member of my tribe, were rounded up, forced to undress, shot into deep pits and buried like garbage, while many locals participated. Even their children ran along and chose to watch their neighbours, their school friends, murdered in broad daylight.

So where did I belong? What location on this pale blue dot of a planet could I claim as my own? I'd spent most of my life in North America—my childhood and adolescence in the United States, my adulthood in Canada. I loved and appreciated each of these countries for what they offered, despite their flaws, and felt the great good fortune of freedom and acceptance. I benefited from many opportunities to pursue my dreams, and still do. My father had indeed given his children the favour of comfortable lives, entirely different from his own dark life before America. But I never fully felt the birthright; I have always identified as an immigrant, successfully passing as a native. Once, about ten years after moving to British Columbia, I was visiting Salt Spring Island and enjoying its famous market. I chatted with a vendor there; he was a potter and I was admiring his raku bowls. As we bantered, he asked me, "Where's home?"

"How far back do you want me to go?" I answered.

He wasn't expecting me to take him back to Poland, Germany, or Ukraine, or Belarus—and I didn't want to go there, in the lighthearted moment we were in. It felt so inappropriate. Yet what seemed like an innocent question was far from it, and at the time I couldn't even think of stepping foot in those places. I had the curiosity, but the emotional baggage was beyond heavy. It made my guts tremble just to imagine it.

And now my guts were trembling again as I thought about returning to Poland. I truly enjoyed the time we had spent visiting Krakow, Lodz, Warsaw, Wroclaw, and Poznan, which deepened our connections with Krzystof and Paulina, and Kasia. I felt very close to them, actively loved them and wanted to spend more time with them and their families. I rubbed the mottled stone in my hand, feeling its heat, while memories of recent Polish films we'd seen rose up before my eyes. *Aftermath* and *Ida* were such different films,[1] yet the core of each was all about the tormented Polish psyche because the nation has never come to terms with its crazed relationship with Jews. And the blood on its hands. But then I pictured Krzysztof and Paulina. We'd had a Skype conversation the week before, and I couldn't get their stricken faces out of my mind, when I told them that I honestly didn't think I could come back to Poland after this law that criminalizes the telling of historical truth had been passed, and all the antisemitism it has released. It wasn't even underground, this hatred; it was out there in the public square. They were devastated by what was happening but felt powerless. They'd already signed countless petitions but had no faith that the government would budge. They and their friends and colleagues were completely disheartened. Of course I knew that antisemitism was far from finished in Poland, and my attitude adjustment felt more like magical thinking than reality. Wiped out was my notion that a loving world could emerge from my ancestral homeland, if only we worked on it, face to face. What hurt so much was the refusal to honestly face the past, to own up and say *yes, we suffered, but many of us were monsters too, when it came to our Jews.*

I put the stone down to release the tightness in my hand, as the conversations I'd had with Tomasz Różycki in Victoria came back to me. I felt grief that my dangerous love affair with the notion of Poland was over, but I refused to turn off my love and admiration for my friends. Loving and respecting them was my antidote against the awful human tendency to condemn every human just because they happened to belong to a collective, be it tribe, religion, or nation. Wasn't that precisely the insanity that leads ultimately to genocide? More than ever, I had to remind myself to resist this.

I couldn't help but compare Poland's official stance with what we experienced in Berlin. All the museums, memorial sites, public displays, engraved stumbling stones embedded in pavement, even cafés dedicated to historical reckoning. Owning it. I found it overwhelming, to be honest, but necessary. Then the farther east we travelled, to Poland and then Ukraine, we were stricken by the diminishing acknowledgement of what had happened. It wasn't just the lack of recognition of the Holocaust, and the antisemitism that enabled it, but avowal of Jewish existence, period. I had read about the erasure of Jewish memory in many parts of Poland and Ukraine, but it didn't prepare me for the total eradication that we witnessed in Kostopil.[2] It was utterly demoralizing.

But on the other hand, less than thirty kilometres away, we'd experienced Poliske, where we were greeted like long-lost family. The night Nataliia announced that the whole village was waiting to meet us, I couldn't believe my ears, but it was absolutely true. Even now, when misery about the horrible state of the world rises up and floods me, I recall our encounters with Oksana, Larissa, and Nadezhda and feel the closest to what I can call redemption. It was as necessary for them to meet us as it was for us to meet them, and in that forest clearing, where we feasted and danced together, we knew that we were braiding the strands of our histories into a story that had been lost for much of a century, and none of us would ever again be the same. It was our living moment of *tikkun*, or repair.

I HAD A TASK TO do. I needed to prepare a package for mailing to Tamar Lewinsky at the Jewish Museum in Berlin. When organizing our last trip, I'd written to Tamar to let her know that we'd be in Berlin, and how I would love to meet with her to talk about my parents' experiences as Jews who'd survived because of deportation to the Soviet Union. It was her paper that had helped me understand the context and complexity of my parents' place in the hierarchy of DP camp life, and had alerted me to Meir Grinszpan's Yiddish book of poetry about Kostopol.[3] I was anxious to meet Tamar, who was now curator of postwar Jewish life in Germany at the museum. Over a long lunch in the museum's café, she made it known that her greatest challenge was finding objects that could concretely demonstrate what real life looked like for Jewish survivors in the DP camps. "Would your family have anything saved from that period, besides the photos and documents you've brought?" Tamar asked. There were plenty of pictures and documents that survived—they were small and easy to carry—but what about objects and artifacts? Most were left behind, too cumbersome or unimportant to bring along at the time of departure. I mentioned my mother's snowflake-patterned sweater, but I had no idea where it was, or if anyone in the family still had it. It was only in a casual conversation with my sister Mayim, much later, that I found out.

We'd just finished dinner and were talking about some childhood memory, which prompted me to bring out an old photo album to refer to. As I turned the pages, I came upon the photo of our mother dressed in her beloved sweater.

"Mayim, do you have any idea about what happened to this sweater?" I asked.

"It's in my cedar chest," she said.

It took me a few seconds to understand what she was telling me. I could picture the chest in her bedroom, pillows on top, a nice piece of furniture. My sister lives in her own suite in our house; all we had to do was walk out our back door and into hers, and up a flight of steps. When Mayim shook out our mother's green and yellow sweater, snowflakes going up each sleeve, I got the shivers. I clutched it close and buried my face in it. Throughout the experience of writing this book, the same thing happened over and over again: friends and family members had held on to a photo or object of such value, without realizing its importance. The sweater had been lying in Mayim's cedar chest since the day our mother gave it to her, years before.

"Is this useful to you or anybody?" Mayim asked.

When I told Mayim more about Tamar's challenges to find artifacts of meaning for the museum's collections, she was as keen as I was to donate the sweater to the museum.

Tamar raised many questions, the primary ones being who knit the sweater, and how did our mother acquire it. We had no idea, at first, so consultation with our Israeli cousins began. Slowly, we gathered that it must have been Manya, our mother's sister who appears in the photograph with her, who had knit the sweater. We surmised that there had to have been a sentimental reason why our mother saved the sweater from the DP camp for the rest of her life, and it filled us with pride that the stories of these two beloved women would be told to posterity in an important museum, in the very country that set out to exterminate them.

As I carefully wrapped the sweater in tissue paper, I couldn't stop thinking about what this all meant. A few days before, I'd taken the sweater to my local yarn shop, bursting with the story, and asked for help to reproduce the snowflake pattern so I could try to knit a version of the sweater myself someday. My knitting friend, Carol, was so taken with my story that she dropped what she was doing and sat down with graph paper and pencil to copy the pattern stitch by stitch. I'd often questioned whether all my labour to dig up family history would matter to anyone beyond family; Carol's rousing response chased away my doubt. Yes, I'd grown closer to those with whom I share this history, and an ever-expanding circle of friends, and through this work I'd reconnected with far-flung cousins and family members I never knew I had. From them and other sources, I'd collected fragments, snippets, shards, and images, pasting them together to make something of substance from the little shreds left behind. Now I was about to send this wabi-sabi object—moth-eaten and stained yet still so poignant—back to the place where it was created. Images of the Lodz *Umschlagplatz* memorial, where rusted bits of scissors and broken buttons displayed in special frames so hauntingly told the story of what was done there, flashed behind my eyes.

EVENING HAD COME. I WAS reading in bed and came across some lines in a poem by Szymborska: *I'm working on the world/revised, improved edition*; they set me off thinking about what I wouldn't give to be able to revise this story, which began with my search for Basia's poems.[4] I realized that I still couldn't let go of my dream of finding them, to hold them in my trembling hands and shout out to the world that here is Basia, my ghost aunt, speaking to us from oblivion. *Don't give up* repeated in my head—the message the scholar had called out to me from the audience of the Holocaust conference at UVic, back in 2015, when I was describing my quest.

Now I was in a reverie, reviewing all the efforts I'd made to locate Basia's poems, and the remarkable people I'd met along the way. I felt a faint hope that maybe I'd overlooked something or someone who held the missing key. Kasia had tried so hard, combing through every page of every journal that might have been the one, and was willing to keep searching further and further afield. But it had all come to naught. I remembered how I'd sobbed when she sent me the disappointing news, not because she hadn't succeeded, but because she'd asked if I would consider including a poem written by a Jewish child, in honour of Basia and all the children murdered in the Holocaust. Kasia's heart hurt too much from the pain of it. That's what made me cry—the compassionate soul that she was. Of course I would include a poem, I'd answered, and she sent me a few that she'd translated into English, with the proviso that I should make a better, poetic translation. I didn't need to.[5]

Wiosna [Spring]

Golden dreams
And longings.
Hidden ember,
trembling heart.
Sweet fear
desire of caress ...
Something wakes up,

something weeps out there ...
Sparks, fires
And flames.
—Something burns!
I don't know what.
Clear form.
Quiet breath.
Someone's coming!
I don't know who.
Smile—tears.
Something strangely hurts,
Strangely makes me happy.
I don't know what.
Someone's lips ...
Falcon eyes.
Someone calls me;
I don't know who.
Fairy tales—fogs,
fogs and delusions.
Something wakes up.
I don't know what.
—You! Who are you?
Miracle—dream.
Someone loves me,
I don't know who.

A Chapter in Three Movements

18

The Birthday Party

2006

MY SISTERS AND I AGREED that we shouldn't wait a year to celebrate our mother's big birthday. She would be eighty-nine in February and her health was failing. We should celebrate now, while we all could. She was living in New London, Connecticut, with Estera and Stephen, since 2001, when they'd bought a huge house that was going to seed. My mother lobbied for the purchase as a co-owner; she was adventurous when it came to real estate. Estera and Stephen were good at home renovations, and ready to give up their academic careers in Iowa City.

At this point in her life, it didn't matter much to her where she lived, as long as there was a synagogue near enough to attend Shabbat services, and kosher food available for her meals. She'd made the best of living in Iowa City since our father died, and being back in New England suited her. The synagogue was her comfort place, where she found a few close friends, including the rabbi and his wife, who were devoted to her. She continued to be fiercely proud of her Jewish self, and the best way she could manifest this in assimilated America was to eat kosher and celebrate the Sabbath and the Jewish holidays. She'd long given up on expecting her godless daughters to do the same.

We were a far-flung family, coming from many directions for this special party. Robbie and I lived the farthest away, not just on the west coast, but the west coast of Canada. My three children lived in Montreal. Estera's two daughters were again living in Boston, while our youngest sister, Mayim, had moved from Oregon to Colorado for graduate school; her two daughters lived there as well. The big house on Ocean Avenue accommodated us all.

While the seven cousins enjoyed the rare opportunity to get together and catch up on one another's' lives, we sisters focused on planning the menu and getting ready for the birthday party. It was mostly Estera's doing; she was a great cook, and it was her kitchen that we had invaded. It was her nature to be in charge, so we obeyed as we bantered back and forth about the current issues of our lives and reminisced about our childhoods. And as we bickered over asparagus versus green beans, roast chicken instead of a winter stew, our mother was like a small bird that flitted from branch to branch. One moment she would swoop a couple of her granddaughters under her wing, and take them on a tour of her now extensive jewellery collection. "Ea, this is for you; Sita, if you like this, it's yours," she'd say, dropping a ring, a brooch, a necklace, or a bracelet into a grateful palm. She'd open her closets and say, "Take what you like." Anna would go for her fancy shoes, many pairs dating back decades—perfect retro styles hard to find in vintage shops. Even her two grandsons enjoyed the closet forays. To them she passed on their Zaide's shirts and sweaters, rings and gold chains. Malachy loved the Chai pendant she gave him, and he wears it to this day.

Although he was also a fine cook, Robbie knew enough to hold back from the kitchen, because it was Estera's domain. He would make a pot of tea upstairs, in his mother-in-law's kitchen, put his arm around his tiny *shviger*, whose head only reached his armpit; she would put her arm around her *eydem*'s waist, and they would sit down and joke about how good his Yiddish was. They had taken to calling each other by their Yiddish descriptors years before, and did so every Friday night during our Shabbos phone call. Simply being together and exchanging stories is what they liked best. Theirs was a loving relationship based on mutual admiration and respect, unclouded by old history. She gave him a gold bracelet and elegant tie clip in the form of a dove bearing an olive branch, which she'd brought back from Israel the last time she was there.

My ritual was to retire to her cozy sitting room and drag out her heavy cardboard box filled with photos. While my mother would crochet—she was determined to make an afghan for all ten of her children and grandchildren before she died—I would pull out handfuls of photos to review. The old pictures were my favourites. "Who is this?" I'd ask, and she'd patiently fill me in on what she remembered, telling me how we were related, or the last time she'd been in touch, adding stories as we went along. I knew that I should write them down, and sometimes I did, but that ruined the flow of these exquisite moments when she was relaxed enough to share her memories. We talked about so much more. She told me that she was ready to die, that she'd lived a long life, much longer than she'd ever expected, and that she wasn't afraid. She believed that souls didn't die, like bodies did; souls were gathered up by God somewhere in the universe, in some form that was beyond imagination. She was curious about the world to come, *olam ha-ba*, because that was where her next reunion would take place.

As evening came for the birthday dinner, we sisters decided that it would be best to have the seven grandchildren and their spouses surround our mother at the dining table, while we would sit at the smaller table in the next room.

We would be close enough to be part of the party, but we wanted our mother to feel the full effect of the next generation's deep love and respect flowing to her, which would lift her spirits like nothing else could. Between her mother, Mica, and her father, Joe, sat two-year-old Elea, our mother's first great-grandchild. A bouquet of yellow roses, her favourites, adorned the table, illuminated by tall silver candlesticks. The dinner was as delicious and festive as we all had wished; the conversations were lively and punctuated by much laughter. Observing it from our slight remove, we sisters couldn't have been happier with the celebration of our beloved mother, who had overcome so much grief to make a life for her family. How could she not be proud? Her three daughters all had master's degrees and were recognized in their fields. We'd struggled, but we had succeeded in making solid lives for ourselves while raising our children. She loved her sons-in-law, who loved her back and took such good care of her. All her grandchildren were university graduates, with bright futures ahead. One of her granddaughters taught at Harvard; another was an MD/PhD. But her greatest *nakhes,* what gave her the most joy and satisfaction, was that they were such fine people. All that she'd worked for and suffered was worth it, she thought, as she feasted her eyes on each of their loving faces.

It was getting late, and she was tired, but we still hadn't brought in the birthday cake—a lemony confection swirled with vanilla icing and yellow roses. We decided to skip the candles, for obvious reasons; Estera simply held the cake high as she advanced toward our mother, and we sang a hearty "Happy Birthday, Dear Bobie" because at this point in our lives, we all called her Bobie. Setting down the cake before her, we each marvelled at our dear Bobie's remarkable life; that she had managed to live eighty-nine years, given her history, seemed to us a great miracle. This was the moment when she started to cry. I thought her tears were about missing our father, who'd died nine years before. Of course his absence was a chronic ache, but with their children and grandchildren all present and surrounding her, his absence had to be especially painful. Daniel, who was sitting near her, asked, "Bobie, why are you crying? We're all here celebrating your amazing life, and we love you so much."

"I know, but I miss my sister," she sobbed. "Every birthday I have reminds me of the life she did not have."

I hate to admit how stunned I was to hear this, in that I had never considered how deep and irretrievable was the loss of a twin.[1] And I was a mother of twins. Much later, when I talked with Daniel about this, I wondered if his Bobie had ever spoken with him about being a twin, because she had hardly ever raised this with me. "No," Daniel answered, she didn't speak with him about it. Nor did she speak with Malachy, nor Mica nor Nira, I learned, when I inquired. Twinship was so fraught a subject for her that she didn't speak of it with anyone, not even her twin grandchildren, who would be the ones who could best understand. But maybe she withheld this talk because she knew how much it hurt to even think about, and she didn't want to inflict this pain on them. Daniel told me that it was unimaginable for him to even consider living without his twin brother. It was that awful.

So I'm left with such a deep regret that I never acknowledged to my mother that I understood, or tried to understand, this sorrow, which she endured in silence throughout her long life. Every birthday filled her with guilt and reminded her of all that she had lost. I realized that I had failed her by deliberately blinding myself to what should have been obvious to me. Being psychologically minded, I could only explain this as protecting myself from her grief, or not wanting to stir the pot of anguish that could awaken the ghosts that plagued her. What I didn't appreciate was that these ghosts never slept.

It took an outsider to make this clearer to me. It was a journalist who'd written a profile of my mother, along with other survivors who lived in New London, for Holocaust

Remembrance Day.[2] The first surprise was to hear that my mother didn't think of herself as an authentic survivor. "Maybe you just want to talk with the ones that were in the concentration camps," she suggested. "My husband and I were deported to the gulag in Russia. We were lucky."

"Survivors have a frame of reference that can be difficult for others to contemplate," the journalist wrote. But the segment that popped out and smacked me was when my mother talked about the killing of her twin sister and her two-year-old son. She told this, the journalist reported, "weeping as if she had got the news yesterday." So near the surface was her torment, sixty years later, yet she kept it hidden from her closest family, not wanting to hurt us by speaking directly about her pain.

But my mother did speak in many other ways, and through her stories and songs she transmitted her pride and attachment to Jewish identity that no one could destroy. Suffering is suffering, she would say, and it's impossible to escape your fate. This was how she came to understand and accept her own astonishing life. She taught us that it's what you make of your life that counts.

19

Home

2018

I'D BEEN WORKING ON THE desk in my sewing room, writing on my old laptop for much of the last year. It was a place where composition, cutting, and piecing happened naturally, so as quirky a psychological choice that it was, it was effective because I needed this metaphorically appropriate space to revise and complete my project.

Could it really be almost five years that I'd been working on this book? I hated to count the time that I'd spent cooped up, wrestling with words, and the time Robbie and I had spent travelling together on this long journey, as enriching as it was. Had I known how long it would take and how difficult it would be, I don't think I would have embarked upon it. My ignorance was a good thing, it turned out; despite all the disappointments, and the pain of opening myself to the horrors (because I had no choice if I were to write about them), I had met such remarkable people with enormous goodwill that often my eyes filled with tears when I thought of them. I wouldn't have missed this experience for the world.

But on this day, not even turning a worry stone in my hand helped me to settle down. It was spring and I had to get outside. Robbie was in the garden and he'd invited me to join him in his domain, where I seldom ventured. I put on my dirty old loafers and hurried down the back stairs. Robbie stood not far from the plum tree, his jeans muddy at the knees.

"I didn't think you were coming down, but I'm glad you're here."

I breathed in the cool air, the unmistakable smell of earth turned over and ready to do its work. The desiccated linden leaves had served as good mulch, and some of the beds were already putting forth nipples of green. I rolled my shoulders and stretched, aware of the tightness in my body and my need for release.

"Here's where the peas will go, and the spuds will be over here." Robbie pointed with his trowel. "Tomatoes and lemon cukes in the octagonal bed, and more tomatoes over there by the shed."

As he spoke, I had a memory of my mother standing where I stood, the summer she spent with us, back in 2001. She loved puttering around here, picking raspberries and checking on the potatoes. It brought her back to her childhood in Pohorelowka, she would say, as we would sit on the sunny deck, feasting on cherries, while we shelled beans for dinner, her silver hair gleaming. I felt that familiar pang of loss whenever a sharp image of my mother rose up. As it passed through me, I turned my head toward the far end of the garden.

"Oh my gosh. Look, sweetheart," I called out.

The almond tree we'd planted in her memory was pinking up with buds. It was a beautiful sight. I'd always admired the idea of planting a tree in memory of someone you loved, to be reminded by its cycles—from bloom, to fruit, to rest— how life renews. We were fortunate to have a big garden and just the place for a new tree. We'd discussed what kind of tree would do her honour, and decided on a *mandelboym*, a quintessential tree of the Yiddish songbook and kitchen. I'd been addicted to Chava Alberstein singing "Ikh Shtey Unter a Bokserboym," a ravishing song about a carob, a fig, and an almond tree—each a leafy refuge, a consolation, but no escape from the pain of living after what happened.[1] Almond trees were uncommon here, so it took us a while to locate one. Now, ten years later, its long thin branches reaching skyward, it had grown taller than everything around it. So immersed had I been in writing that I'd forgotten about this tree and what it represented, and I felt ashamed by my forgetting. All my labours excavating the past, trying to recover the story buried beyond reach had brought me to this moment of clarity. On this tiny sliver of earth, we'd planted our own memorial. My mother was the holder of deep family memory, which among her many gifts was the prize gift she passed on to me. For all the erasure of our history in a far corner of eastern Europe, here in our own backyard we honoured those we loved and those we never had a chance to know. I suddenly understood that for all that is lost and cannot be recovered, what remains is love, and by love we carry on.

Afterword: Afterlight

2019

UNGRY FOR A GOOD READ, I was happy to discover
that *Jabotinsky's Children*, Daniel Heller's book
about the Betar Zionist youth movement in Poland,
had finally landed in the library at the University of Victoria.[1]
Given that my parents, Basia and Pesach, and my aunt Pola
had all been active members of this movement, I thought I
would gain more insight about their lives during the interwar
years. Good background material, I figured. Even though I'd
finished writing this memoir, my passion for this history had
not lessened.

I turned to the index, curious to see if any places or individuals key to my story were listed. There was nothing under
Fishman, Milman, Kostopol, nor Stolin, but I was halted by
the last listing under "K": Kremer, Batya, page 197. What
were the chances? It's a pretty common name, I told myself,
so it most likely wouldn't be my Basia. But Batya was her
Hebrew name.

On page 197, an excerpt from a letter by Batya Kremer
from Kostopol is quoted. The letter was published, in Yiddish,

in the Betar newspaper, dated 1935. How many Batya Kremers from Kostopol were members of Betar in 1935? My heart started to race, but I didn't want to get carried away without confirmation. If this was indeed my aunt, she would have been eighteen years old, writing a feminist lament about how young women were treated by the Betar movement, and how it needed to change. "Why did men in Betar despise women?" she asked. What other reason could explain why women weren't included in any positions of leadership or given opportunities to develop their organizational abilities? "Were they only biologically capable of cooking, washing, and sewing?" What about their intelligence, and their capacities to contribute all their skills, since they shared the goal of re-establishing a Jewish homeland in Palestine?

Daniel's swift reply to my email sent goosebumps down my spine. "I would say that it's almost certain that Batya Kremer is your aunt," he wrote, and included the original Yiddish version of her entire letter, which he kindly translated for me. "I can't tell you how moved I am to receive your note, including her picture. She's no longer an abstract name to me, but a person I can fully picture now." Although he was truly saddened to learn about Batya's fate, he was as excited as I was to make this connection.

Finally, unexpectedly, gloriously, Basia's voice is unearthed. Not the poems I had hoped to find, but her insightful, progressive thoughts have risen from oblivion. I'm pinching myself as I write.

Batya Kramer's letter in *Ha-medina*, Poland, March 1935:[2]

One of the greatest problems in our organisation is the "women's question" in general and the problem of the young woman on hachshara [training] specifically.

Much has been written and said about this problem, but no practical solutions have been found to this day.

The relationship to the young woman in hachsharot is not correct, and does not fit Betar's image of chivalrous behaviour ("hadar betari").

In most of the Betar units, young men treat young women in the well-known fashion, and this sort of behaviour has more than once created bitterness among the women. If in the hachsharot there are unsatisfied women, it's a product of the way they are being treated.

We young women are angered that we are not counted in Betar's leadership, and we are not given any major organisational tasks. None of us have been given the opportunity to develop our organisational abilities, or to use our intelligence. The reason that young women are not trusted in the movement makes no sense to us. Are we really not able to do anything else other than cook, wash, and sew? Has nature truly degraded us? Looking at the history of humanity, one comes to another conclusion.

There are many women who take on roles of tremendous responsibility in different movements and demonstrate that their abilities are no less than those of men. The woman in Betar also wants to achieve important tasks in different work situations. The Betar movement should pay attention to the instances in which women are degraded by young men, and should uproot this behaviour the moment it appears in the hachsharot. Truth be told, when members of the hachshara are doing their daily work, the young woman doesn't have the time to think about her own improvement; but with some good will, the situation would get better. But the first condition for this to happen is: the young men have to have a better attitude and relationship towards us.

One must admit that in the hachsharot one can also find the "negative type" of young women, who bring their lack of order into the plugah [troop]. Such a young woman should not be pushed away; on the contrary, one should get closer to her and help her improve. It often happens that the young women who come to the hachsharot have suffered a great deal in their lives. She behaves as if she wants to distance herself from the group. One must understand this type of young woman. One shouldn't bombard her with questions that might harm her psychological state. On the contrary, one must form a sisterly relationship with her, and help introduce her to the interests of the plugah.

The plugah must be a home for the sisters and brothers who strive to work for the same goal, which we all know; but one must also remember that the revived Jewish nation depends on conscious, bold and proud mothers, and the Betar education must help fulfill this goal.

Acknowledgements

FIRST, TO MEMBERS OF MY family who provided living memory as well as documents and photos to get this story onto paper, and for their critical reviews and feedback along the way. I am enormously indebted to my cousins Ilana Malah, David Malah, Barbara Baumgarten, Janina Elmaleh, Rachel and Victor Ben Cnaan, and Avi Shadmi; my sisters Estera Milman and Sepora Mayim Jacobson, my daughter Anna Phelan, and my niece Mica Pollock and her husband Joe Castiglione, who did all of the above as well as join me on our adventure in Poland and Ukraine. In addition, Joe Castiglione's map-making has added another dimension that illustrates my parents' astonishing journey. I can hardly thank you enough.

For believing in this story and encouraging me to keep going, because they felt my voice was important, I extend my thanks to my writing community: Lynne Van Luven, Betsy Warland, Wendy Morton, Yvonne Blomer, Eve Joseph, Patricia Young, Anne Simpson, Don McKay, Heidi Garnett, Patrick Lane and Lorna Crozier, and my beloved Webbles poetry collective: Arleen Paré, Terry Ann Carter, Sue Gee,

Barbara Herringer, and Beth Kope. Above all, I am indebted to Laurie Elmquist for her steadfast assistance and astute critiques, chapter by chapter, as this book took shape and final form. To Barbara Pulling I offer my thanks for her editorial brilliance, even if it meant starting this book all over.

I am forever grateful for the support, active encouragement, and critical assistance of the writers and scholars in the academic world, some of them friends from long ago, and others whom I've met in the long process of research and writing: Goldie Morgentaler, Esther Frank, Norm Ravvin, Helga Thorson, Charlotte Schallié, Serhy Yekelchyk, Olga Pressitch, Kristen Semmens, Roberta Kremer, Olga Medvedev-Nathoo and Khadim Nathoo, Alex Ramon, Krzysztof Majer, Paulina Ambroży, Kathleen Gysells, Steven Zipperstein, Kenneth Moss, Nathalie Belsky, Eliyana Adler, Atina Grossmann, Tamar Lewinsky, Antony Polonsky, and Jared McBride. For sharing her expertise on twins, I'm especially grateful to Nancy Segal.

This book would be a shadow of itself without the assistance of skilled translators of Hebrew, Yiddish, Polish, and Ukrainian. Dahlia Beck was my Hebrew tutor/translator par excellence, who not only reviewed most of the pages of *Sefer Kostopol* with me, but even brought back Hana (Nussenblatt) Bat-Ami's volume from Israel and highlighted the most important passages for my story. Elise Polkinghorne worked with me page by page to translate Meir Grinszpan's book, as well as accomplished the impossible by translating handwritten Yiddish scribbles into text. I'm grateful to Allan Rutkowski for his initial research of Polish literary archives. Seymour Levitan generously provided me with his translations of Rokhl Korn's poems from her time in Fergana, for which I am very grateful. Of the many editorial gifts I've received from him, I acknowledge and thank Krzysztof Majer. Katarzyna Kacprzak in Warsaw began with translations of family documents and continued with multiple searches for Basia's poems and family history. Her knowledge and guidance through Warsaw and

Praga left indelible impressions, and her subsequent aid in identifying landmarks critical to this story is beyond measure. I am forever grateful for our enduring friendship. Serhy Yekelchyk's correspondence and research of Ukrainian sources were instrumental in enabling the connections we made in Poliske, while our discussions about the gulag and my parents' experiences as displaced persons provided much insight. Daniel Heller's translation of Basia's essay from the Yiddish couldn't be more praised. This book would not be what it is without all their brilliant aid.

In Poland, I had the good fortune of help from many great people. My thanks go to Anna Przybyszewska Drozd at the Jewish Historical Institute, genealogical division, for finding key family documents, and to Helise Lieberman, who played an important role in enabling our trip to Ukraine. To Anna Landau and Eugenia Prokop-Janiec, my appreciation for guidance in searching for Basia's lost poems. Jonathan Webber, from Krakow, provided inspiration on "cultural diplomacy" which helped enormously in how best to prepare for Ukraine. At the conference in Lodz, meeting Barbara Kirshenblatt-Gimblett was not only memorable but inspiring to my search.

I thank the Jewish Federation of Victoria and Vancouver Island for contributing financial support for my first trip to Poland, where I began my research. I am grateful to the YIVO Institute in New York for providing me a copy of Meir Grinszpan's book, and for responding to my numerous requests for archival assistance. Yahad-In Unum, Father Patrick Desbois's organization, was very helpful in providing interview records of eyewitness accounts of the murder of the Jews of Kostopol, and I am humbled by the important work that they do in honouring the memory of those who were erased from history. Elizabeth Anthony at the US Holocaust Memorial Museum in Washington was instrumental in unearthing family documents from the International Tracing Service which I didn't even know existed. To all, I extend my sincere thanks and appreciation.

A special thank you to Jared McBride, a fellow at the USHMM at the time I approached him. In answer to my query, he proceeded to contact his colleagues in Rivne to enlist their assistance for our visit. Nataliia Ivchyk acted as guide, translator, and friend. We are forever in her debt. Oksana Dzjubuk, Larissa Gergelyuk, and Nadezhda Nesterivina in Poliske opened their hearts to us and brought the whole village of Poliske into ours. In Rivne, we benefited from the guidance of Vika Chymshyt, and archival research from Tetiana Samsoniuk, who found family records we never imagined still existed. Kuba Łusiak, our skilled guide and driver from Warsaw to Rivne and back, made our travels comfortable and memorable. You are forever a part of our story.

I couldn't complete this thank you list without acknowledging Tomasz Różycki, poet and humanist, and friend. Our conversations still resonate, as do particular poems. Thank you for allowing me to include one in this volume.

A special thank you to Darcy Buerkle, who admonished me to not give up my search, despite my doubts. She was right. Daniel Heller's reference to Batya Kramer's published essay was an astonishing and unexpected discovery. Our whole family is very grateful for his research and his generosity with translating her words. We now have a sample of her thoughts, and how significant they are as her manifesto for a better world for women at such a tumultuous time in history.

To Lara Kordic, Nandini Thaker, and all the folks at Heritage House, I extend my deep gratitude in believing in my book, and working so hard to bring it into print.

This journey would never have happened without the love and complicity of my husband, Robert McConnell. With him I had the good fortune to share this life for thirty years, and I can't find better words to express my eternal gratitude. His unexpected death in 2019 plunged me into grief from which I am gradually emerging. His memory shall always be a blessing.

Notes and Sources

Maps

1. The map of Sabina's escape from Warsaw to Kostopol in late fall of 1939 uses geospatial data from Stanford University's Spatial History Project, "Building the New Order: 1938–1945," and from the European Environment Agency.
2. The map of Sabina and Olek Milman's deportation to Siberia, relocation to Uzbekistan, and repatriation to Poland, 1940–1946 uses geospatial data from ArcGIS Online and WorldMap Harvard University.
3. The map of Flight from Poland to the US zone in Germany, 1946–1950, uses geospatial data from Nils Weidmann and the European Environment Agency.

Chapter One—OPENING THE BOX OF HISTORY

1. There were a number of Zionist youth movements in Poland in the interwar years. For more detail about *Betar*, the movement described here, see: Hillel Halkin, *Jabotinsky: A Life*, New Haven: Yale University Press, 2014, and more recently, Daniel Kupfert Heller, *Jabotinsky's Children: Polish Jews and the Rise of Right-Wing Zionism*, Princeton: Princeton University Press, 2017.

Chapter Two—THE LONGING FOR POLAND

1. *Ashkenaz* refers to the vast swath of Eastern Europe where most Jews lived until the twentieth century. Ashkenazim made up the vast majority of Jewish immigration to North America. (Sephardim, the other branch of the Jewish people, originated in Spain in Biblical times.) Poland did not exist as a nation state at the turn of the twentieth century, but belonged to the German, Austro-Hungarian, and Russian empires. Modern Poland was created in 1920 by treaties at Versailles after the First World War.

2. Isa Milman, *Prairie Kaddish*, Regina: Coteau Books, 2008.

Chapter Three—OUTBREAK

1. This chapter is based on a 1994 video interview of Sabina Milman, recorded in Boston, by Isa Milman and Mica Pollock.

2. Countless books have been written about the outbreak of World War II. *Isaac's Army*, by Matthew Brzezinski, New York: Random House, 2012, is particularly compelling, especially in describing the plight of Warsaw's Jews and their experience in the Warsaw ghetto.

3. Thanks to Katarzyna Kacprzak, my Warsaw-based researcher, for identifying the location and photo of Zeliszew Koscielny.

Chapter Four—MISTLETOE

1. For a comprehensive bilingual text of the proceedings of the conference, see: *Kanade, di Goldene Medine?: Perspectives on Canadian Jewish Literature and Culture*, edited by Krzysztof Majer, Justyna Fruzińska, Józef Kwaterko, and Norman Ravvin, Leiden: Brill, 2018.

2. Mike Usiskin's original Yiddish book, *Oksn un Motorn* (Toronto: Vochenblat, 1945) was translated by his niece, Marcia Usiskin Basman, and published as *Uncle Mike's Edenbridge: Memoirs of a Jewish Pioneer Family*, Winnipeg: Pegius Publishers, 1983.

3. Robert Pogue Harrison, *Dominion of the Dead*, Chicago: University of Chicago Press, 2003, 39–40.

4. Ronald S. Lauder Foundation is dedicated to rebuilding Jewish life in the part of Europe where the destruction of the Holocaust was followed by the oppression of Communist rule.

Chapter Five—WARSAW

1. Information about the keeping of Polish civil records for marriage was provided by Katarzyna Kacprzak, and indirectly from Anna Przybyszewska Drozd.
2. Janusz Korczak (Henryk Goldszmit) was a Polish Jewish pediatrician, writer, and pedagogue who chose to accompany the children in his orphanage to Treblinka, rather than accept the offer to escape deportation from Warsaw and save his own life.
3. Yad Vashem, Israel's World Holocaust Remembrance Centre in Jerusalem, houses a museum, archives, education centre and a campus dedicated to remembering all who were lost, and all who acted to save the lives of Jews during the Shoah.
4. Since my visit to the Warsaw zoo in 2014, there is now a museum in the zoo. It can be visited online at http://zoo.waw.pl/villa/wirtualna-wycieczka.
5. This clipping is from *Księga Adresowa Polski (wraz z w. m. Gdańskiem) dla handlu, przemiosłu i rolnictwa; Annuaire de la Pologne (y Compris la V. I. de Dantzig) pour le Commerce, L'Industrie, les Metiers et L'Agriculture,* 1926.
6. In his memoir, *Dos mayse-bukh fun mayn lebn (The Storybook of My Life)*, Vol 2, Tel Aviv: I.L. Publishing House, 1975, 520, Melekh Ravitch described Warsaw as "a dark and mighty word, simply 'Var-she' in Yiddish, but in Polish, three black, heavy syllables fraught with destiny and drama and perhaps also with tragedy: 'War-sza-wa.'"

Chapter Six—FIVE GOOD MONTHS

1. The events described in this chapter are based on a video interview with Sabina Milman, recorded by the Holocaust Documentation and Education Center in Hollywood, Florida, 1998. This recording is also on file at the United States Holocaust Memorial Museum in Washington DC.

2. *Kostopol: The Life and Death of a Community*, edited by Arie Lerner, (Tel Aviv: Irgun Yotzei Kostopol B'Israel, 1967) is the *Yizkor* (memorial) book that provides a history of Jewish Kostopol and details the destruction of its Jews during the Second World War. Written in Hebrew by survivors, it lists the names of all the Jewish victims. The description of the Soviet army's arrival in Kostopol appears on page 176.

3. Much has been written about the history of Soviet forced migrations and deportations during the war. One source is Pavel Polian's *Against Their Will: The History and Geography of Forced Migrations in the USSR*, translated by Anna Yastrzhembska, Budapest/NY: Central European University Press, 2004, 119.

    The following outstanding volumes about the establishment of the Soviet prison camps and the experience of deportation in the Soviet Union informed my understanding immeasurably:

    - Anne Applebaum, *Gulag: A History*, New York: Anchor Books, 2003.
    - Timothy Snyder, *Bloodlands: Europe Between Hitler and Stalin*, New York: Basic Books, 2010.
    - Lynne Viola, *The Unknown Gulag: The Lost World of Stalin's Special Settlements*, Oxford: Oxford University Press, 2009.

4. *Kinderlekh*, a Yiddish term of endearment, means "dear children." *Bashert* means "fate" or "destiny."

5. Many thanks to Dr. Natalie Belsky for this reference to find the location and photos of Itatka: https://aos1986.livejournal.com/11030.html.

6. Rebecca Manley's *To the Tashkent Station: Evacuation and Survival in the Soviet Union at War* (Ithaca: Cornell University Press, 2009), tells this story extremely well.

Chapter Seven—SURPRISE IN AMSTERDAM

1. Susan Sontag, *On Photography*, New York: Farrar Straus and Giroux, 1977.

Chapter Eight—FERGANA

1. Much of the personal history described in this chapter is based on the two video interviews of Sabina Milman, recorded in

Boston, 1994, and Hollywood, Florida (Holocaust Documentation Center), 1998.

2. Rebecca Manley's *To the Tashkent Station* provides much insight into the experience of those displaced. Another source is the poetry of Rokhl Korn: *Heym un Heymlozikayt (Home and Homelessness)*, 1948, translated from the Yiddish by Seymour Levitan, 2013, which include poems written in Fergana during the war.

3. This remarkable paper by Olga Medvedeva-Nathoo details the life of Polish Jews in Central Asia and describes such unlikely reunions: "Certificate of Birth, Certificate of Survival," from the cycle *Scraps of Lives: Polish Jews in Central Asia during the Second World War*, The American Association for Polish Jewish Studies, aapjstudies.org.

4. Thanks to Dr. Natalie Belsky for explaining how the office of the Red Cross in Buguruslan operated in the Soviet Union.

5. Details of the killing of Kostopol's Jews are from eye-witness testimony of survivors, recorded in Hebrew in *Sefer Kostopol: Kostopol, The Life and Death of a Community*. In addition, Father Patrick Desbois and his team from Yahad-In Unum have sought out and interviewed surviving eyewitnesses, and uncovered many killing sites, including Kostopol. I relied on their video interviews of eyewitnesses, and the text by Father Patrick Desbois, *The Holocaust by Bullets: A Priest's Journey to Uncover the Truth Behind the Murder of 1.5 Million Jews*, New York: Palgrave Macmillan, 2008.

6. Paul Celan's famously understated expression is quoted from his Bremen Prize Speech of 1958 (cited in John Felstiner's *Paul Celan: Poet, Survivor, Jew*, New Haven: Yale University Press, 2001, 113).

7. Keith Lowe details the harrowing history of the postwar experience of Europe in his excellent volume: *Savage Continent: Europe in the Aftermath of World War II*, New York: St. Martin's Press/ Picador, 2012.

Chapter Nine—SEARCHING FOR BASIA

1. Isa Milman, "Searching for Wallenberg," in *The Malahat Review*, issue 139, Summer 2002.

2. Anda Eker, *"O pewnym domku"* ("About a Certain Little House"), in Eugenia Prokop-Janiec's *Polish-Jewish Literature in the Interwar Years*, Syracuse: Syracuse University Press, 2003; © Syracuse University Press (reproduced with permission from the publisher).

3. Isa Milman, "Hanging the Star of David on Blashard Street," in *Between the Doorposts*, Victoria: Ekstasis Editions, 2004.

4. Skamander poets are discussed in Eugenia Prokop-Janiec' illuminating history: *Polish Jewish Literature in the Interwar Years*, translated by Abe Shenitzer, Syracuse: Syracuse University Press, 2003.

Chapter Ten—REUNION

1. Albert Kaganovitch, "Stalin's Great Power Politics, the Return of Jewish Refugees to Poland, and Continued Migration to Palestine, 1944–1946," in *Holocaust and Genocide Studies* 26, no. 1 (Spring 2012): 59–94.

2. Norman Davies & Roger Moorhouse, *Microcosm: Portrait of a Central European City* (London: Pimlico, 2002) is a great reference about the history of Breslau/Wroclaw, including the Second World War and immediate postwar period.

3. A great thank you to Dr. Eliyana Adler for answering my question about how survivors found each other after the war. Posting notices in cafés was one of the most popular and effective means used throughout Europe.

4. For a comprehensive review of this history, and the Polish treatment of Jews during and after World War II, see Jan T. Gross, *Fear: Anti-Semitism in Poland After Auschwitz*, New York: Random House, 2006, and Jan Grabowski, *Hunt for the Jews: Betrayal and Murder in German-Occupied Poland*, Bloomington: Indiana University Press, 2013.

5. *Brichah*, meaning "escape" or "flight" in Hebrew, was made up of Jewish resistance fighters who'd survived the war in Poland, along with members of the Jewish Brigade of the British army, and the *Hagana*, the clandestine Jewish army in Palestine. Yehuda Bauer's definitive history can be found in *Flight and Rescue: Brichah*, New York: Random House, 1970.

6. Hana (Nussenblatt) Bat-Ami's book, *M'ever L'Skhakha* (*Beyond Remembrance*), Ministry of Defense, Israel, © 1992, describes the situation in Vienna and the escape to the US Zone in Germany. The photos in her book include my parents standing at Herzl's grave.

7. For an astute and vivid review of the complexities of the history preceding the establishment of Israel, I recommend Jonathan Schneer's *The Balfour Declaration: The Origins of the Arab-Israeli Conflict,* New York: Random House, 2011.

Photo Insert

1. Palac Zeliszew. Photo by Jerzy Szandomirski, Pracownia Konserwacji Zabytków, published in *Stolica: warszawski tygodnik ilustrowany,* R. 28, 1973, nr 32 (12 VIII). (Every effort was made to locate the photographer's estate to request copyright permission. Pracownia Konserwacji Zabytków no longer exists.)

Chapter Eleven—MOTHER TONGUE

1. Thanks to Dr. Kenneth Moss for recommending this wonderful book, in answer to my question about what books would have been found in the Kramerovkes' home: Jeffrey Shandler, editor, *Awakening Lives: Autobiographies of Jewish Youth in Poland Before the Holocaust,* published in cooperation with the Yivo Institute for Jewish Research, New Haven: Yale University Press, 2002.

2. Katka Reszke, *Return of the Jew: Identity Narratives of the Third Post-Holocaust Generation of Jews in Poland,* Boston: Academic Studies Press, 2013.

3. Stanley Kunitz, "Touch Me," from *The Collected Poems of Stanley Kunitz,* New York: W.W. Norton & Company, 1995.

4. Malgorzata Niezabitowska & Tomasz Tomaszewski, "Remnants: The Last Jews of Poland," in *National Geographic* 170, no. 3, September 1986.

5. Don McKay, *The Speaker's Chair: Field Notes on Betweenity,* the 2010 E.J. Pratt Lecture, Running the Goat Books & Broadsides, St. John's Newfoundland, © Don McKay, 2013.

6. Anna Kamienska, "A Prayer That Will Be Answered," translated from the Polish by Stanislaw Baranczak and Clare Cavanagh,

from *A Book of Luminous Things*, edited by Czeslaw Miłosz, San Diego: Harcourt Brace & Company, 1996.

7. Tomasz Różycki, "Scorched Maps," from *Colonies*, translated by Mira Rosenthal. Copyright © 2013 by Tomasz Różycki. English translation copyright © 2013 by Mira Rosenthal. Reprinted with permission of The Permissions Company, LLC on behalf of Zephyr Press, zephyrpress.org.

Chapter Twelve—DISPLACED PERSONS

1. My primary source about the Jewish experience in the Displaced Persons camps in Germany is the scholarship of Atina Grossmann: *Jews, Germans and Allies: Close Encounters in Occupied Germany*, Princeton, NJ: Princeton University Press, 2007, and "Entangled Histories and Lost Memories: Jewish Survivors in Occupied Germany, 1945-49," in *We Are Here: New Approaches to Jewish Displaced Persons in Postwar Germany*, edited by Avinoam J. Patt & Michael Berkowitz, Detroit: Wayne State University Press, 2010.

2. This illuminating paper helped me understand the conundrum my parents faced: Laura Jockusch & Tamar Lewinsky, "Paradise Lost? Postwar Memory of Polish Jewish Survival in the Soviet Union," in *Holocaust and Genocide Studies* 24, no. 3 (Winter 2010): 373-399. In addition, my discussions with Dr. Serhy Yekelchyk helped clarify the situation that Jewish deportees to the Soviet gulag were forced to grapple with postwar.

Chapter Thirteen—RETURN

1. The revised title of the manuscript by Jared McBride is: *Webs of Violence: Occupation, Revolution and Terror in Western Ukraine, 1941-1944*; manuscript in progress.

Chapter Fourteen—EXILE

1. The foundation of the State of Israel was traumatic for all; the terrible irony of displacement and exile of many Palestinians haunts the country to this day. So much has been written and debated about the creation of the State of Israel and the imme-

diate aftermath that I can't possibly do justice to the subject here. A few titles to refer to:

- Anita Shapira, *Israel: A History*, Lebanon, NH Brandeis University Press, 2012.
  - Martin Gilbert, *Israel: A History*, New York: Doubleday, 1998.
  - Benny Morris, *Righteous Victims: A History of the Zionist-Arab Conflict, 1881–2001*, New York: Random House, 1999.
  - Tom Segev, *The Seventh Million: The Israelis and the Holocaust*, translated by Haim Watzman, New York: Farrar Straus Giroux, 1993.
  - Tom Segev, *1949: The First Israelis*, New York: Henry Holt, Owl Books, 1998.
2. The International Tracing Service in Bad Arolsen has now digitized over 30,000,000 wartime and immediate postwar records.

Chapter Fifteen—KOSTOPIL

1. *Yizkor* (which means "remember") is a communal prayer for the dead, recited a few times a year during important Jewish holidays. *Yizkor* books were written by survivors of Jewish towns and villages after the Shoah, to commemorate what was lost, and honour those murdered. Over two thousand *Yizkor* books are known to exist.
2. W.H. Auden, "Musée des Beaux Arts," from *Another Time*, London: Faber & Faber, 1940.
3. For a detailed description of how mass murder was carried out, see: Father Patrick Desbois, *In Broad Daylight: The Secret Procedures behind the Holocaust by Bullets*, translated from the French by Hilary Reyl and Calvert Barksdale, New York: Arcade. Publishing, 2018.
4. Meir Grinszpan, *Majn Sztetl Kostopol: Poeme*, Neu-Ulm, Deutschland, 1947.

Chapter Sixteen—FINALLY

1. *Hoshomer Hatza'ir* is a Socialist-Zionist secular youth movement, founded in 1913; Betar, founded by Ze'ev Jabotinsky in 1923, was far more to the right, politically.

Chapter Seventeen—A CHAPTER IN THREE MOVEMENTS

1. Wladyslaw Pasikowski, writer and director, *Aftermath* (Poklosie), 2012; Pawel Pawlikowski, writer and director; Rebecca Lenkiewicz, writer, *Ida*, 2013.
2. For a deeper understanding, I recommend this book by historian Omer Bartov: *Erased: Vanishing Traces of Jewish Galicia in Present Day Ukraine*, Princeton, NJ: Princeton University Press, 2007.
3. Laura Jockusch & Tamar Lewinsky, "Paradise Lost? Postwar Memory of Polish Jewish Survival in the Soviet Union," in *Holocaust and Genocide Studies* 24, no 3 (Winter 2010): 373–99.
4. Wislawa Szymborska, "I'm Working on the World," from *Poems: New and Collected, 1957–1997*, translated from the Polish by Stanislaw Baranczak and Clare Cavanagh, Harcourt © 1998.
5. Mirjam, "Winosa" (Spring), *Mały Przegląd*, 19 Czerwca (June) 1931, Warszawa.

Chapter Eighteen—BIRTHDAY PARTY

1. Following are excellent sources that helped inform my understanding of twinship:
   - Nancy L. Segal, *Indivisible by Two: Lives of Extraordinary Twins*, Cambridge, MA: Harvard University Press, 2005.
   - Anna Van der Wee, *Lone Twin*, Documentary Film, 2011, lonetwinfilm.com.
   - Joan Woodward, *The Lone Twin: Understanding Twin Bereavement and Loss*, London: Free Association Books, 1998.
2. Bethe Dufresne, "To Never Forget: The Stories of Six People in Southern Connecticut Who Survived the Holocaust to Bear Witness Today," in *The Day*, New London, CT, April 18, 2004.

Chapter Nineteen—HOME

1. Chava Alberstein and the Klezmatics, "*Ikh Shtey Unter a Bokserboym*" ("I Stand Beneath a Carob Tree"), by Zhame Telesin, in *The Well*, Cambridge, MA: Rounder Records, 2001.

Afterword—AFTERLIGHT

1. Daniel Kupfert Heller, *Jabotinsky's Children: Polish Jews and the Rise of Right-Wing Zionism*, Princeton, NJ: Princeton University Press, 2017.

2. Batya Kramer, "*Di Bahura oyf hachshara*," *Ha-medina*, March 30, 1935.

Index